SPORTS IN ZION

SPORT AND SOCIETY

Series Editors
Benjamin G. Rader
Randy Roberts

*A list of books in the series appears
at the end of this book.*

SPORTS IN ZION

Mormon Recreation, 1890–1940

RICHARD IAN KIMBALL

UNIVERSITY OF ILLINOIS PRESS

Urbana and Chicago

The illustrations in this book appear courtesy of
the LDS Church Archives.
Library of Congress Cataloging-in-Publication Data
Kimball, Richard Ian.
Sports in Zion : Mormon recreation, 1890–1940 /
Richard Ian Kimball.
    p.   cm. — (Sports and society)
Includes bibliographical references (p.   ) and index.
ISBN 0-252-02857-0 (cloth : alk. paper)
    1. Mormons—Recreation—History.
    2. Recreation—Utah—History.
    3. Mormons—Social life and customs.
I. Title. II. Series.
GV54.U8K56   2003
790'.088'283—dc21   2002156585

For Bird

CONTENTS

Acknowledgments   ix

Introduction: Religion, Reform, and Recreation   1

1. "Not Playing without a Purpose": The Construction of a Mormon Recreation Ideology   21

2. "A Strong Arm to the Church": Recreation Building Boom   57

3. "For the Uplifting and the Betterment of the Youth of Israel": Athletics, Socialization, and the "Selling of the Word of Wisdom"   88

4. "A Means of Preserving the Memory of the Mormon Pioneers": LDS Recreation in the Great Outdoors   125

5. To Make the Most of Leisure: Recreation Responds in a Depression Decade   162

Conclusion: Recreation Recedes   185

Bibliography   193

Index   213

Illustrations follow page 124

ACKNOWLEDGMENTS

A Chinese proverb advises that "when you drink from the stream, remember the spring." For many years I have guzzled from an intellectual stream without stopping to recall its headwaters. Intellectually and socially, I have many springs to acknowledge.

Thanks first must go to Dr. Nancy F. Gabin, who shepherded me not only through my dissertation but through graduate school. As a friend, employer, confidante, and sounding board, she has served me well and earned the title of mentor. I also benefitted immensely from other faculty members at Purdue—Professors Jon Teaford, Michael Morrison, and Frank Lambert. Their help unquestionably improved the final document, and their friendship improved my life. Other professors in the Department of History, including Harold Woodman and Ariel de la Fuente, enriched my studies by introducing me to ideas and methodologies outside of my field. Other friends and scholars at Purdue were there from the beginning of the project—Richard Lindstrom, Robert Cousins, and Chris and Julie Porter. Timothy Berg deserves special recognition for his advice and dear friendship. Tim read every word of the initial manuscript and gave invaluable help with his edits and his example as a first-rate scholar and teacher.

Others at my new academic home, Brigham Young University, also deserve recognition for their contributions. My neighbor and friend Gary Daynes offered not only useful criticism but support in the form of unstructured conversations, trips to Tommy's Burgers, and regular boosts in self-confidence. In our case, at least, bad fences made for good neighbors. His departure left a great hole in our department. Members of the BYU history department writing group let me know that I was on the right track but still had work to do. Susan Sessions Rugh, Ignacio M. Garcia, Brian Q. Cannon, Thomas G. Alexander, Jenny Hale Pulsipher, and Neil L. York each read portions of the manuscript and prodded me to do my best work. Depart-ment head Frank W. Fox provided much-needed research support as the manuscript neared its deadline. Eric E. Tuten and Rodney D. Bohac proved most amiable companions in the neverending search for jazz music in the mountain West. The BYU history department has proven to be an altogether collegial location throughout the book's final preparations. Thanks also to Julie Radle, the only indispensable member of the history department.

A summer stipend from the National Endowment for the Humanities allowed me to spend the summer of 2002 in Chicago studying with the sports historians Steven A. Riess and Patrick B. Miller. That experience rounded many of the corners of the manuscript and cleared away many of the final intellectual hurdles before publication. The University of Illinois Press has made the publications process a joy. Elizabeth Dulany, Terry Sears, and Matt Mitchell have been unerringly professional and saved me from a multitude of mistakes. Thanks also to two astute and anonymous reviewers for the University of Illinois Press. Their comments cut me down to size but hope-fully expanded the range of the book.

Most importantly, my parents, James L. Kimball Jr. and Joan Hunt Kimball, parents-in-law, and family members supported and cajoled me through a long process that largely occurred from a long distance. My fa-ther, an outstanding Mormon historian, probably saw the genesis of this project long before anyone else. But he never mentioned it. For that, I thank him. My brothers and sisters knew about the book but also understood that we had more important things to do, too. Debts have been incurred that can never be repaid. Thanks to Mark and Melissa Gardner, James and Mary Kimball, Mark and Lisa Kimball, Amy and Carlos Caro, Corky and Kay Carbon, Steve and Ginger Ross, and Marie Burt.

Since I began the book, our family received our most precious gifts (and both on the same day!)—Abigail and Solomon Chase. Their presence proves that *more* recreation does not necessarily lead to a more fulfilling life. Above all, my wife Suzanne did just about everything else to make this possible. Her professional excellence and seemingly boundless energy marvel me. It is for her.

SPORTS IN ZION

Religion, Reform, and Recreation

> Recreation of whatever nature or form, under the direction of
> the Church, should make true Latter-day Saints. It should in-
> crease the spirit of brotherly love and sympathy, break down
> undesirable class distinction, develop leadership, promote
> health, direct and develop the power of self expression, direct
> the emotional expression and develop culture and refinement.
> —JOHN T. WAHLQUIST (1923)

The growth of the city, throughout the nineteenth century but especially as
"new" immigrants migrated to American urban areas after 1880, provoked
"an authentic, intense, and growing fear of the threat urbanization posed
to society itself."[1] Efforts to reform city dwellers (particularly immigrants
living cheek by jowl in slum-ridden inner cities) reached a crescendo as the
nineteenth century passed into the twentieth. Referred to by historians and
others as the "Progressive Era," the period from 1890 to 1920 saw reform
activists transplant the moral concerns of antebellum reformers to the bus-
tling cities of industrial America. Whether organizing settlement houses,
where middle-class professionals worked to "Americanize" immigrants
newly arrived from eastern and southern Europe, or creating action groups
to democratize state and federal politics, Progressive reformers sought to
bring order to the complex and often confusing city. Armed with sociological statistics, Progressives tried to transform the physical landscape of the
city in the belief that physical modifications would naturally lead to social
and moral improvements.[2]

Although the concept (or even the existence) of a "Progressive Movement"
remains contested, most historians agree that the decades surrounding the
turn of the twentieth century witnessed important changes that transformed
society as Americans encountered modernity. In the words of the historian
David M. Kennedy, "The progressive era, in sum, was an era of transition,
and that transitional character is one of its most significant aspects. We
cannot look to it for the source of all aspects of our modern life, nor can

we make the progressives the heroes or the scapegoats for the triumphs or failings, as the case may be, of the rest of the century. Progressivism, after all, is past, and must be so treated. But past does not mean irrelevant, and certainly does not mean nonexistent."[3]

If the Progressive Era was a time of transition for Americans generally, the decades after 1890 marked a momentous transformation for the Church of Jesus Christ of Latter-day Saints (hereafter the Mormon or LDS Church), both within the church and between the religious organization and the world outside of LDS-dominated Utah. As the last decade of the nineteenth century began, Mormons had been in the throes of federal persecution for more than thirty years. Attempting to force the LDS faithful to fall in line with the standards of Victorian America, the federal government outlawed polygamy (a deeply held though controversial LDS doctrine)[4] in 1862 and thereafter passed increasingly punitive measures. Captured in antipolygamy raids, hundreds of Mormon men and women received jail terms in state and federal prisons. Other church members, including church president John Taylor and various apostles, avoided the long arm of the federal law by hiding in "underground" safe homes throughout the Mormon region. Eventually, the church reached its breaking point with the passage of the Edmunds (1882) and Edmunds-Tucker (1887) acts, which dissolved the church as a legal corporation, forced the forfeiture of all church property over fifty thousand dollars, disenfranchised all polygamists and ended female suffrage in Utah, and allowed the federal government to assume control over the territory's schools.

Rather than continue to antagonize the federal government, church president Wilford Woodruff announced in 1890 the official end of church-sanctioned polygamy. That profound change in Mormon practice (the theological doctrine has never been officially disavowed) began the church's first major accommodation to the main currents of American behavior. The next several decades witnessed the general, though not absolute, acceptance of Mormons into conventional American Protestantism.[5]

The Mormon movement into the mainstream was neither quick nor painless. According to the historian Thomas G. Alexander:

> Conditions during the period of the 1890s constituted for the Latter-day Saints a challenge to the paradigm under which they had operated at least since 1847. The previous paradigm necessitated the integration of religion, politics, society, and the economy into a single non-pluralistic community and adopted polygamy as a means of solving the traditional problem of the marriage relationship. This was simply unacceptable to Victorian America, so in the 1890s the Mormons began groping for a new paradigm that would save essential characteristics of their re-

ligious tradition, provide sufficient political stability to preserve the interests of the church, and allow them to live in peace with other Americans.

Seeking the temporal salvation of the religious body, church leaders began to emphasize nuances of LDS doctrine that had previously been overshadowed by polygamy. The dietary code (known as the Word of Wisdom), tithing (pegged at 10 percent of a member's income), and the construction of sacred temples helped fill the void created by President Woodruff's prohibition of polygamy.[6]

Mormon leaders at the beginning of the twentieth century faced a double dilemma. Not only did they have to construct new distinctions between their religious group and the outside world, they also had to deal with the problems confronting their contemporaries—namely, urbanization, immigration, and industrialization.

During this period of transition, when Mormons were seeking for methods to maintain their unique way of life while accommodating to the American mainstream, the LDS Church first utilized organized recreation as a means of teaching morals and Mormon values to adolescents. As part of the effort to maintain the cultural distinctiveness of Mormons, church leaders organized a massive recreation program designed not only to keep young men and women interested in church attendance but to inculcate a sense of "Mormonness" in the rising generation. The creation of intrachurch athletic meets and leagues as well as the addition of gymnasiums to local meetinghouses and the construction of a state-of-the-art athletic training facility in downtown Salt Lake City furthered the work of the church by teaching lessons of cooperation and teamwork through sporting events. A close alliance with the Boy Scout organization and the construction of elaborate Girls' Camps also helped church leaders instill frontier values in a generation raised in the city. Undergirding the creation of the wide-ranging recreation program was the development of an LDS recreation ideology based on Mormon theology and the writings of twentieth-century play theorists. Recreation offered a malleable social device that could teach religious values to adolescents and prove to outsiders that Mormons fit in with other religious denominations.

An unmistakable gendered emphasis pervaded Mormon recreation in the first decades of the twentieth century. In the main, Mormon leisure-time programs were clearly designed to appeal to boys. Like other Progressive recreational reformers, Mormon leaders believed in what the Congregational minister William Forbush described in his popular book, *The Boy Problem*.[7] Changes in the American social landscape—immigration, the rise of professional women, and the luxury and ease of city life—seemed to affect young

men disproportionately, and reformers feared that the rising male generation was particularly susceptible to degeneracy. Girls, however, had no
"problem," as it were. Though young women were similarly buffeted by
social change, they were somehow less amenable to illegal and immoral
activities and were therefore much less often the focus of Progressive, and
Mormon, reformers.[8]

The emphasis on male activities within the LDS Church is reflected
throughout *Sports in Zion*. Though I have tried wherever possible to include
leisure-time programs directed toward young women, Mormon recreation
in the early twentieth century primarily aimed at inculcating morality into
young men and socializing Mormon boys into the institutional church.[9] The
church program imitated the goals and tactics developed by advocates of
"Muscular Christianity" in the nineteenth century. In effect, "Muscular
Mormonism," defined as the desire to instill masculinity and the religious
tenets of Mormonism, was at the heart of Mormon recreation.[10]

The Mormon use of recreational programs to right the wrongs of urban
life places the religious group firmly in the broad category of Progressive
reformers that Paul S. Boyer identifies as "positive environmentalists." This
brand of reformers, in Boyer's formulation, "took their cue from the more
hopeful and visionary side of late nineteenth-century urban reformism. Their
goal was to create in the city the kind of physical environment that would
gently but irresistibly mold a population of cultivated, moral, and socially
responsible city dwellers."[11] Although Mormon leaders also participated in
some efforts typical of "negative environmentalists"—most notably the
eradication of saloons—generally the church sought to raise downtrodden
urban dwellers by adding uplifting activities to the variety of urban offerings. Like settlement-house workers, playground advocates, and park planners, Mormon recreation leaders worked to provide replacement activities
to lure boys away from street corners. Mormons may not have exemplified
the "typical" Progressive reformers, but their concerns about the social dis-
location caused by urbanization and their reliance on sociological expertise
mark them as much more similar to than different from their Progressive
counterparts in American cities.

Progressive-Era social reformers were interested in much more than merely
protecting the urban poor. In many cases, the recreational elements of reform activities were thinly veiled mechanisms of "Americanization"—the
quest to transform immigrants from southern and eastern Europe into red-
blooded, true-blue Americans. Reformers believed that games and other
playground activities would instill democratic values, patriotic feelings, and
industrial discipline in the teeming masses of immigrants. Steven A. Riess

asserts that reformers "hoped to use parks to raise the moral level of urban folk, improve their character, and Americanize them, or, if that did not work, to use playgrounds as a source of social control."[12]

The concept of Progressive reformers as social-control specialists—like so many puppeteers forcing their subjects to salute the American flag—no longer seems appropriate to describe the give and take of urban reform efforts in the early twentieth century. Rather, as Paul S. Boyer has written, any effort to shape social behavior "involves considerable mutuality, with a nexus of shared social assumptions and aspirations linking the 'controllers' and the 'controlled.'"[13] The shared social assumptions and aspirations in the Progressive Era are evident in many recreation programs of the early twentieth century. Reformers used sports and recreational activities as instruments to teach social values; participants, however, were eager to join the games not to learn proper behavior but because the games provided diversion, competition, and fun. Programs proved popular to both reformer and reformee, albeit for different reasons.[14]

Around the turn of the twentieth century, a variety of social forces combined to create a unique opportunity for the rise of recreational reform efforts. Concern over the plight of urban children, a desire to reform or "Americanize" immigrants, and the formation of a guiding play ideology turned parks and playgrounds into centers of socialization for Progressive-Era children. Building on a long history of urban reform efforts, Progressive reformers often turned to play programs as the antidote to urban disorder. Similarly, in the Mormon community, the problems caused by urbanization led directly to the creation of church-sponsored recreation programs.

"Progressive" Salt Lake City

In the early years of the twentieth century, Salt Lake City was not only the home of the Mormon church, it was a thriving city, the economic and social hub of the intermountain West. Though located in the isolated Great Basin and populated primarily by a unique religious subgroup, Salt Lake resembled other American cities. By 1911, as one history of the city records, Salt Lake had assumed the appearance of a "generally typical American city." Long considered abnormal among American urban areas because of distinctive Mormon-Gentile antagonisms, historians now regard cultural and religious conflict as a commonplace of American city life. The presence of such conflict (though not necessarily the terms) might qualify Salt Lake City as typical rather than aberrant. Furthermore, the City of the Saints had been integrated into the national economy at least since the completion of the transcontinental railroad in 1869. In no sense an "island" community of the type famously described by Robert H. Wiebe,[15] the Mormon capital city had taken on the characteristics of most cities of the industrial era: department stores, dance halls, newspapers, theaters, sports, and other urban amenities flourished by the end of the nineteenth century.[16] The impacts of urbanization, immigration, and industrialization shaped the Mormon capital in the decades after 1890 as much as they did other "Progressive" cities.

Like other American urban areas, Salt Lake City experienced massive growth between 1890 and 1930. Six years before Utah gained statehood, the 1890 census enumerated 44,843 persons living in Salt Lake City. By the turn of the century, the city boasted 53,531 residents (an increase of 19.4 percent). From 1900 to 1910, the city's population expanded to 92,777, an increase of over 70 percent. Salt Lake's 1910 population placed it in the same rank as cities like Reading, Pennsylvania (96,071), Dallas, Texas (92,104), and Lynn, Massachusetts (89,336). Augmented by immigration and in-migration from rural areas, the population continued to grow, reaching 118,110 in 1920 and 140,267 in 1930.[17] In the forty years following the renunciation of polygamy, the population of Salt Lake City more than tripled (312 percent increase). For the same period, the state's population expanded from 210,779 in 1890 to 507,847 in 1930, an increase of 240 percent. (See table 1.)

Not only did the city's growth rate typically outpace the population growth rate of the state as a whole, urban areas gradually siphoned a majority of the population away from rural locations. See table 1 for the growth of other urban areas in Utah. Although the majority of Utah's population resided in rural areas until 1930, the percentage of the population in the cities increased significantly after 1880, as table 2 indicates. By 1930, Salt Lake City had not entered the first (or perhaps even the second) rank of Ameri-

Table 1. Population of Selected Cities and Decade Growth

	1880	1890	1900	1910	1920	1930
Salt Lake	20,768	44,843	53,531	92,777	118,110	140,267
% growth	n.a.	115.9	19.4	73.3	27.3	18.8
Ogden	6,069	14,889	16,313	25,580	32,804	40,272
% growth	n.a.	145.3	9.6	56.8	28.2	22.8
Provo	3,432	5,159	6,185	8,925	10,303	14,766
% growth	n.a.	50.3	19.9	44.3	15.4	43.3
Utah	146,963	210,779	276,749	373,351	449,396	507,847
% growth	n.a.	43.4	31.2	34.9	20.3	13.0

Source: *Statistical Abstract of Utah*, 4, 28.

Table 2. Rural and Urban Population in Utah

	Total Population	Percent Urban	Percent Rural
1880	143,963	23.4	76.6
1890	210,779	35.7	64.3
1900	276,749	38.1	61.9
1910	373,351	46.3	53.7
1920	449,396	48.0	52.0
1930	507,847	52.4	47.6

Source: *Statistical Abstract of Utah*, 11.

can urban places, but urbanization had transformed Utah's capital from a Mormon outpost to a regionally important social and economic center.

On the streets of nineteenth-century Salt Lake City, one would have expected to meet European immigrants at nearly every turn. One report estimates that 69 percent of households in Salt Lake County were led by immigrants, the majority having come from English-speaking countries. Salt Lake's "average family" in the second half of the nineteenth century consisted of foreign-born parents and their children. Anglo-Saxon and Celtic surnames dominated city directories, though a smaller number of Scandinavian, central European, and Italian surnames are evident.[18] Most Mormon immigrants quickly assimilated to the dominant culture. Though church publications and activities were available in many languages, most immigrants attended worship services in English. Nearly all second-generation residents of Salt Lake City became fluent in English, and "relatively little sense of ethnic community survived beyond the generation of immigrants themselves." In fact, when immigrant descendants served as missionaries to their ancestral homes, most had to learn the language in order to communicate.[19]

Notwithstanding the long tradition of European immigration into LDS communities throughout Utah, the face of immigration modified slightly after 1890. Similar to changes in immigration occurring nationwide, Utah received a larger number of newcomers from southern and eastern Europe. Immigration from Great Britain and Scandinavian countries continued to dominate (in terms of population and cultural impact), but an influx of "new" immigrants permanently altered the ethnic composition of Utah. As shown in table 3, the total population of all immigrants in Utah remained largely static, except for a noticeable rise of more than twelve thousand between 1900 and 1910—an increase of 22.3 percent. The stability of the total immigrant population, however, obscures the unprecedented growth of several ethnic groups during the period. Though the population of the newer immigrant groups would never approach the size of the groups from

Table 3. Country of Birth of Selected Immigrant Populations in Utah, 1890–1920

	1890	1900	1910	1920
Austria	109	272	1,870	987
Denmark	9,023	9,132	8,300	6,970
England	20,905	18,879	18,083	14,839
Germany	2,121	2,365	3,953	3,589
Greece	3	3	4,039	3,029
Italy	347	1,062	3,117	3,225
Japan	5	419	2,050	2,358
Russia	290	154	568	684
Total Utah population	53,064	53,777	65,822	59,200

Source: Information collected from the United States Census for 1890, 1900, 1910, and 1920.

northwestern Europe, it is instructive to note which ethnic groups grew the fastest in Utah during the Progressive Era.

Without question, the most remarkable expansion occurred within Utah's Greek community. Virtually nonexistent until 1900, Greek immigrants flooded into Utah in astounding numbers between 1900 and 1910. The 1900 census enumerated only three Greeks in the state, but only ten years later the Greek population had reached 4,039, a growth rate of 1,346 percent for the decade. Though most did not settle in the urban areas along the Wasatch mountains—they were bound for the mines of central Utah or for work on the railroads—the Greek culture visibly changed Salt Lake City. From the erection of the Holy Trinity Church in the city's center to Greek coffeehouses, the immigrants transplanted Peloponnesian culture in their new homeland.[20] Other ethnic groups experienced similar, if not quite as meteoric, increases in their numbers. The population of Italians in Utah nearly tripled from 1,062 in 1900 to 3,117 in 1910; the number of state residents born in Japan grew from 419 at the turn of the century to more than two thousand in 1910; Austrian immigrants likewise expanded their numbers from 272 to 1,870 in the first decade of the twentieth century. Interestingly, due to deaths and a decrease in immigration, the immigrant communities from Denmark and England decreased in size from 1900 to 1910, though they remained the largest immigrant groups in the state (see tables 3 and 4).

Immigrant communities transformed Salt Lake City by introducing new languages, religions, fashions, and ways of life. Greek coffeehouses, Asian restaurants, and ethnic business enterprises evidenced not only the reality of relocation but the immigrants' desire to replicate their home cultures. In addition to changing the social landscape, the presence of immigrant communities also recast the physical environs of Salt Lake, as ethnic groups congregated in particular corners of the city. The Chinese community, for

Table 4. Country of Birth of Selected Immigrant Populations
in Salt Lake City, 1910

	1910
Austria	355
Norway, Sweden, and Denmark	379
England, Scotland, and Wales	621
Germany	2,102
Greece	7,532
Italy	4,662
Russia and Finland	214
Total Salt Lake City population	19,544

Source: U.S. Census 1910, 213.

example, was concentrated in the heart of downtown in an area bordered by Main and State Streets and First and Second South. To the south of the Chinese lay African American neighborhoods between Main Street and Third East. Japanese Americans lived just west of the Salt Lake Temple along First South. Syrians, Italians, and Greeks likewise lived in ethnic enclaves, often close to the railroads and typically in the poorer sections of the city.[21] With ethnic neighborhoods and institutions adding new flavor to Salt Lake City, the wave of "new" immigrants propelled urban growth.

While Salt Lake City was growing in population and diversity, the city underwent the process of industrialization. As the percentage of Utahns living in rural areas gradually declined, the number working in manufacturing industries expanded rapidly. Statistics alone fail to convey the day-to-day realities that followed in the wake of industrialization in Utah and elsewhere; perhaps the best method of apprehending the lives of industrial workers is found in social and labor histories of the period.[22] A statistical portrait, however, clearly outlines the growing importance of industrial manufacturing to Utah's economy.

As table 5 indicates, growth in Utah's manufacturing sector kept pace with the state's expanding population. Already well established by the turn of the twentieth century, industrial manufacturing became a staple of Utah's economy during the Progressive Era. Concentrated in the emerging urban corridor from Ogden to Provo, the number of manufacturing firms—not including extractive industries like mining—grew from 619 in 1904 to 1,089 fifteen years later, an increase of 76 percent. Moreover, the number of industrial workers expanded 139 percent during the decade and a half, with 9,650 industrial employees in 1904 and 23,107 workers by 1919. Wage-earning workers (those paid by the hour or by piece rate rather than salary) comprised the vast majority of Utah's industrial workers in the century's

Table 5. Industrial Workers, Utah, 1904–19

	People in Industry	Wage Earners	Proprietors and Firm Members
1904	9,650	8,052	619
1909	14,133	11,785	688
1919	23,107	18,868	1,089

Source: U.S. Census, 1910, 527; U.S. Census, 1920, 1258–59.

first decades. Figures for 1904 indicate 8,052 wage earners, while fifteen years later the number had grown to 18,868—an increase of 134 percent. Eighty-six percent of wage-earning workers during the period were adult male, 13 percent adult female, and approximately 1 percent were children under the age of sixteen. Seasonal employment, however, affected the number of wage-earning Utahns. For example, in April 1919, only 16,196 wage earners found employment, compared to 22,592 workers employed in October of the same year, a difference of 39 percent. Many of the fluctuations in the availability of wage work can be attributed to the ebb and flow of seasonal demand and the agricultural cycle.

White-collar employment reached significant levels by 1919 as well. Salaried officials of corporations numbered 266 across the state that year, while 880 worked as superintendents and managers. More than two thousand clerks worked in the offices of the state's industrial companies. Unlike the situation on the factory floor, however, women made up nearly 30 percent (572 of 2,004) of Utah's clerks.

At least in terms of the three major markers of the Progressive Era—urbanization, immigration, and industrialization—Utah's urban areas kept pace with the developments occurring in other regions of the country. Rural folk flocked to the cities, factories lured farmers from their fields, and the addition of "new" immigrants broadened the ethnic diversity in urban and rural areas.

Mormon Society at the Crossroads

Mormon cities were not alone in experiencing profound change in the decades surrounding the turn of the twentieth century. During this period, LDS society underwent significant change as well. Still reeling from federal persecution and the end of polygamy, Mormonism faced its most severe crisis since the martyrdom of its founder, Joseph Smith. In the estimation of the historian Jan Shipps, Mormons after the Manifesto stood at a crossroads:

At stake was the sheer survival not of the LDS Church itself, but of a Mormonism that continued to preserve its exclusive claim to be the sole corporate body in possession of the holy priesthood and invested with the status of God's chosen people. Without boundaries to set them apart, without "gentiles" to stand over and against, a chosen people cannot exist; their very identity depends on their perception of specialness; and that specialness, in turn, depends on their being separated in some way from that part of the population that is not special. The United States government had made it clear that institutionally established and maintained boundaries could not be tolerated in this nation, and this meant the Latter-day Saints were faced with a serious internal problem. Somehow the responsibility for boundary maintenance had to be shifted from the corporate body to the individuals within that body, and that shift had to be legitimated in such a way that it would gain general acceptance.[23]

Mormons were caught between a past where plural marriage provided a strict border with the outside world and an uncertain future where boundaries would have to be carefully constructed to satisfy the mainstream world while maintaining the unique aspects—the "specialness"—that the faithful had enjoyed throughout the nineteenth century. Boundaries had to be set that allowed the religious organization to maintain its integrity; however, those borders needed to be permeable enough to permit the passage of ideas and trends that would lead to acceptance by the world outside of the church community. The scriptural injunction that directed Christians to be in the world but not of the world not only became a prescriptive catchphrase for Mormons, it described the church's challenge on the eve of the twentieth century.[24]

Although Mormonism's transition from religious pariah to peaceful coexistence with other Americans took decades, after 1890 the church experienced a mighty change, an unanticipated thrust into the modern world. No geographical relocation was required, but the psychological, cultural, and spiritual transformation was every bit as wrenching as immigration had been for other Progressive-Era Americans. Immigrants and Mormons faced a new world where new vocabularies had to be mastered, rules adjudicated, and identities forged. Just like many Progressive reformers determined to "Americanize" immigrants, LDS recreational leaders sought to "Mormonize" the rising generation of post-polygamy young men and women. The desire to inculcate values, teach morals, and model exemplary behavior energized the recreational reforms sponsored by the Church of Jesus Christ of Latter-day Saints.[25]

The LDS Church's accommodation to the outside world after 1890 has been well chronicled by historians, within and outside of the faith. Most have noted that outside forces—primarily political—impinged on the church, wore down its resistance, and eventually convinced and coerced Mormon officials to set aside their separateness, renounce polygamy, and enter the mainstream currents of American thought and behavior. According to this view, the church was changed enormously through contact with the outside world. In large measure, especially in the political realm, this interpretation provides insight into the "Americanization" of the Mormon church and people.

Focusing only on the intrusion of unwanted power from the outside, however, fails to tell the whole story. As this analysis of LDS recreation during the early twentieth century shows, the church's contacts with the outside world were often complex and ambiguous. In designing and implementing recreation programs, church officials turned to outside "experts" to acquire ideas and techniques that would meet more adequately the recreational needs of church members.[26] In no way forced to seek or accept assistance from outside sources, Mormon leaders willingly cultivated contacts to help them solve their problems. Even though officials sought advice from non-LDS professionals and organizations, the church consistently used those borrowed techniques to strengthen church membership. Rather than wholesale "accommodation" to non-Mormon groups or value systems, Mormon recreation offers an example of "creative adjustment" that bolsters the historians Leonard J. Arrington and Davis Bitton in their contention that the church used worldly knowledge and contacts to insure the continuity of the group's unique institutions. Not "selling out" to Gentile experts, LDS leaders were cautiously "buying into" ideas that they could manipulate to their own ends.[27]

In many ways, the use of recreation to aid the creative adjustment of Mormons to the modern world closely resembles the role that sports played in the Americanization of many immigrant Jews in the early twentieth century. As detailed by Peter Levine, the children of Jewish immigrants "turned sportive experiences to their own ends in ways that paid attention both to traditional Jewish communal purpose and mainstream American values." Levine describes how sports became a "middle ground" where Jews could alter and adapt a "significant American cultural institution to serve ethnic community ends while encouraging their own enthusiasm for full integration into American life."[28] During the Progressive Era and beyond, sports and recreation programs allowed Jews and Mormons to accommodate to American culture without completely surrendering their "ethnic" identity.

As only one part of a complex religious organization, the recreational programs of the LDS Church ranged widely over the years and involved millions of Mormons at play. It would be foolhardy to suggest that any one study could cover the vast terrain of Mormon recreation in any period. Even in surveying such a small field as the decades between 1890 and 1940, volumes of material have been left out. Rather than create a catalog of activities, events, participants, and final scores, the following chapters represent an in-depth treatment of how particular programs in the church used recreation and sports to communicate Mormon morals, attitudes, and expectations. As an instrument of social persuasion—a method of teaching proper behavior—recreation programs instructed adolescents in what it meant to *be* Mormon. Though many other lessons were learned along the way, LDS leaders hoped that morals learned from games, hikes, and social activities would instill the faith of the nineteenth-century Mormon pioneers into the church's first urban generation.

To ascertain the depth and breadth of Mormon recreation, we will first turn to an examination of the development of a rationalized recreational philosophy within the church. Borrowing from myriad outside sources, church leaders organized a system of thought to guide recreational leaders in devising worthwhile activities. Next follows a discussion of the evolution of the articulation of sacred and secular space with the introduction of gymnasiums into LDS meetinghouses. As the demand for recreation increased in the early years of the century, Mormon leaders responded with a massive construction program that eventually incorporated gymnasiums as a major feature of LDS worship space. As part of chapter 2, the Deseret Gymnasium is analyzed as the Mormon "Temple of Health" where young Mormons learned the principles of physical salvation as well as the outlines of proper gender roles within the church. Chapter 3 explains what happened inside the newly constructed LDS gymnasiums and describes the important social role played by athletic programs in local and general church organizations. Moreover, the connection between prominent Mormon athletes and the construction of the new interpretation of the Word of Wisdom is used to explain the central role that athletics played in forging a new boundary between church members and the outside world. Moving beyond LDS gymnasiums, the Boy Scouts and Girls' Camps receive treatment in chapter 4. Hoping to link urban adolescents with their pioneer forebears, LDS leaders sponsored programs that temporarily removed young men and women from the city for rest, recuperation, and a recapitulation of the frontier experience of early Mormonism. The final chapter considers LDS recreational programs during the Great Depression of the 1930s. Forsaking the thematic approach, this chapter offers an example of the church using all of its recreational weapons to fight a particular challenge—economic depression. This chapter provides a fitting conclusion by tying all of the various strands together and showing the full-fledged LDS recreation program in action.

An analysis of Mormon efforts to organize recreation in the early twentieth century illuminates the evolution of Mormon society. Although federal persecution may have pushed some Mormons into the modern world, most went willingly. They often looked to outside sources for ideology and direction and then combined that knowledge with the inspiration they found within the church. By the Second World War, Mormons enjoyed social acceptance among mainstream Americans while maintaining an aura of slight separation from the larger society. No longer viewed as threatening polygamists or crackpot communitarians, Mormons joined the American middle class with its emphasis on private property, accumulation of wealth, and political conservatism. The church's recreational ideologies and activities help us comprehend the Americanization of the Latter-day Saints. As the historian Bruce C. Daniels describes, play patterns often reveal details about a social group that otherwise remain hidden: "Everyone plays; the need to do something for relaxation is built into the biology and psychology of human beings. The forms of play, however, are not universal but are a social construction shaped by specific physical circumstances, values, and history." Most importantly, Daniels continues, "A culture at play should tell much about itself. Patterns of leisure and recreation are manifestations of a society's core identity."[29] Just as Daniels deciphers the core elements of early New England religion by studying "Puritans at play," examining Mormon recreation reveals much about that religious group's "core identity."

Although this analysis of LDS recreation spans from the renunciation of polygamy in 1890 until the eve of the Second World War, the adjective "progressive" applies throughout. Scholars often mark the end of the Progressive Era with the First World War; for our purposes, however, the term "progressive" should not be considered merely in chronological terms. Rather, the recreational programs of the LDS Church, built on progressive principles and philosophies, persisted well into the 1930s and beyond. This is not meant to argue for a new periodization of the Progressive movement. It is meant to contend that ideas and concepts expounded during the Progressive Era continued to influence Mormon recreation well beyond the traditional death of progressivism around 1920. As shown by many of the programs of the New Deal, progressive philosophy was not a casualty of World War I, even though the Progressive Era might have been.[30]

Moreover, by analyzing a "progressive" recreation program far removed from the typical venues of Progressive social histories like Chicago and New York City, we learn that progressive philosophy had an impact well beyond

Hull-House and the huge metropolises. Progressive ideas are shown to have been plastic enough to shape the programs of a unique religious subgroup in a midsized western city. Although they will never be considered alongside Jane Addams and Lillian Wald, LDS leaders like Lyman R. Martineau and Amy Brown Lyman were engaged in the same "progressive" conversation as their more renowned counterparts.[31] By looking at LDS recreation schemes, it is clear that Mormon leaders followed the Progressive norm by applying the findings of social scientists to remake their urban world. Mormon leaders hoped that by instructing play leaders and constructing play spaces, young Mormons could find a moral alternative to the typical urban fare of corruption and wickedness. That such a wide-ranging program of recreational offerings was organized in Salt Lake City by a conservative religious organization reorients slightly our historical fixation with eastern urban areas. New York, Boston, and Chicago will certainly remain the historical settings of much Progressive-Era recreation scholarship. In the future, however, historians must widen their lens to include cities of lesser renown that were home to similar recreational reform efforts.

Finally, a note on Mormon terminology. The church's hierarchical organization is capped by the president of the church, a man revered as a modern-day prophet who leads the church through revelation from God. The president with two counselors forms the First Presidency, which, along with the Twelve Apostles, compose the ruling body of the organization. During the early twentieth century, the apostles were assisted by the First Council of the Seventy, men responsible for missionary work who were often called upon to assist the apostles in spiritual and administrative matters. A Presiding Bishop, assisted by two counselors, oversaw the church's temporal affairs. The men who led the church were considered "general authorities" in church matters, an ambiguous term that denotes official sanction. The church's auxiliary organizations (the women's Relief Society, Young Women's and Young Men's Mutual Improvement Associations, Sunday School, and children's Primary) were each run by a general board overseen by a president (or superintendent) and two counselors.

The church is organized into geographic domains known as stakes (like parishes) and wards (congregations). Several wards (the smallest denominational unit) compose a stake. Local lay leaders, called and confirmed by general authorities, officiate in presidencies (president and two counselors) on the stake level and bishoprics (bishop and two counselors) in each ward. Local leaders continue to hold outside jobs and work in the church on a volunteer basis. The lay priesthoods typically include worthy male members over the age of twelve. The lesser or Aaronic priesthood contains three offices (deacon, teacher, and priest, in ascending order) as does the superior Melchizedek priesthood (elder, seventy, and high priest). Organizational and spiritual direction is given in general conferences held each April and October. During the Progressive Era, the auxiliaries for the Young Men and Young Women held an annual conference in Salt Lake City each June.

Notes

1. Paul S. Boyer, *Urban Masses and Moral Order in America, 1820–1920* (Cambridge, Mass.: Harvard University Press, 1978), 130.

2. On the Progressive movement, see Steven J. Diner, *A Very Different Age: Americans of the Progressive Era* (New York: Hill and Wang, 1998); Nell Irvin Painter, *Standing at Armageddon: The United States, 1877–1919* (New York: W. W. Norton, 1987); Vincent P. DeSantis, *The Shaping of Modern America, 1877–1916* (Arlington Heights, Ill.: Forum Press, 1973); Robert H. Wiebe, *The Search for Order, 1877–1920* (New York: Hill and Wang, 1967); Richard Hofstadter, *The Age of Reform: From Bryan to F.D.R.* (New York: Vintage Books, 1955); Allen F. Davis, *Spearheads for Reform: The Social Settlements and the Progressive Movement, 1890–1914,* 2d ed. (New Brunswick, N.J.: Rutgers University Press, 1984); Jane Addams, *Twenty Years at Hull-House* (1910; rpt., Urbana: University of Illinois Press, 1990); Don S. Kirschner, "The Ambiguous Legacy: Social Justice and Social Control in the Progressive Era," *Historical Reflections* 2:1 (1975): 69–88; Daniel T. Rodgers, "In Search of Progressivism," *Reviews in American History* 10 (Dec. 1982): 113–32; Peter G. Filene, "An Obituary for the Progressive Movement," *American Quarterly* 20 (1970): 20–34.

3. David M. Kennedy, "Overview: The Progressive Era," *The Historian* 37 (May 1975): 468.

4. On Mormon polygamy, see B. Carmon Hardy, *Solemn Covenant: The Mormon Polygamous Passage* (Urbana: University of Illinois Press, 1992); Jessie L. Embry, *Mormon Polygamous Families: Life in the Principle* (Salt Lake City: University of Utah Press, 1987); Richard S. Van Wagoner, *Mormon Polygamy: A History* (Salt Lake City: Signature Books, 1986).

5. For the definitive biography of Wilford Woodruff, consult Thomas G. Alexander, *Things in Heaven and Earth: The Life and Times of Wilford Woodruff* (Salt Lake City: Signature Press, 1993). The announcement that ended church-sanctioned polygamy can be found as Official Declaration No. 1 in the Doctrine and Covenants.

6. Thomas G. Alexander, *Mormonism in Transition: A History of the Latter-day Saints, 1890–1930* (Urbana: University of Illinois Press, 1986), 14. Alexander's work is an indispensable resource for the history of the LDS Church in the twentieth century. Another examination of the post-polygamy church can be found in James B. Allen and Richard O. Cowan, *Mormonism in the Twentieth Century,* 2d ed. (Provo, Utah: Brigham Young University Press, 1967).

7. William B. Forbush, *The Boy Problem: A Study in Social Pedagogy* (Boston: Pilgrim Press, 1907).

8. For more on the "boy problem," see Clifford Putney, *Muscular Christianity: Manhood and Sports in Protestant America, 1880–1920* (Cambridge, Mass.: Harvard University Press, 2001), 99–105.

9. For more information on the history of gender relations in the church, see Maureen Ursenbach Beecher and Lavina Fielding Anderson, eds., *Sisters in Spirit: Mormon Women in Historical and Cultural Perspective* (Urbana: University of Illinois Press, 1987); Maxine Hanks, ed., *Women and Authority: Re-emerging Mormon Feminism* (Salt Lake City: Signature Books, 1992); Jill Mulvay Derr, Janath R. Cannon, and Maureen Ursenbach Beecher, *Women of Covenant: The Story of Relief Society* (Salt Lake City: Deseret Book, 1992).

10. Putney's *Muscular Christianity* offers an insightful look at how Protestant Americans used sports and other leisure-time activities to teach morals and masculinity to young men. Putney situates LDS recreational activities on the extreme edge of Protestant recreation. He writes, "The Mormon Church was the first to support Boy Scout troops, the first to erect a recreation hall wherein athletic competitions were held. . . . Why exactly they pioneered these forms of organized uplift is difficult to explain. Possibly it devolved somehow from their belief in familial, as opposed to individual, salvation: the notion that more important even than inner goodness was outward conformity to the laws of God and society" (53).

11. Boyer, *Urban Masses and Moral Order,* 190.

12. Steven A. Riess, *City Games: The Evolution of American Urban Society and the Rise of Sports* (Urbana: University of Illinois Press, 1989), 133–34.

13. Boyer, *Urban Masses and Moral Order,* 59.

14. One should not conclude, however, that participants in recreation programs did not use the games to "Americanize" themselves. In the Progressive Era, as today, sports were used as a means to gain entrance into the dominant American culture.

15. On "island communities," see Wiebe, *Search for Order,* 44–75.

16. Thomas G. Alexander and James B. Allen, *Mormons and Gentiles: A History of Salt Lake City* (Boulder, Colo.: Pruett Publishing, 1984), 159, 8–9. On the concept of island communities, consult Wiebe, *Search for Order.* On the elements of city life, see Gunther Barth, *City People: The Rise of Modern City Culture in Nineteenth-Century America* (New York: Oxford University Press, 1980). For cities with religious and cultural conflicts, see Carl V. Harris, *Political Power in Birmingham, 1871–1921* (Knoxville: University of Tennessee Press, 1971); Richard J. Jensen, *The Winning of the Midwest: Social and Political Conflict, 1888–1896* (Chicago: University of Chicago Press, 1971); Paul Kleppner, *The Cross of Culture: A Social Analysis of Midwestern Politics, 1850–1900* (New York: Free Press, 1970); and Paul Kleppner, *The Third Electoral System, 1853–1892: Parties, Voters, and Political Cultures* (Chapel Hill: University of North Carolina Press, 1977).

17. *Statistical Abstract of Utah, 1996 Centennial Edition* (Salt Lake City: Bureau

of Economic and Business Research, David Eccles School of Business, University of Utah, 1996), 28.

18. Alexander and Allen, *Mormons and Gentiles,* 105. For additional detail, consult Dean L. May, "A Demographic Portrait of the Mormons, 1830–1980," in *After 150 Years: The Latter-day Saints in Sesquicentennial Perspective,* ed. Thomas G. Alexander and Jessie L. Embry (Provo, Utah: Charles Redd Center for Western Studies, 1983), 39–69.

19. Richard L. Jensen and William G. Hartley, "Immigration and Emigration," in *Encyclopedia of Mormonism,* 5 vols., ed. Daniel H. Ludlow (New York: Macmillan, 1992), 2:673–76 (quote on 675).

20. Alexander and Allen, *Mormons and Gentiles,* 135.

21. Ibid. For more on Utah's ethnic groups, consult Stanford J. Layton, ed., *Being Different: Stories of Utah's Minorities* (Salt Lake City: Signature Books, 2001); Helen Z. Papanikolas, *The Peoples of Utah* (Salt Lake City: Utah State Historical Society, 1976); Richard L. Jensen, "Immigration to Utah," in *Utah History Encyclopedia,* ed. Allan Kent Powell (Salt Lake City: University of Utah Press, 1994), 270–73.

22. See Leonard J. Arrington and Thomas G. Alexander, *A Dependent Commonwealth: Utah's Economy from Statehood to the Great Depression* (Provo, Utah: Brigham Young University Press, 1974); Leonard J. Arrington, *The Changing Economic Structure of the Mountain West* (Logan: Utah State University Press, 1963); Allan Kent Powell, *Next Time We Strike: Labor in Utah's Coal Fields, 1900–1933* (Logan: Utah State University Press, 1985); Thomas G. Alexander, "From Dearth to Deluge: Utah's Coal Industry," *Utah Historical Quarterly* 31 (Summer 1963): 235–47; Owen Franklin Beal, *The Labor Legislation of Utah: With Special Reference to the Period of Statehood* (Logan, Utah: N.p, 1922); Helen Zeese Papanikolas, "The Great Bingham Strike of 1912 and the Expulsion of the Padrone," *Utah Historical Quarterly* 38 (Spring 1970): 121–33; Gunter Peck, "Padrones and Protest: 'Old' Radicals and 'New' Immigrants in Bingham, Utah, 1905–1912," *Western Historical Quarterly* 24 (May 1993): 157–78; Glenn V. Bird, "The Industrial Workers of the World in Utah: Origins, Activities, and Reactions of the Church of Jesus Christ of Latter-day Saints" (Master's thesis, Brigham Young University, 1976).

23. Jan Shipps, "In the Presence of the Past: Continuity and Change in Twentieth-Century Mormonism," in *After 150 Years,* ed. Alexander and Embry, 11–12.

24. See John 17:11–18.

25. This is not to say that Mormons, and Utahns generally, had not previously used sports contests and leisure activities to teach morals and values. For instance, Mormons and Gentiles played competitive baseball in the late nineteenth century to bolster Salt Lake City's image and to fit into the American mainstream. See Kenneth L. Cannon II, "Deserets, Red Stockings, and Out-of-Towners: Baseball Comes of Age in Salt Lake City, 1877–79," *Utah Historical Quarterly* 52 (Spring 1984): 136–57.

26. For our purposes, the terms "church leader" and "church official" are used to describe both the general authorities of the LDS Church and recreation program

leaders, like Mormon Boy Scout officials or Mutual Improvement Association (MIA) committee members. I have tried to include sufficient explanations about each historical actor to describe his or her connection to Mormon recreation.

27. The concept of "creative adjustment" is found in Leonard J. Arrington and Davis Bitton, *The Mormon Experience: A History of the Latter-day Saints* (1979; rpt., Urbana: University of Illinois Press, 1992), 243–61.

28. Peter Levine, *Ellis Island to Ebbets Field: Sport and the American Jewish Experience* (New York: Oxford University Press, 1992), 25. For an excellent collection of articles on the Jewish sporting experience, see Steven A. Riess, ed., *Sports and the American Jew* (Syracuse, N.Y.: Syracuse University Press, 1998). For more information on how ethnic groups used sports to assimilate into American society while maintaining group distinctions, consult the following: for the assimilation of French Canadians in Woonsocket, Rhode Island, see Richard Sorrell, "Sports and Franco-Americans in Woonsocket, 1870–1930," *Rhode Island History* 31 (Fall 1972): 117–26; Gary Ross Mormino describes how the Italian community in St. Louis used sports in "The Playing Fields of St. Louis: Italian Immigrants and Sport, 1925–1941," *Journal of Sport History* 9 (Summer 1982): 5–16.

29. Bruce C. Daniels, *Puritans at Play: Leisure and Recreation in Colonial New England* (New York: St. Martin's Press, 1995), xi.

30. The historian Daniel T. Rodgers argues that many of the innovations associated with the New Deal of the 1930s were influenced by progressive thought. He contends that "to a striking degree the New Deal enlisted its ideas and agenda out of the progressive past. Old-age and unemployment insurance, public housing, the National Labor Relations Act, the Fair Labor Standards Act, emergency work relief, rural electrification, banking and securities regulation, holding company legislation, and agricultural reform all had precrisis roots. In style, in urgency, in federal-state relations, and in political alliances there was no missing the administration's new departures. But as a legislative program, it is far more accurate to see the New Deal as a culmination: a great gathering in from the progressive political wings of a generation of proposals and ideas." See *Atlantic Crossings: Social Politics in a Progressive Age* (Cambridge, Mass.: Harvard University Press, 1998), 415. Sean Wilentz echoes Rodgers by describing "the emerging progressive era that culminated in the New Deal." See "A Scandal for Our Time," *American Prospect* 13 (25 Feb. 2002). For a different view on the continuities linking the Progressive Era and the New Deal, see Otis L. Graham Jr., *An Encore for Reform: The Old Progressives and the New Deal* (New York: Oxford University Press, 1967).

31. For more on the life of Amy Brown Lyman, see David Roy Hall, "Amy Brown Lyman and Social Service Work in the Relief Society" (Master's thesis, Brigham Young University, 1992).

CHAPTER ONE

"Not Playing without a Purpose"

The Construction of a Mormon Recreation Ideology

> It is my play, in my leisure hours,
> That I burst my bands and divert my powers;
> It is there that I enter false or true,
> To match my good or my bad with you;
>
> It is there that I score for pride or shame,
> As I tally square or foul the game,
> My best, my worst is released and free,
> And I play debased or gloriously!
> —BERTHA A. KLEINMAN, "In My Play" (1927)

To understand the hardscrabble early years of the Church of Jesus Christ of Latter-day Saints, a focus on recreation, merrymaking, and amusements might seem completely out of place. Compared with the organization's need to find new members, forge a hierarchical structure, and create settlements in the frontier West, the desire to have fun and relax paled in necessity and importance. Or so it would seem. Mormon leaders, however, beginning with Joseph Smith, recognized that recreation and wholesome amusements were not only necessary but beneficial. To create communities, whether religious bodies or frontier settlements, Mormon leaders stressed the positive aspects of uplifting diversions. By encompassing all aspects of life—including body, mind, and spirit—Mormonism represented a "new religious movement" that evinced a new religious attitude toward recreation.[1]

With the publication of the Book of Mormon in 1830, Joseph Smith announced to the world a bold departure from traditional Christianity. Relating the story of a group of Old World Jews that settled in the New World around 600 B.C.E., the book of scripture contains revelations, divine directives, and historical narrative. The highlight occurs near the book's conclusion, when a resurrected Jesus Christ visits the American continent and preaches many of the messages found in the Bible. This new scripture was the foundation on which Smith declared his prophetic calling and represented the earliest theological statements of the emerging religion. Not only did the book attempt to reorient the historical traditions of Christianity, it pronounced the attitude of the new religion toward pleasure. In fact, the Book of Mormon placed human happiness at the center of existence. In a crucial passage near the beginning of the book, the ancient prophet Lehi (the man in charge of the original group of immigrants in 600 B.C.E.) succinctly states the purpose of life: "Adam fell that men might be; and men are, that they might have joy."[2] The kernel of life, the very crux of creation, was human happiness. Religion, which provided for the ritual worship of God, was the critical element in the Mormon quest for "joy"; recreation, though secondary, would likewise help church members find religious joy. Religious recreation, even in the nineteenth century, played an integral role in the formation of the LDS Church and proved important to early church leaders.

The Prophet Joseph Smith fits more comfortably in the tradition of the rugged outdoorsman of the frontier than the retiring religious cleric of Puritan fame. Fond of jokes and quick with a laugh, the jocular prophet's muscular physique seemed more suited to frontier fields than to urbane divinity schools. His religion suited his personality. Convinced, as an 1832 revelation detailed, that "the spirit and the body are the soul of man," Smith set out to nourish both halves of his eternal soul.[3] So much for the Western religious supposition pitting spirit against body; in fact, in Smith's formulation, to find redemption for the soul, the spirit and body have to work together. It follows that what is good for the body is good for the soul.

Smith's penchant for the physical marked him as a new breed of religious leader. Wilford Woodruff's first contact with the prophet demonstrated Smith's unique approach to religion. Woodruff, who would later become the fourth president of the LDS Church, wrote of that initial meeting in his journal: "'Here for the first time in my life I met and had an interview with our beloved Prophet Joseph Smith. . . . My first introduction was not of a kind to satisfy the preconceived notions of the sectarian mind as to what a prophet ought to be, and how he should appear. It might have shocked the faith of some men. I found him and his brother Hyrum out shooting at a mark with a brace of pistols.'"[4] Perhaps even Woodruff himself was a little "shocked" at Smith's behavior. Such activities were not unusual for the prophet, however. Stories about him pulling sticks, wrestling, reading, and riding are legion in the lore and the history of the church. One account from Smith's *History* evinces the array of activities that filled a typical day. On 8 February 1843 the prophet recorded: "This morning, I read German, and visited with a brother and sister from Michigan, who thought that 'a prophet is always a prophet'; but I told them that a prophet was a prophet only when he was acting as such. After dinner Brother Parley P. Pratt came in: we had conversation on various subjects. At four in the afternoon, I went out with my little Frederick, to exercise myself by sliding on the ice."[5] Intellectual, spiritual, and physical exercise filled the prophet's day and comprised the major elements of Mormon cultural and spiritual life. As Smith's journal describes, there were no clear-cut boundaries separating spiritual, mental, and physical health. Mormonism combined all of the elements of life—just as the soul combined the spirit and the body.

Joseph Smith's belief in the positive power of play continued to influence the church after his death in June 1844. Brigham Young, who assumed authority as the head of the church after Smith's assassination, followed in the prophet's footsteps by extolling the virtue of wholesome recreation. Not athletic like his predecessor, Young pursued pleasure through drama and dance. Although amusements were curtailed for a time after the prophet's death (Young counseled the Saints in October 1844 that "it is not now a time for dancing or frolics but a time of mourning and of humiliation and prayer"), it did not take long for dancing and merrymaking to be renewed.[6] Childhood religious strictures regarding recreation had not inured the young Brigham to pleasure seeking; rather, they had increased his desire to join in appropriate activities as he matured. Looking back on his youth, Young recognized that forbidding fun was anathema to a religion that required both body and spirit:

> When I was young, I was kept within very strict bounds, and was not allowed to walk more than half-an-hour on Sunday for exercise. The proper and necessary gambols of youth having been denied me, makes me want active exercise and amusement now. I had not a chance to dance when I was young, and never heard the enchanting tones of the violin, until I was eleven years of age; and then I thought I was on the high way to hell, if I suffered myself to linger and listen to it. I shall not subject my little children to such a course of unnatural training, but they shall go to the dance, study music, read novels, and do anything else that will tend to expand their frames, add fire to their spirits, improve their minds, and make them feel free and untrammeled in body and mind. Let everything come in its season, place everything in the place designed for it, and do everything in its right time.[7]

Young feared that children who were not allowed to indulge in play were "more fit for companions to devils," because without the diversion offered by recreation, their "duty becomes loathsome to them."[8] Everything, including uplifting and wholesome recreation, had a proper time and place. Susa Young Gates recorded that her father's motto was, "Eight hours work, eight hours sleep, eight hours recreation."[9] All too familiar with the effects of proscribing recreational activities, Young made sure that church members were allowed to enjoy themselves.

Brigham Young's first revelation to the church, given at Winter Quarters in January 1847, instructed the Saints not to forget the important role of recreation. Despite the poverty and deprivation that overflowed the streets and shacks of their winter resting place on the central plains, the new prophet reminded the migrating Mormons: "If thou art merry, praise the Lord with singing, with music, with dancing, and with a prayer of praise and thanksgiving."[10] The ability to pray and to play helped the Saints cope with the treacherous conditions at Winter Quarters.[11]

To Brigham Young, the key to recreation was found in the word itself—diversionary pleasures actually re-created individuals, making them more fit for their daily labors. When asked why he permitted fiddling and dancing, Young replied, "that my body may keep pace with my mind. My mind labors like a man logging, all the time; and this is the reason why I am fond of these pastimes—they give me a privilege to throw every thing off, and shake myself, that my body may exercise, and my mind rest. What for? To get strength, and be renewed and quickened, and enlivened, and animated, so that my mind may not wear out."[12] On another occasion, Young advised, "Recreation and diversion are as necessary to our well-being as the more serious pursuits of life. There is not a man in the world but what, if kept at any one branch of business or study, will become like a machine. Our pursuits should be so diversified as to develop every trait of character and diversity of talent." Ironically, men and women needed recreation so that they could concentrate on the "more serious pursuits of life."[13]

Not all recreational activities were equal, however. Music, dancing, holiday parties, swimming, and picnicking among the Saints all received Young's approbation. Nonetheless, on many occasions, he warned church members against allowing innocent amusements to become illicit. Young knew from personal experience that merrymaking could quickly get out of hand. After asking, "Is there anything immoral in recreation?" he turned to his own family for a prescriptive example. "If I see my sons and daughters enjoying themselves, chatting, visiting, riding, going to a party or dance, is there anything immoral in that? I watch very closely, and if I hear a word, see a look, or a sneer at divine things or anything derogatory to a good moral character, I feel it in a moment, and I say, 'If you follow that it will not lead to good, it is evil.'"[14] Guarded carefully by the righteous, recreation could have a positive impact on the individual and society. Let loose among the wicked, however, and recreation had the potential to destroy character as well. Young seemed especially concerned that Mormons seek pleasure within the fold whenever possible. Mormon travelers far from Zion received a stern warning regarding their leisure time: "Never suffer yourselves to mingle in any of these recreations that tend to sin and iniquity, while you are away from the body of the Church, where you cannot so fully control yourselves."[15] In Young's mind, the license to recreate was restricted by the requirement that appropriate pleasure seeking was best regulated within the church.

A belief in restricted recreation—conducted within church parameters—prevailed among Mormon leaders throughout the nineteenth century. As the twentieth century dawned, however, and secular and religious authorities perceived a need for rationalized recreation, leaders of the LDS Church pursued a recognizable, comprehensive philosophy regarding the proper use of leisure time. From 1900 to 1930 they made a conscientious effort to define a recreational ideology and to disseminate it throughout the church through workshops, pamphlets, and educational opportunities.

Rise of Rational Recreation

As the nineteenth century waned, the proper use of leisure time became a major concern not only for Mormons but for many Americans. Beset by the social problems caused by urbanization and industrialization, Progressive-Era Americans looked to rationalized recreation to counteract the destructive tendencies toward the idleness, delinquency, and exploitation fostered by city life.

According to observers, an expansion of free time was at the root of many urban problems. While it seemed that there was never enough time for farmers and their families to finish their myriad tasks, city dwellers were confronted with the opposite problem—they found themselves with too much time on their hands. A combination of industrial and social factors had freed many urban workers from the twelve- and fourteen-hour days that had been commonplace a generation earlier. Labor organizations such as the Knights of Labor and the American Federation of Labor emphasized the shortening of the workday, and in the first decade of the twentieth century state governments began to cooperate with labor groups to limit the number of hours that women and children were allowed to work. The Supreme Court, in *Mueller v. Oregon* (1908), validated this type of governmental regulation by upholding an Oregon law limiting maximum working hours for women. By 1920 the average work week in the United States was fifty-one hours, down from sixty hours in 1890.[16]

In addition to the increasing amount of time away from work, the quest for rational recreation was advanced by the rise of sociology as a respect-

able and scientific field of study. America's burgeoning cities became labo-
ratories for newly minted sociologists. Particularly attuned to the importance
of environment, urban social scientists took recreation seriously and accorded it major prominence in their schemes to make urban spaces more
livable. Whether it was Jacob Riis's muckraking photographs or Jane
Addams's Hull-House, turn-of-the-century sociologists brought attention to
the shame of the cities and preached wholesome, directed recreation as a
form of salvation for urban dwellers, especially children.[17]

Settlement-house workers noticed the popularity of recreation programs
and used them to attract neighborhood children. Hull-House in Chicago
offered calisthenics, gymnastics, boys' clubs, and billiard tournaments.
Activities coalesced around the Hull-House gymnasium, which housed a
popular women's basketball team in addition to many other programs. Jane
Addams articulated the centrality of recreational programs in the settlement-
house movement but realized that volunteer reform efforts could not reach
all of the needy: "The young people in our clubs are comparatively safe, but
many instances come to the knowledge of Hull-House residents which make
us long for the time when the city, through more small parks, municipal
gymnasiums, and schoolrooms open for recreation, can guard from disas-
ter these young people who walk so carelessly on the edge of the pit."[18]
Supervised athletics even proved a recuperative salve to settlement-house
subjects who had already fallen into the proletarian pit of industrial America.
"Young people who work long hours at sedentary occupations, factories,
and offices," wrote Addams, "need perhaps more than anything else the
freedom and ease to be acquired from a symmetrical muscular development
and are quick to respond to that fellowship which athletics apparently afford more easily than anything else."[19] Parks, playgrounds, school sports,
church recreational programs, and settlement-house activities combined to
form a protective web around inner-city immigrant groups.

Building on developments in sociological theory, urban social reformers
constructed a "scientific" play philosophy to guide their efforts in the parks
and playgrounds of American cities. Dominick Cavallo, the foremost historian of the urban play movement, writes that play organizers, the reformers
in charge of rationalizing urban recreation, "did not want children to relax, or nonchalantly pass the time of day on playgrounds. Organized play
was a means of shaping mental and moral faculties: it had little in common
with the escapism of either sport or casual recreation. Organized play, as
play advocates were fond of pointing out, was educational, not recreational:
it was related to physical and psychological development as well as to political socialization."[20] Organized play was serious business to social reform-

ers who created a comprehensive play ideology that borrowed elements from the emerging disciplines of adolescent psychology and sociology.

Organized play's ideological centerpiece was psychologist G. Stanley Hall's concept of recapitulation. Hall asserted that each stage in an adolescent's social, psychological, and physical development "recapitulated" experiences of the child's ancient forebears. For example, the restless energy of ten- and eleven-year-olds corresponded to the nomadic era of human history; likewise, the adolescent's attachment to peer groups re-created the tribal experience of the distant past. Because ancient men and women relied on their muscles and instincts for moral direction, wrote Hall, the best way to inculcate morality was through muscle development. Marching, physical drills, and supervised play habituated children in the ways of proper social behavior. Although the scientific basis of Hall's conclusions was widely challenged, his core concept of instilling morality through muscles found widespread acceptance. Other play theorists, like James Mark Baldwin and John Dewey, built on Hall's conception of play as the mediator between child and society. Baldwin maintained that organized play efforts should be designed to take advantage of the child's innate desire to imitate. Ripe with the potential for social control, play (and especially team games) taught children proper social roles and the need to subsume personal desires to the expectations of the social group. Dewey's instrumental theory of knowledge held that play situations permitted children to "act out" social roles until they became habitual.

Though the theories of organized play operated on different principles, most play theorists agreed that "mind, body, and emotions were not distinct, separate 'faculties' but existed on a fluid continuum, interpenetrating each other." The belief that "external conditioning could change the child's inner world" challenged the nineteenth-century separation of mind and body and the assumption that the mind was superior. Taken together, these psychological theories provided the ideological basis undergirding the call for rationalized recreation.[21]

In their quest to shape the modern moral landscape, sociologists and reformers converged on the need to create green urban space where children could play, far away (in attitude if not geography) from alleys and street corners. Sensing that a "back-to-the-farm" movement would affect at best a small percentage of the swelling urban masses, reformers brought the farm to the city. Urban green spaces—often directed by trained social workers—became the linchpin of what was termed the playground movement. While creating a space for children to amuse themselves, play experts likewise created a space for themselves in new professional organizations. In 1906, the Playground Association of America (later the National Recreation Association) was founded to advocate supervised children's play in municipal playgrounds across the United States.[22]

Siren Songs of Salt Lake City

The social problems that beset American cities likewise struck at the Mormon community, which was concentrated in the Mountain West states primarily along the Wasatch mountains in northern Utah. As the twentieth century dawned, Salt Lake City (the headquarters of the church since its arrival in Utah) was experiencing the pains of urban growth. As elsewhere, growth in population meant an increase in social problems and adolescent delinquency. Moreover, expanding city boundaries fostered opportunities to perpetrate sins of commission by participating in urban evils and sins of omission by remaining idle and lazy. City street corners seemed to sing a two-versed siren song that lured youngsters toward illicit activities and idleness.

While it was not quite Gomorrah, Salt Lake's urban attractions included myriad opportunities for lounging and more lascivious behavior. Daily attendance at the city's eighteen movie houses ran as high as fifteen thousand, with as many as 35 percent of attendees under the age of eighteen. One sociological survey of Salt Lake in the 1920s worried that "many of the pictures offered . . . are unwholesome to a dangerous degree, by reason of their emphasis upon and vivid portrayal of sex indulgence, drunkenness, burglary, robbery, suicide, murder, and other forms of vice and lawlessness." When young men and women were not attending the movies in Salt Lake, they could find other entertainment at five public dance halls or a variety of smaller roadhouses. After a night of drinking and "dating up" at a roadhouse, couples commonly drove off "into some lonely or poorly-lighted part of town and indulge[d] themselves sexually." In some places, prostitutes, pimps, and bootleggers openly sold their products. Additionally, many adolescents sought refuge in the sixty pool halls around the city. Particularly popular with teenage boys, the halls provided a less-than-wholesome venue for "hanging out."[23] With population growth came the urban problem of commercialized recreation, and the Mormon capital was no exception.

Though similar to social reformers in other urban areas, Mormons in Salt Lake City had some unique concerns about the rise of urban life. First, some Mormons feared that the ease of city life had destroyed the physical and spiritual vitality of the rising generation. Like the Puritan divines more than two centuries earlier, Mormon spiritual leaders wondered how they would be able to hold onto third-generation members of the church. Adolescents around the turn of the century were less likely to respond to the "bloody shirt" of Joesph Smith's martyrdom. Rather, new methods of attraction and retention were needed to lure young people off the streets and into meetinghouses. Cataloging the urban vices that young Mormons faced, Joseph F. Smith, the first counselor in the First Presidency and a nephew of the Prophet Joseph, firmly focused on the errant generation:

> I hope . . . that we will, above all other things, look after the welfare and salvation of the souls of our young men who are wandering in darkness, being left by their parents to grow up like weeds. We have more work to do right here in Zion, in the way of instructing the youth of Zion, and in preaching the gospel to our own children, than out in the world. . . . Right here at home, under the very droppings of the sanctuary, where we ought to see eye to eye, and where our children ought to be growing up true to the covenants of the gospel and interested with the people of God, we find them by the hundreds in the different stakes of Zion associated with the elements that are of the world. We see them smoking their cigars, their pipes, their cigarettes, and chewing their tobacco; we see them loitering around the whiskey saloons and places of amusement.

As if to affirm the declension that separated the mischief makers from their pious parents, Smith pointed his finger at the unconverted generation. "Inquire who they are," the apostle intoned, "and you will find that they are the children of parents who have joined The Church in the old world, perhaps, or in different parts of the United States, and have gathered to Zion for the love of the gospel, and yet their children are growing up in this way. . . . What a field there is for us right here at home, and how necessary it is for us to do something to reclaim these young men, and bring them to a realization of their condition."[24]

Several years earlier, Elder Smith spoke in similar terms in denouncing "a class of young men growing up in the cities":

> They have broken loose from all healthy restraint; they do as they please; they incline to deviltry and rowdyism; love fast living; visit the restaurants for their meals; rent quarters in the business part of the city, so that they can come and go at all hours of the day and night without being disturbed or questioned, and have abandoned home living and influence because it abridges them in their revelries. No common pleasures satisfy them; each day must see new sensations to thrill the passions and appetites. To mention the society of the Saints, Sunday schools, meetings, improvement associations, as places where the happiness may be enjoyed, is to them like bidding a king to feed on husks. They despise these institutions and the society therein as simple, fit for children, old folks and fools, not for "bloods" and their style of citizen.

Smith, though, was quick to remind the young men that rural areas also contained trouble spots—restaurants, the corner grocery, the post office, and the town loafing place were specifically indicted. Rural sins, however, were not cast in the same light as their urban counterparts; the "light-mindedness and indifference" of country boys did not exact the same stinging rebuke given to city dwellers.[25] Examples abound of LDS adults questioning the dedication and the hardiness of adolescents in the century's first decade.[26]

A fictionalized account, edited by Susa Young Gates, captures the perceived problem of indolence and ease caused by urban living. Writing a letter to a son traveling to a distant mission field, the fictional mother chastises her boy for grumbling about not being able to take a sleeper car on the train ride east. The mother writes:

> You are city-bred, my son, and have been reared in a comfortable home; and this fact may often be a drawback to you. Your father has spent so many nights on the far off hills, alone, with but the bark of the coyotes for company and his saddle for a pillow, that he thought your velvet-cushioned seat was a splendid place for a night's rest. I, too, have lain many nights on the ground, in the early days of Utah, as we traveled to and fro; and I am glad, now, that I have had all such experiences. Never complain at circumstances; first, because it is useless; and, second, because they are provided especially for your trial and, therefore, for your development.[27]

Unlike the pastoral scenes of nineteenth-century Utah, where coyotes sung ranchers to sleep and stiff saddles forged strong character, Mormons in twentieth-century cities too often fell victim to urban predators that preyed on adolescents and devoured physical and spiritual strength. Twentieth-century Mormons, however, had no halfway covenant solution to insure that a wayward generation would remain in the fold. Instead, inventive methods of inviting youngsters to church were the order of the day. Church-sponsored recreation, rationalized by academic study and sociological principles, became a potent weapon in the war against youthful "declension."

But, as Joseph F. Smith indicated, the sole blame for wayward children could not be placed on the broad-shouldered city. Parents in urban Zion had been shirking their responsibility to raise righteous offspring. After listing a litany of youthful offenses, including smoking "miserable cigarettes," loafing, creating trouble, and acting "smart," the editor of the *Improvement Era* asked, "why should such characters grow up in the midst of the Saints?" Answering his own question, he pinned the problem on parents: "I say it is due to the infidelity, indifference and neglect of parents. They certainly do not live in conformity with the Gospel which we have embraced, for in that case the result with their children would be widely different. Or, if they believe the precepts of the Gospel, they certainly have neglected to practice and teach the young people these things, which is a proof in itself that they have miserably failed in obeying one of its vital teachings."[28]

Children were not the only ones going astray on the streets of Salt Lake City. Parents had problems, too; namely, mothers and fathers were not paying enough attention to their children. Throughout the 1920s, articles in the *Improvement Era* bemoaned the negligence of parents. One poignant poem captures the impact that a father might have had:

> What's that you say: "The same old tale,
> Father a stranger to his boy."
> "Joe's idle, leisure time sent him to jail,
> And wrecked his father's pride and joy."
>
> Oh, men, when will you ever see
> That minutes make the hour—the day.
> That what your boys will finally be
> Is what they think and act and play.
>
> He was a boy, a wee small lad,
> With smiling eyes and ruddy face.
> A stranger to his busy dad,
> Allowed to run most any place.[29]

Along the same lines, a "college senior" wrote about memories that he wished he had—memories of a caring, involved father. Striking a sad chord, the young man longed to remember "just one talk in which we had discussed together the problems and facts that trouble every growing boy, on which his clear and vigorous viewpoint might have shed such light and comfort, instead of leaving me to pick up the facts haphazardly as I might, and to solve the problems as best I could."[30] Absent and uninvolved parents (especially fathers) provided another problem that pushed Mormon leaders toward an increased emphasis on church-sponsored recreation.

Of particular concern to observers in the Mormon community was the increasing laxity toward Sabbath observance. The vices of the city and the pervasive fear of declension in the rank and file appear in the struggles of church leaders to regulate Sunday behavior. One *Improvement Era* editorial spelled out some of the reasons that young (as well as middle-aged) Mormons gave for missing their meetings. To explain the "apathetic feeling about attending meetings," the editor argued that the primary cause was a "breakdown of the traditional obligations to attend [Sunday worship services], which earlier in the Church was rightly set down and considered as a duty." The fact that Mormons now suffered no social penalty for Sabbath breaking was a far cry from the days when "a member who failed to attend his meetings was often severely criticised by his teachers and bishop, and even considered to be a backslider." Clearly, at least in the eyes of the editor, the LDS community had lost the ability to apply social pressure to keep members on the straight and narrow. The second cause of Sabbath breaking was an increase in the "number and variety of Sunday amusements." Such Sabbath diversions included trips to the lakes and canyons, music halls, buggy or carriage rides into the country, parties, socials, and other entertainments. "You have noticed how time for diversion and amusement can always be found by people who can find no time for religious worship," wrote Joseph F. Smith in one sharp condemnation.[31] Sabbath breakers seemed to be winning the spiritual war for control of the Lord's day, and the control over wholesome recreation was at the heart of the battle.

Though Mormons recognized honoring the Sabbath day as one of the cardinal commandments of Christianity, LDS leaders believed that inappropriate Sunday activities were not only spiritual sins but caused social problems as well. First, Sabbath breaking often was the first step toward other illicit activities. Warning parents that "sons and daughters have been led astray through their being turned loose at night, going to miserable shows, dance halls, resorts, and cheap penny entertainments," Joseph F. Smith argued that the road to such immoral activities often began with the breaking of the fourth commandment. "Many of these abominable habits," the church leader claimed, "are started by failure to properly observe the Sabbath day."[32] The pathway of salvation led to the chapel door on Sunday morning; the primrose path of destruction started when one stepped away from Sabbath observance. Furthermore, Sabbath breakers not only stunted their own spiritual growth, they also provided a bad example that might lead others into improper activities. When asked by a young brother what harm there was in breaking the Sabbath, Dr. James X. Allen replied that such behavior placed a "stumbling-block in the path of those who are jealous of the Lord's day."[33] Breaking the Sabbath was often a social activity. The greatest impact might be felt in the inner life of the sinner, but the community also paid a price for desecrating the holy day.

Most histories of Progressive-Era recreation conclude that industrialization and urbanization led to the call for more wholesome and socially beneficial recreation. Viewed from the widest perspective, these social changes also played an important role in motivating Mormons to take recreation more seriously. Other local factors, however, including declension from pioneer fortitude, parental neglect, and laxity in keeping the Sabbath, prompted LDS leaders to place recreational pursuits under the agency of the church. Although efforts to rationalize Mormon recreation proceeded haltingly at first, the first quarter of the twentieth century witnessed the development and dissemination of a comprehensive leisure-time philosophy based on the seven theoretical "urges" of humankind.

Melange of Early Ideas

Although a singular ideology would eventually dominate Mormon recreation, a variety of ideas persisted as the LDS play philosophy developed. Around the turn of the twentieth century, many commentators feared that leisure time led to physical and spiritual decay. Believing that work was the best palliative to leisure-time problems, they thought it was better to avoid leisure time than to manage it to good ends. One article in the *Era* claimed:

> It is the man of voluntary or compelled leisure who mopes, and pines, and thinks himself either into the mad house or the grave. Motion is all nature's law. Action is man's salvation, both physical and mental. And yet nine out of ten are wistfully looking forward to the coveted hour when they shall have leisure to do nothing, or something only if they "feel like it"—the very siren which has lured to death many a successful man. He only is truly wise who lays himself out to work till life's latest hour; and he is the man who will live the longest, and will live to the most purpose.[34]

A stark contrast was drawn between work and leisure. Work produced the mental and physical health of a fulfilling life, while leisure often lured the successful man toward death. This perspective, however, was only one of many philosophies about work and leisure that made up the melange of Mormon recreational beliefs.

Three months later, in September 1898, another statement in the same church magazine presented an altogether different leisure-time ideology. Rather than avoid free time, recreation was to be taken in moderation to refresh the mind and reinvigorate the body. While this statement similarly contended that the "idler is never happy," persons filling their free time with wholesome recreational activities were not considered idle. Work was no longer the only productive pursuit. In fact, work that was not leavened with wholesome diversion was harmful. Moderation—the key word in Mormon recreation in the early part of the century—constituted the central element of a full life. The article advised,

> To take no amusement is bad, for it deprives the mind of needful rest and recreation; so likewise is it bad to be altogether given up to amusement, for then all se-

rious objects are lost sight of. The true plan is to take amusement in moderation. To be very much in society is sure to cause the human character to deteriorate, making it frivolous, and incapacitating it for taking abstract and elevated views; on the other hand, a perfect solitary life weakens the mind, lays it open to odd fancies and eccentricities, if not to hypochondria, and ends in some instances by altogether throwing it from its balance. The medium here is alone found salutary. Even in the simplest points of behavior an extreme is to be condemned. To be excessively gay, in a world where so many onerous things call for our attention, is wrong; so is it to be always serious, seeing that the world also contains material for much happiness, and that gaiety to a certain extent is positively salutary.[35]

The call here is for all things in moderation. If too much work makes for dull boys, in other words, then so might too much play. Neither work nor play is privileged to stand alone; they must work in tandem. The article concludes that those who take pleasure in both occupation and recreation are less likely to submit to temptation.

The relationship between occupation and recreation reflects the ideological preeminence of work among early twentieth-century Mormon leaders. The connection was articulated by the LDS educator George H. Brimhall in October 1899: "Leisure is purchased by labor, and the person who endeavors to possess the former before the latter lives the life of a down-going debtor from start to finish."[36] Work and play were connected, but it was perfectly clear which was master and which was servant. Work was championed because it helped youngsters ward off the evils of idleness. "Aside from financial considerations," wrote Lewis A. Merrill, a professor of agriculture at the Utah Agricultural College (UAC), "every young man in Zion should have an occupation, because of the security it furnishes against all those evils which result from idleness and a luxurious mode of life; or, in other words, because of its influence on the moral and social natures." Work not only produced in the economic sense, it helped boys to stay out of trouble. "[T]he young man who finds regular employment is not found around street corners, indulging habits which tend to his moral degradation," promised the professor.[37]

Though productive employment qualified as the superior virtue, all jobs were not created equal. Some jobs were not desirable, according to Edwin F. Parry, especially those involving sports and recreation. "While such occupations [in sports and amusements] are all right for the sake of recreation or entertainment, they are not the most preferable callings for our young people to follow as business. . . . With many an aspiring youth there seems to be a desire to acquire talents that can be displayed before the public in preference to others of more real value." As evidence of his assertion, Parry argued, "Some men display wonderful skill in marksmanship with a gun, or in performing upon a trapeze or a tight rope, and yet the only use to which they apply this ability is that of giving public exhibitions with perhaps less practice and perseverance, they might have learned to run a locomotive or to even engineer the construction of a railway." Leisure was integrally connected to work, but young men should not let their leisure become their work—work's "real value" should not be tinged by too close an association with play.[38]

To Mormons living at the turn of the twentieth century, the sometimes complementary relationship between work and leisure assumed a lower priority than the often antagonistic connection between leisure and salvation. As Apostle Francis M. Lyman described in 1899, "We do not live simply for enjoyment or to occupy our time in some certain direction to amuse or be pleasant to us in this life, but for the salvation and redemption of the children of God."[39] Spiritual exigencies superceded physical and social interests. Mormons have never questioned the priority of the spiritual. In the two decades after Elder Lyman segregated the spiritual and the social, other Mormon leaders created a philosophy that more fully integrated leisure-time pursuits into the community's spiritually based worldview. By the mid-1920s, recreation was accepted not only as socially redemptive but as spiritually salvific as well.

Inching toward Organization

The definition of a "Mormon" philosophy of recreation and the creation of an institutional approach to providing leisure-time activities proceeded in fits and starts after 1900. Mormons have always sought recreation, and from time to time LDS leaders had made pronouncements concerning the appropriateness of certain leisure-time pursuits. At the close of the nineteenth century, however, the church lacked a coherent, recognizable ideology concerning the human need for recreation. Moreover, little had been done within the organization to foster a permanent role for the church in providing wholesome recreation for church members. From 1900 to 1930, the church underwent a sea change as a recreation philosophy emerged and church-sponsored recreational activities flourished as never before.

The first offensive maneuver in the Mormon battle against illicit recreation was announced at the MIA's conference in June 1906, when the officers of the church-wide Young Men's Mutual Improvement Associations (YMMIA) were instructed to cooperate with ward amusement committees in overseeing the leisure-time activities of each local unit. The announcement offered an appropriate mix, acclaiming the importance of recreation and denouncing the pastiche of improper activities presented to too many young members of the church. The amusement committees provided an organizational base within the church where recreation could be brought under control. Outlining "pernicious habits" that had infected the church's young people, the announcement lamented, "We learn with much regret that from various causes some of our young men have fallen into evil habits, such as profanity, using tobacco, and liquor, frequenting saloons and pool rooms, and spending considerable time loafing on street corners, all of which is demoralizing." Card playing, buggy riding, and playing baseball on the Sabbath rounded out the list of undesirable activities. The statement argued that misguided recreation was more than a social problem; spiritual values were also at stake. Young men were "to assist in eradicating these evils, and we urge them not to countenance unprofitable, nay *sinful* recreation on the Sabbath day." Recreation itself was not sinful, but improper activities at inappropriate times could not be condoned. Local amusement committees could help counterbalance the tendency toward such "*sinful* recreation."[40]

The rationale for the formation of ward amusement committees bespoke the growing importance accorded to recreational activities. In language that would become the cornerstone of church-sponsored recreation, the YMMIA leaders proclaimed: "Recreation and amusement are indispensable to our social and moral development, but should be under the same vigilance and control as our religious training." The time had come to pull in the reins on recreation, and the "best method for this control is to co-operate with the ward amusement committee for each ward, under whose direction excursions, picnics, dances, etc., should be given." Again playing on the ability of leisure time to uplift or to destroy, the announcement prescribed, "Excursions to canyons and other resorts, should always be conducted by proper chaperones. Dancing parties, beginning and ending at reasonable hours, are proper enough, if not indulged in to excess; but we regard the public dancehall, with its promiscuous and unselected patrons as a menace to the morals of any community. Too much dancing is not commendable. It encourages late hours, mental lethargy, and intellectual laziness." To reorient recreational behavior, the new ward committees stressed more vocal and instrumental music, drama, and uplifting literary works. Leaders hoped that "all our members can engage in these better recreations and thereby gather more zeal for the more serious spiritual work."[41] The first steps had been taken on the road to rational recreation in the church.

Wards and stakes quickly organized activities, programs, and institutes that were designed to increase church control over leisure time. Church officials from northern Utah's Weber Stake prepared a course of study for the summer of 1907. Leaders feared that during the summer months—when the Mutual Improvement Associations traditionally took a hiatus—young men and women encountered more opportunities for illicit pleasure seeking. Following closely the injunction given to amusement committees, Weber Stake created a program with a "literary and musical rather than a theological character, even though there is a religious element about it."[42] Summer evenings were spent singing, encouraging the young people in their church work, and reading good literature. Local association officials reported beneficial returns, particularly when young men and women worked together.

As the demand for local church-sponsored recreation grew, so did the need for church members who had the ability to run programs effectively. Accordingly, the General Boards of the YMMIA and the Young Ladies' Mutual Improvement Association (YLMIA) offered training courses in sports and recreational leadership. At least three separate courses were held in 1912 alone. A circular letter sent in November 1912 to the superintendents of stakes and to bishops outlined "the immediate need in all the wards of the Church for leaders and trained men in athletics, field sports and boy scout work" and announced a four-week training program. The costs for tuition, books, and board were expected not to exceed thirty-five dollars.[43] A course for leaders of the young women was held at the same time. Under the direction of Anne Nebeker, seven women attended the conference held at the Deseret Gymnasium in Salt Lake City.[44]

Because the training institutes required a significant commitment from participants, organizers worried that young men with "sufficient education and ability to become leaders" would be unable to attend because they were "so engaged in business and professional duties" that they could not afford the time away from the office. Rather than forego the opportunities for recreational training, church leaders set their sights on young men who were not involved with either business or church activities. "Young men who may not be identified with Mutual work, and who may now be spending their time to very little purpose at home," they thought, could benefit from this course and "develop into successful leaders and trainers." To young men seemingly uninterested in worldly or spiritual affairs, "the nature of the work [in recreation] is such that it becomes fascinating to boys who ofttimes find little or no interest in other activities." To underscore the importance of training young men to serve their wards as recreation experts, the MIA Normal Training Course in Athletics was compared to the most important Mormon rite of passage—missionary service for the church. "Many young men are neither able nor qualified to go on foreign missions," read an announcement for the training session, "but could and would, if they were called, take this course, and we are safe in saying that no other brief mission would be of greater benefit to them." Every ward was requested to send at least one young man to receive intense instruction in track and field events, scout work, swimming, games, and dancing.[45]

Mormon leaders made church recreation a high priority as well. B. H. Roberts, one of the Seven Presidents of Seventy, made clear the important place of recreation in the church in a 1912 address entitled "Physical Development." To create a viable ideology regarding leisure time, Elder Roberts borrowed from the old philosophy that linked a sound mind with a sound body. From his address:

> I would urge upon the officers of the association to regard this work of physical development as a very essential part of our labors, and just as sacred as when our efforts are devoted to the spiritual and the moral. Of course it is a commonplace that a "sound mind in a sound body" is the acme of human desire; and the thought is growing, that you cannot have a completely sound mind, nor can that mind attain to its best functions and highest development, without the accompaniment also of a sound body. And that, parents of the youth of Israel, is what we are working at in our play. We are not playing without a purpose. We are not seeking to take the youth of Zion and direct their physical activities in their amusements, we are not working at that, without a purpose, and that purpose is the development of the spirit of manliness in your sons and the spirit of womanliness in your daughters.[46]

Recreation in the church, according to Roberts, was not only about keeping young men and women out of trouble. Instead, church leaders and youth organizations should harness the positive power of recreation to foster spiritual growth in young Mormons; there was a purpose to church-organized play. Although by 1912 the LDS Church was sponsoring recreation events and training local recreation leaders, there had yet to develop any coherent leisure-time ideology. There may have been a purpose in play, but only in embryonic form. Following Roberts's call, the church entered a phase in which the purpose of play was intensively investigated, a philosophy of recreation was pronounced, and recreation training opportunities flowered. From 1912 to 1929, concerns about recreation took center stage for Mormon adolescents and adults.

The next effort to place recreation more securely under the control of church leaders was the appointment of traveling secretaries in the YMMIA to oversee the recreational activities of young men throughout the church. An athletic director, Dr. John Harris Taylor, was installed in September 1911 to administer the sports and amusement program in the church youth organization. In June 1913, Oscar A. Kirkham was named as the first traveling secretary for the organization. As the "mental and spiritual director" of the boys, Kirkham had the responsibility to "inspire and guide the higher activities of our young men . . . [and to] direct the reading, debating, the class work, and very much of the convention work of the organization."[47]

In framing a leisure-time philosophy, church leaders looked beyond their local borders. Although there were some recreation guidelines delineated in LDS scripture, they were for the most part too vague to use as the foundation for a comprehensive recreational program. With little to draw from in the LDS canon, Mormon leaders turned to outside experts for advice, authority, and recreational dogma. The first attempt to cull methodically from knowledgeable sources outside the church was the publication of *Parents' Bulletin No. 1: Recreation and Play* in 1914.

Published by the Deseret Sunday School Union (church recreation would not come under the control of the MIA and Primary until 1923), the bulletin was designed for use in the parents' classes of the Sunday School. Compiled by Dr. E. G. Gowans, the superintendent of the State Industrial School and a member of the Parents' Class Committee of the General Board, the pamphlet contained excerpts about play written by nationally prominent sociologists, social workers, and play theorists. Recognizing that much of the Mormon situation differed from the problems reported by many of the experts, the preface insisted: "[W]e can find in their discussions many things of worth to us and to our children. . . . [T]heir thoughts will stimulate our discussions, and make us better able to solve our particular problems." Parents and leaders were to make the modifications necessary to fit local needs. "Read it thoughtfully and with discrimination," the preface advised, "and extract from it those things which are in keeping with our Gospel and apply in your daily lives the good things you find therein."[48]

Parents' Bulletin No. 1 repeated the fears of turn-of-the-century Mormon leaders—urban commercialized recreation and the lack of parental involvement at home. On both fronts, the Sunday School Union believed that church members were "paying very dearly today for our pleasures." "Are not most of the evils that trouble us today an outgrowth of improper play?" asked Gowans. Such a potent force could not be left unchecked. Arguing that schools had been created to train the minds of children and churches had been established to take care of their spirits, it was now time to focus on controlling the physical side of children—the "most important phase of life." Rather than relinquish recreational control to the money mongers of commercialized play, Mormons needed to place recreation within the confines of the church. Dr. Gowans could not have been more emphatic: "The time is on us when we must take this phase of life into our own hands and provide wholesome pastimes for our children just as systematically, just as religiously, as we provide for their educational instruction and their religious training."[49] *Parents' Bulletin No. 1* enlisted expert help from outside the church to bring recreation back inside the fold.

Bulletin No. 1 also chastised parents. After all, the pamphlet was designed to help them do a better job of raising their children. Mothers and fathers—consumed by home duties, work, and religious responsibilities—had allowed other attractions to lure their attention from their children. Parents were reminded of the importance of play for both children and adults. Wholesome leisure within the family played a critical role in creating responsible children and functional families. Parents neglected play at their peril. "Play is just as natural as work," the pamphlet advised. "Parents who lose the play spirit are likely to lose their children's souls. Our parents must get out of the bad habit of growing old; they must learn how to keep the spirit of youth; they must play with their children." Maintaining the spirit of play prepared a child to receive the Spirit of God. Recreation had become a religious obligation. Gowans made the connection explicit: "Our homes will be happier and more spiritual just in proportion to the spirit of play that is kept within them. . . . The father who plays with his boy, or mother who plays with her girl, are far more likely to save their souls than those who merely clothe and feed and school. . . . [I]f [parents] apply the suggestions that come from the study, our homes will reflect the spirit of good cheer, true companionship, and holiness."[50] Whereas most recreation proponents sought to save the city, Mormon recreational leaders wanted to save souls.

The experts quoted in *Parents' Bulletin No. 1* comprise a who's who list of important play theorists in the early twentieth century. Recreation advocates, including Joseph Lee (vice president of the Massachusetts Civic League), Jane Addams, William Byron Forbush (child expert), and Dr. Luther H. Gulick (the president of the Playground Association of America) appear on the pages of the bulletin. Topics covered included the eroticism of popular songs;[51] the evil side of the dance halls of Chicago; the relationship between the movies and juvenile crime; sex education through dance; and the moral value of play. Mormon parents found further opportunities to learn from recreational experts in a list of reference books provided at the back of the pamphlet. Works ranged from Edward Alsworth Ross's *Sin and Society* and Edwin Asbury Kirkpatrick's *Fundamentals of Child Study* to William Arch McKeever's *Farm Boys and Girls*. Parents were even directed to study *Hans Brinker*.[52] No stone was left unturned in the Mormon quest for expert advice that would promote wholesome recreation.

Of particular interest to LDS leaders may have been the discussion of recreation's ability to integrate individuals within larger groups. As part of a continuing effort to encourage individuals to identify with and be loyal to the church, leaders sensed the possibilities that play might provide. In an article describing "Play and Democracy," Dr. Luther H. Gulick spoke in terms that youth leaders could easily apply to the church:

> The older children learn lessons in the mutual relationships by sharing the use of swings, by having to play by the rules of the game. Later on, as they form into teams, they learn that self-sacrifice which is involved in the team game. They learn that the social unit is larger than the individual unit, that individual victory is not as sweet as the victory of the team, and that the most perfect self-realization is won by the most perfect sinking of one's self in the welfare of the larger unit—the team. Thus the child learns to control himself because he is not externally controlled.[53]

What worked for the "team" would surely succeed in the church as well. Expert advice modified to fit local situations formed the backbone of the emerging LDS leisure-time philosophy, as shown by the Sunday School Union's *Bulletin No. 1.*

The Sunday School Union did not stand alone in its concern about the social behavior of Latter-day Saints. Joseph F. Smith, in a January 1917 *Improvement Era* article, proclaimed, "Direction in social conduct and proper control of amusements are really among our most pressing problems at this time." Discussing proper dress standards and conduct at social gatherings and dances, the church president called for "[d]eportment that will lead to clean, innocent, genuine pleasure, and steer far away from the kind that in the end leaves a sting of sin, sorrow and regret—deportment that will herald the making of true men and women of character."[54] For years, President Smith and other church leaders had asked for such reforms. At the YLMIA-YMMIA conference in June 1915, the subject of dress and dancing had been discussed, and a joint meeting of Young Men and Young Women had agreed to a series of regulations governing their social gatherings. By December 1916, however, there had been "little improvement in this line." Outraged that even after the MIA guidelines had been created LDS daughters continued to go "half-naked before the public," Smith and the First Presidency commissioned a joint committee to direct the church on matters of social policy. The Social Advisory Committee (SAC)—with members from the Relief Society, Primary, and YLMIA—created "unified plans and a systematic course of actions" to reform individual and church activities.[55]

The project was placed under the leadership of the Relief Society, a female organization. In this assignment, the First Presidency followed the long-standing gender ideology that placed women in the home, where they would raise virtuous children while men worked to support the family. The "Mothers in Israel" were the "exemplars" in regard to dress standards because it was the "home influences that, above all others, should direct in moral, social and dress reforms."[56] The Social Advisory Committee would assist the home because some mothers allowed their girls to go about immodestly, even indecently. It followed then that a reform movement designed to influence young women was best placed under the direction of mothers and wives— pure vessels seemingly untouched by the world outside of the home.[57]

As a part of their reform efforts, the Social Advisory Committee examined the recreation of the Saints. In the summer of 1920, the committee sponsored a month-long course on "Social and Recreational Leadership" during the summer session at Brigham Young University (BYU). A letter from the First Presidency advised each stake president to assign one person to enroll in the course.[58] According to a published synopsis of the course, seminar participants focused on finding ways to promote church activity among the young: "The available facts indicate clearly that increasingly large numbers of our children, particularly adolescents, are becoming inactive in all forms of church activities." If the church could not retain young Mormons, future membership growth was impossible. Rather than trying to convert the world, the committee suggested, it was time to proselyte among Mormons through recreation and social activities. "According to present indications," the synopsis warned, "the future growth and membership of the Church depends upon the conversion of 'Mormon' children, rather than upon proselytes from outside: hence the welfare of the rising generation in the Church is paramount, and therefore second to no other consideration."[59]

Although not a great deal is known about the training that occurred during the recreation institute, the speakers in the daily "Special Lectures" reveal the intense interest of leading church officials. Talks ranged from church president Heber J. Grant's message on "The Gospel and Social Work" to Salt Lake City recreation manager Charlotte Stewart's "Leisure Time Needs of the Adolescent Girl."[60] Other prominent Mormon speakers included Apostle Stephen L Richards ("The Social and Recreational Program of the Church"), Adam S. Bennion ("Recreation and the Religious Life"), Milton Bennion ("Moral Development through Recreation"), and Earl J. Glade ("Selling Mormonism to the Young Man").[61] In attracting the attention of leading church figures, the recreation institute rivaled the semiannual general conferences of the church.

Apostle David O. McKay's lecture on "Religious Instruction in Relation to Recreation" offered seminar participants a glowing recommendation of the positive power of recreation but also cautioned that unchecked leisure activities could lead to vice and immorality. Citing statistics that one-third of church members had no interest in standard church work, Apostle McKay noted that even those who would not consider attending a worship service would "either directly or indirectly participate in the various forms of recreation and in social functions." Therefore, the apostle concluded, "In as much . . . as this one third will not come out of the recreation field to receive religion, religion must be taken into the recreation field." Leisure-time activities had a great power to impart religious sensibilities and sensitivities. Courage, reputation, willpower, health, self-control, self-reliance, kindness, friendship, and devotion were all products of proper play. When left unsupervised, however, positive play could degenerate. "The great duty of the social worker," McKay advised the gathered recreation leaders, "is to convince wayward boys and girls that there is in many forms of amusement and recreation a definite line beyond which they cannot go with impunity. In other words, some things are virtuous up to a certain point, beyond which they become vices." The wisdom of trained recreation leaders was necessary to decide which activities promoted virtues and which promulgated vices. The recreation seminar fostered that necessary discernment among the local recreational officers of the church.[62]

To create a program that would be effective on the local level, seminar attendees regularly split into smaller groups to do "intensive work on specific problems." Each group then made recommendations to the Social Advisory Committee. Many of these ideas and initiatives were collected in a newsletter published after the institute closed in July 1920. The recommendations from the small group that studied the adolescent girl (ages fourteen to twenty-one) were typical. First the group noted a number of social and psychological tendencies that defined the behavior of young Mormon women. They concluded that the cohort possessed a "desire to indulge in reverie and day dreams, self-consciousness, tendency to incorrigibility, affectations and mannerisms." "Freakishness," pranks, the desire to show off, and awkwardness also loomed large in the social lives of adolescent girls. On the positive side, girls were thought to be susceptible to religious influences, to love reading, and to have a taste for adventure.

Armed with this information about young women, the group created a program to channel adolescent tendencies toward positive outcomes. First, group activities should satisfy the love of adventure and foster cooperation among the girls. Music, storytelling, sewing, hiking, tobogganing, and horseback riding were mentioned as appropriate. Second, the leisure-time program needed to provide an example of high ideals by choosing the right kind of teachers and leaders, companions, and books. Finally, church-sponsored recreational activities must "appeal to the heart as well as to the intellect." Moreover, the study group recommended that girls be given a supervised recreational period each week.[63] The group studying adolescent boys came to similar conclusions but recommended that a church-controlled social center be placed in every ward. Open and supervised during all leisure hours, the centers would resemble city-run playgrounds.[64] Each of the small groups at the summer recreation institute followed the same pattern: determine the tendencies of the age group under question and then create a program to direct those tendencies toward wholesome outcomes. The committee newsletter helped publicize the recommendations throughout the church.

Following the success of the SAC recreational conference in 1920, opportunities for instruction in recreational theory and technique abounded in Mormon Utah. Both Brigham Young University and the Utah Agricultural College offered summer courses in leisure-time leadership; annual summer conferences of the YLMIA and YMMIA often focused on recreational issues; and recreational institutes led by trained Mormon experts were conducted in clinics throughout the intermountain West. During "Leadership Week" at BYU in 1923, thirty-five hundred persons from fifty stakes learned about recreational theory from national and local experts. At one session, L. H. Weir, a field representative of the Playground and Recreation Association of America, expounded on the place of recreation in the life of a people. Following Weir, Dr. George H. Brimhall and BYU President Franklin S. Harris spoke on the importance of leisure and the demands of leisure-time leadership.[65] That same year, BYU announced that Knute K. Rockne, the football coach and director of athletics at Notre Dame University, would be among the guest faculty members during the summer session.[66]

Other well-known figures in athletics and recreational leadership spent their summers teaching at the UAC in Logan. For the summer session in 1924, the college president, Elmer G. Peterson, invited "church recreational leaders, Boy Scout leaders, teachers and physical education directors" to enroll in a summer recreational leadership course offered by Dr. Emmett D. Angell of the University of Wisconsin. Angell—called the "most eminent leader in America in recreation and play"—was a distinguished coach in track, basketball, and football as well as the author of several high school– and college-level texts on sports.[67] In 1927, the UAC summer course included instruction in coaching techniques from Rockne and Forest C. ("Phog") Allen of the University of Kansas. Charlotte Perkins Gilman was also on the faculty that summer.[68] The following year, young coaches received training from the father of modern football, Glenn Scobey "Pop" Warner.

Learning at the feet of the recognized masters not only provided expert training for Mormon recreation leaders but also legitimized the pursuit of wholesome leisure-time activities. The renowned sociologist (and member of the summer faculty at UAC in 1926) Edward A. Ross complimented the Mormon approach: "I don't know any other place where the young people are so well provided for as here in [Utah]. I don't understand how the 'Mormon' Church got the idea of providing so well for the recreational and social needs of people so much earlier than we sociologists got the idea. The Church was way ahead of us in making this discovery."[69] Learning from experts and modifying their teachings to fit local situations helped Mormons meet the social and recreational needs of church members.

The universities were not alone in supporting recreational leadership training programs. Stake officials from the Salt Lake area, for example, participated in a recreational leadership course that met weekly from 31 October to 19 December 1923. The course promoted the improved organization of recreational work, trained ward leisure-time leaders, and gave "those directing this work a clearer vision of the entire movement." The aim of the course captures the essence of Mormon recreation as it evolved in the early twentieth century—"not *more* recreation, but *better* recreation." Expert lectures were given in the fundamental principles of recreation work, and more specific instruction was available in drama, dancing, music, and special programs. Similar courses were held in the four stakes of Weber County, Utah, and at Brigham Young University. An abbreviated version of the course appeared in twenty other stakes.[70] In 1925, a group of Mormon recreation experts traveled throughout Utah instructing local recreation leaders from Logan to Payson. Under the direction of the executive director of the YMMIA, Oscar A. Kirkham, the experts gave general advice in recreational supervision and specific guidance in meeting the recreational interests of children, adolescents, adults, and communities.[71]

The knowledge gained in these courses was subsequently transmitted to others on the local level. In Granite Stake (Salt Lake City), where eighty delegates had attended the Deseret Gym course, the newly trained recreational leaders "returned to their stake ready to pass on to the home folks the lesson learned at headquarters." A series of local institutes taught music, special activity work, and dance to members of each ward in the stake. More than five hundred persons attended the conferences.[72] The need for recreation—and the organization of leisure-time activities—was quickly becoming institutionalized within the church.

The annual June conferences sponsored by the YMMIA and YLMIA also provided a site for instruction in leisure-time leadership and the further institutionalization of recreation. At the conference in June 1923, only months after the assignment of recreational leadership to the MIA, clean recreation was emphasized. In the report of the conference, one can detect a developing dichotomy concerning the role of religious recreation. As the editor of the *Improvement Era* reported, on the one hand, church-sponsored leisure activities were dedicated to "the preservation of health, clean amusement, proper employment of leisure hours and social cooperation." On the other hand, Mormon recreation needed to "encourage reverence for and faith in our religious obligations."[73] Which of these two objectives was preeminent was not always clear; as the June 1923 conference indicates, a wide divide on this question developed between church recreational authorities and LDS ecclesiastical officials.

Apostle Melvin J. Ballard, who acted as YMMIA superintendent, made it clear in his address to the June conference that the spiritual took precedence over the social in church-sponsored recreational programs:

> The men and women who are chosen to head this recreational work must not only be interested in recreational work; they must be spiritual minded individuals as well, seeing the point of view that the ultimate purpose of our being interested in this recreational work is to keep our young people safe, pure, and under the influence of the Church, and keep them in such environment that they ultimately will find their way into some one or other of the Church organizations, Priesthood quorums, Sunday schools and other organizations—the end being to establish in their hearts faith in God, love for his work, desire to serve and keep themselves during their leisure period free from the vices and sins and contaminating influences of the world.[74]

To Ballard, the primary purpose of church recreation was to build the church; ancillary benefits might accrue, but the focus of Mormon recreation was spiritual, not social, indoctrination.

Other church officials, not ecclesiastical leaders but general church committee members, privileged personal and social benefits over the opportunity for spiritual growth through recreation. In his address to the June 1923 conference, the chairman of the Recreation Committee, Ephraim E. Ericksen, who was also a sociology professor at the University of Utah, sought to better society through religious recreation. "Our great purpose," Ericksen contended, was to

> use the recreational facilities and these activities to promote higher ideals, character and better social relationship. We believe that while we come together in a great many ways in a business way, in a political way, in social ways and religiously, perhaps we can increase our sympathy if we meet in places for mere enjoyment,

where we can live our natural selves, that is, where we can laugh and sing and play. . . . I believe we will think more of one another, love one another more, if we get together and laugh and sing and play together.[75]

Spiritual enhancement through recreation was not completely absent from Ericksen's perspective, but it paled next to the lessons of social cooperation taught through supervised recreation. Charlotte Stewart of the YLMIA General Board similarly situated recreation within the physical and social realm, not necessarily the spiritual:

> Recreation is not an antidote for evil; it is not a substitute for vice; it is not a passively good thing to keep people out of mischief; it is the warp and woof out of which a well rounded life can be woven, the material for giving benefit, life, experience, a vital, fundamental means to growth and power, not only as a substitute but it is valuable in itself. If recreation is to fill up a vacancy, just a vacuum, it is not worth while; if it is vibrant with meaningful life value, then it is one of the greatest of national activities.[76]

John T. Wahlquist, an education professor at the University of Utah, likewise weighed in on the social ramifications of LDS recreation. "Recreation of whatever nature or form, under the direction of the Church," Wahlquist argued, "should make true Latter-day Saints. It should increase the spirit of brotherly love and sympathy, break down undesirable class distinction, develop leadership, promote health, direct and develop the power of self expression, direct the emotional expression and develop culture and refinement."[77]

But questions remained about what it meant to be a "true Latter-day Saint." Was the guiding principle in constructing Mormons merely social cooperation, or were Mormons made primarily by spiritual conversion? At least at the June 1923 conference, there was some discord between the pronouncements of the ecclesiastical leader and the recreation experts. While Ballard's vision was riveted firmly on building the kingdom of God, the sociologist Ericksen and the playground manager Stewart seemed to focus on the personal and the social, largely overlooking the needs of the institutional church. Such diverging viewpoints—ideological competition between Mormon recreation authorities and LDS general authorities—may have led to the eventual dissolution of the Social Advisory Committee in 1922.

Satisfying the Seven Urges

The 1920s also saw the rise of the most comprehensive ideological statement about leisure time and how Mormon recreation programs could be used to direct church members toward wholesome activities. Based on a belief in seven fundamental urges that influence human behavior, church recreation proponents outlined the urges and then created a program designed to satisfy each urge for a variety of age groups from childhood through adolescence and adulthood. This program represented the ideological apex of Mormon religious recreation. Far from the ad hoc approach used by church leaders into the twentieth century, LDS officials in the 1920s had a "scientific" foundation underlying their leisure-time efforts.

The philosophy divided human tendencies into seven fundamental urges: physical, rhythmic, constructive, environmental, dramatic, linguistic, and social. Leaders understood that all age groups did not relate to the seven urges in the same way. Therefore, different activities were designed to satisfy the seven urges in five age groups: childhood/preadolescence; youth/early adolescence (ages twelve through fifteen); middle adolescence (fifteen through seventeen); late adolescence (seventeen through twenty-four); and adulthood. These ideas were first published by the MIA in *Recreation Bulletin No. 5* in 1925.[78] By 1928, a slightly modified treatment of the seven urges appeared in the MIA handbook that guided recreational activities throughout the church.

Outlined carefully, each urge helped recreation workers not only understand the rationale behind the leisure-time program sponsored by the Mutual Improvement Associations but also explained why children and adults behaved in peculiar or destructive ways.

Under the heading "Social Urge," the 1928 *MIA Handbook* suggested that "comradeship is a fundamental human need" and that the church had "gone far in bringing our people together in the spirit of fellowship, in helping us to understand, appreciate and enjoy each other." However, like other human interests and desires, the social urge was double-edged—left unchecked, the desire to associate with others could destroy any sense of social cooperation. The manual warned, "The modern tendency of society . . . is toward a breaking up into specialized cliques, groups and cults, which could easily disintegrate 'the common feeling of social relationships,' without which democracy itself cannot exist, because upon it rests the development of that self-control which is related to an appreciation of the needs of the rest of the group." Controlled social interaction was important; democracy could not thrive without it and neither, though it goes unspoken, could a social organization like the church. Proper social behavior—the avoidance of cliques and cults—hinged on individual self-control. If the church, or society, was to succeed, individuals must harness the social urge and remember that they were "bound up with the rest of the community" to such a degree that "we stand or fall together."[79] Proper activities for fulfilling the social urge included picnics, parties, socials, dancing, and reunions. For preadolescents, holiday socials received special emphasis because "every holiday should be a memorable day to children." Older boys and girls should be initiated into social groups like the Boy Scouts, Bee-Hives, or radio clubs. Educational, literary, and scientific societies offered social opportunities appropriate for middle and late adolescents, while adults might productively sponsor or attend family and community reunions.[80]

The philosophical basis for a "rhythmic urge" was straightforward: "We all have, to a greater or less degree, an 'ache' to respond with voice, feet, or body, to an urge or rhythm; to live, create, invigorate, in free, happy, spontaneous dance, song and kindred expressions."[81] Though not recognized by that appellation, the "rhythmic urge" had been at the center of Mormon social life for nearly a century. Dancing was perhaps the most ubiquitous recreational activity of nineteenth-century Mormons[82] and never lost its attraction for the Saints. But dancing was not without faults. Just as earlier church leaders had denounced the sensuality of the waltz, some twentieth-century dance styles failed to measure up to the moral standards of Mormon recreation. After extolling the wholesome virtues of the aesthetic element in many dances, the *MIA Handbook* warned: "[W]hen the emotional appeal becomes so intense as to stimulate those emotions which are fundamentally related to the sex-instinct, social dancing is no longer wholesome. It is therefore recommended that all those factors in dancing which in any way overstimulate the emotions be eliminated, as far as possible." Unless dancing was properly supervised, it was the "most dangerous and most easily perverted social pastime." Dancing, if allowed to flourish unhampered, would lead young Saints away from fulfilling the rhythmic urge and toward satisfying the sex instinct.[83]

Although dancing was the most popular leisure-time activity, LDS recreational workers were directed not to offer dances only for amusement but as functions "through which proper social conduct may be taught and fostered." The rhythmic urge was properly satiated with a combination of music instruction and activity (both vocal and instrumental) and a variety of dancing techniques including folk, social, interpretive, and clog. To insure the wholesome nature of the dance, a dance director—"a competent man, who is tactful, and has influence among the young people"—was to be appointed in each ward. The dance director received specific instructions on how to prepare for an event, choose appropriate music, and set a proper dance atmosphere. Above all else, the director was not only organizing a dance, he was "training men and women."[84]

The dramatic urge extended from the "universal" instinct for self-expression. As a means of escaping from one's everyday surroundings, "playing a part"—whether as an actor in a professional drama or playing dress-up with friends in the basement—offered a healthy respite from daily rigors.[85] The dramatic urge could be met not only by performing but by writing plays and pageants as well. Children were told to act out stories and imitate the activities of daily life. Adolescent and adult activities centered on drama and vaudeville as well as writing plays.

Fulfilling the "linguistic urge" had been part of a decades-long effort to get young Mormons interested in good literature. As early as 1907, the MIA published a yearly reading list for members. Equipping local meetinghouse libraries had also been popular since the turn of the century. Though reading enjoyed the "enviable distinction of being the medium of recreation of the greatest number of people in all the world," reading by itself did not satisfy the linguistic urge.[86] Debating, oratory, and writing plays and stories were needed to satisfy linguistic desires. Wards encouraged linguistic skill by offering prizes in debate and creative writing.

Meeting the "physical urge" involved a myriad of athletic competitions. Stressing the primary importance of sportsmanship and fair play, athletic events were designed to teach young Mormons the value not only of physical excellence but of obeying the rules as well. "Thus and thus only," the manual provided, "will a youth make himself what we all admire and what we class as a thoroughbred, and started right, he will always be a thoroughbred." Athletic events were tailored to the physiological and sociological development of each age group. The youngest groups could safely play tag games or go swimming, while older groups participated in a variety of more strenuous team and individual sports. Local leaders were reminded that if "boys and girls with weak hearts or some physical defect are allowed to enter too strenuous competition, very serious injury may result."[87]

A set of more rigid guidelines governed the athletic participation of young women. Whether in team sports like basketball and baseball or in running games and relays, recreation leaders feared that girls were particularly susceptible to serious injuries through overtaxation. Officials warned local leaders of the effects of menstruation on physical performance: "To promote a reasonable and sane attitude toward certain physiological conditions which may occasion temporary unfitness for vigorous athletics, in order that effective safeguards shall be maintained is one of the duties of the director of girls' athletics."[88] The baneful psychological and sociological effects of sports also concerned athletic leaders. Competitions that emphasized individual accomplishment and winning at the expense of enjoyment and sportsmanship were discouraged. Girls could participate in a wide variety of sports—

often alongside boys—but they required special attention to meet their unique feminine needs.[89]

The "environmental urge" induced people to go outside "to see new sights, to travel, to walk in the woods, to hear the birds sing, to hear the babbling of the water, to fish and hunt." Urged on by this spirit of adventure, adolescents and adults restored much of the energy lost to the "grind of daily routine." Outside activities provided recreation in the truest sense—they re-created the individual by removing her or him from the workaday world. Boy Scouting, Fathers and Sons' Outings, and Mothers and Daughters' Days all encouraged the Saints to refresh themselves in the great outdoors. Children's groups that were too young to camp or travel were encouraged to attend zoos, parks, and museums and to camp out in the back yard.[90]

At the base of the "constructive urge" was the "desire of ownership, a pride in manual activity."[91] From planting gardens to raising pets to needle work, making something by hand registered as a fundamental urge of humankind. Satisfying the urge to construct acquired special importance in an age where many workers no longer toiled in the soil or built handcrafted items. Office workers and factory workers required a recreation program that respected their need to create. The MIAs kept young and old hands busy building handicrafts, raising flowers, making radios, and building homes.

The definition of the fundamental urges of humankind and the creation of a recreational program to satisfy them represented a Mormon foray into the world beyond their borders. The urges were not based on scripture or prophetic pronouncement but relied on knowledge gleaned from the emerging social sciences of sociology and human development. Religious recreation remained a spiritual pursuit, but it now had a "scientific" foundation. The knowledge came from well beyond Zion, but the applications were strictly LDS. Mormons in the early twentieth century were not afraid, or even hesitant, to see what Gentile America had to offer; the purpose of gaining such knowledge, however, was to strengthen Mormon institutions and maintain organizational integrity while increasing personal morality. By the 1920s, recreation was at the center of the church's efforts.

From the days of Joseph Smith, leisure-time activities have always been an integral component of Mormon society. But it was not until the Progressive Era that an LDS ideology of recreation emerged. Far removed from the days when Brothers Joseph and Brigham made occasional announcements regarding recreation philosophy and policy, the church in the 1920s developed a comprehensive leisure-time ideology based on satisfying the seven fundamental urges of human beings. Great effort was spent to create the philosophy and to insure that local leaders were properly trained in the theories and techniques of recreational leadership. In the first three decades of the twentieth century, hundreds of institutes and training sessions helped turn local lay leaders into recreational experts.

Notes

1. For a discussion of Mormonism as a new religious movement, see Jan Shipps, *Mormonism: The Story of a New Religious Tradition* (Urbana: University of Illinois Press, 1985).

2. 2 Nephi 2:25. This quote is taken from a longer monologue that relates the story of the creation of Adam and Eve in the Garden of Eden and the eventual coming of the "Messiah . . . in the fulness of time, that he may redeem the children of men from the fall." See 2 Nephi 2.

3. Doctrine and Covenants 88:15.

4. Qtd. in Matthias F. Cowley, *Wilford Woodruff* (Salt Lake City: Deseret News, 1909), 39. Another contemporary of Joseph Smith told a similar story: "I have been with him at times when approached by a long-faced religious stranger, who seemed to think that it was almost a sin to smile, and that the Prophet should be sedate and as cheerless as himself. The Prophet would challenge someone present for a wrestle— to the utter astonishment of the religious stranger, who would be almost shocked at the mention of a wrestle, but would extol Jacob, who seemed to be an accomplished wrestler and also a great favorite with God." See Hyrum L. Andrus and Helen Mae Andrus, *They Knew the Prophet* (Salt Lake City: Bookcraft, 1974), 117–18. For more on early Mormon attitudes regarding recreation, consult the pathbreaking study by Rex A. Skidmore, "Mormon Recreation in Theory and Practice: A Study of Social Change" (Ph.D. diss., University of Pennsylvania, 1941). Additional detail can be found in Ruth Andrus, "A History of the Recreation Program of the Church of Jesus Christ of Latter-day Saints" (Ph.D. diss., University of Iowa, 1962).

5. Joseph Smith, *History of the Church of Jesus Christ of Latter-day Saints,* ed. B. H. Roberts, 7 vols. (Salt Lake City: Deseret Book, 1970), 5:265.

6. *Times and Seasons* 5 (1 Oct. 1844): 668–70.

7. *Journal of Discourses,* 26 vols. (Liverpool, England: Latter-day Saints Book Depot, 1854–86), 2:94.

8. Ibid.

9. Susa Young Gates, *Life Story of Brigham Young* (New York: Macmillan, 1930), 251. This phrase bears a striking resemblance to the most popular labor song of the late nineteenth century, "Eight Hours." See Philip S. Foner, *American Labor Songs of the Nineteenth Century* (Urbana: University of Illinois Press, 1975), 222–24.

10. Doctrine and Covenants 136:28.

11. For a description of some Mormon recreational activities at Winter Quarters, see Richard E. Bennett, *Mormons at the Missouri, 1846–1852: "And Should We Die . . ."* (Norman: University of Oklahoma Press, 1987), 168–72. See also Richard Ian Kimball, "'Somethin' to Do': Mormon Recreation in Kanesville, 1849–1852," *The John Whitmer Historical Association Journal* 15 (1995): 35–49.

12. *Journal of Discourses,* 1:29–30.

13. Ibid., 13:61.

14. John A. Widtsoe, ed., *Discourses of Brigham Young* (Salt Lake City: Deseret Book, 1925), 365–66.

15. *Journal of Discourses,* 1:48.

16. *Historical Statistics of the United States, Colonial Times to 1970,* pt. 1 (Washington, D.C.: U.S. Bureau of Census, 1975), ser. D 765–78, 168.

17. For a firsthand account of her settlement-house work in Chicago, see Jane Addams, *Twenty Years at Hull-House* (1910; rpt., Urbana: University of Illinois Press, 1990). An example of Jacob Riis's work, complete with classic photographs, can be found in *How the Other Half Lives: Studies Among the Tenements of New York* (New York: Dover, 1971).

18. Addams, *Twenty Years at Hull-House,* 244.

19. Ibid., 304.

20. Dominick Cavallo, *Muscles and Morals: Organized Playgrounds and Urban Reform, 1880–1920* (Philadelphia: University of Pennsylvania Press, 1981), 22.

21. Ibid., 51, 49–70.

22. On the Playground Association of America, see Richard F. Knapp and Charles E. Hartsoe, *Play for America: The National Recreation Association, 1906–1965* (Arlington, Va.: National Recreation and Park Association, 1979).

23. Arthur L. Beeley, *Boys and Girls in Salt Lake City* (Salt Lake City: University of Utah Department of Sociology and Social Technology, 1929), 13–17.

24. "Our Work—The Annual Conference of the Mutual Improvement Associations," *Improvement Era* 4 (Aug. 1901): 790–91.

25. "Talks to the Young Men—The Tendency to Deify Evil," *Improvement Era* 2 (Oct. 1899): 944–46.

26. See "Our Work—Obstacles," *Improvement Era* 9 (Nov. 1905): 72–73. During the annual Young Men's Mutual Improvement Association conference in June 1905, Apostle George Albert Smith enumerated a number of obstacles for adolescent males living in urban areas. "In the city wards," spoke Smith, "first, many young men are engaged in business which ties them up until late in the evening; second, school work—many of our young men being students; third, the constant round of amusements which attracts so many; fourth, the great amount of light and trashy literature; fifth, lack of interest on account of the multitude of meetings."

27. Susa Young Gates, ed., "A Mother's Letters to Her Missionary Son: II.—Letter Posted to Chicago," *Improvement Era* 8 (Mar. 1905): 353. The selfishness of city-born youth was likewise discussed by the ranking Apostle Francis M. Lyman: "In our cities especially, false standards are creeping into the lives of many young men. In their homes, possibly, they have tasted luxury, or they see others about them enjoying the good things of life. Foolishly, they begin to spend everything available, in their effort to live on a higher plane than they belong." See Francis M. Lyman, "Manhood," *Improvement Era* 7 (Jan. 1904): 177.

28. "Editor's Table—Worship in the Home," *Improvement Era* 7 (Dec. 1903): n.p.

29. O. E. Howell, "Play with Them," *Improvement Era* 28 (May 1925): 668.

30. A College Senior, "Five Memories I'd Like to Have," *Improvement Era* 30 (Dec. 1926): 145.

31. "Editor's Table—The Spirit of Religion," *Improvement Era* 6 (Oct. 1903): 945.

32. Joseph F. Smith, "Editor's Table—True Love," *Improvement Era* 14 (July 1911): 829.

33. James X. Allen, "Consistency," *Improvement Era* 10 (July 1907): 747.

34. "Encouragement for 'Busy' Men," *Improvement Era* 1 (June 1898): 621. Additional encouragement for boys and girls to stay busy came from Douglas M. Todd's address: "One of the great purposes we have in view is to keep our young people busy, avoiding the danger that exists when young men and women are not fully and capably employed in some good work." See the report of the address in "Our Work—The Annual Conference of the Mutual Improvement Associations," *Improvement Era* 3 (Aug. 1900): 714.

35. "Notes," *Improvement Era* 1 (Sept. 1898): 853.

36. George H. Brimhall, "Continuity in Character," *Improvement Era* 2 (Oct. 1899): 929.

37. Lewis A. Merrill, "Choosing an Occupation," *Improvement Era* 5 (Jan. 1902): 212.

38. Edwin F. Parry, "On Choosing Life Models," *Improvement Era* 5 (Jan. 1902): 173.

39. Lyman's talk was summarized in "Our Work—The Annual Conference of the Young Men's and Young Ladies' Mutual Improvement Associations," *Improvement Era* 2 (Aug. 1899): 711.

40. "Our Work—To Stake and Ward Officers of the Y.M.M.I.A.," *Improvement Era* 9 (Oct. 1906): 979.

41. Ibid.

42. "Our Work—General M.I.A. Conference," *Improvement Era* 10 (July 1907): 760.

43. "Mutual Work—Class in Athletics," *Improvement Era* 16 (Dec. 1912): 177.

44. See "Mutual Work—The Third Y.M.M.I.A. Normal Training Class," *Improvement Era* 16 (Feb. 1913): 393.

45. "Mutual Work—February Class in Athletics," *Improvement Era* 16 (Feb. 1913): 392.

46. B. H. Roberts, "Physical Development," *Improvement Era* 15 (Aug. 1912): 920.

47. "Mutual Work—The New Traveling Secretary," *Improvement Era* 16 (June 1913): 833.

48. *Parents' Bulletin No. 1: Recreation and Play* (Salt Lake: Deseret Sunday School Union, 1914), 3.

49. Ibid., 3–4.

50. Ibid., 4.

51. One popular 1913 song quoted by George Weston included such racy lyrics as, "He'd feel around and fool around and then they'd kiss again / And then he'd

row, row, row / A little further he would row, oh, oh, oh, oh." Weston was appalled to find such "erotic syncopation" in contemporary love songs. See ibid., 43–44.

52. Ibid., 46–47.

53. Ibid., 9.

54. Joseph F. Smith, "Editor's Table—Social Doings," *Improvement Era* 20 (Jan. 1917): 259.

55. "Editor's Table—Dress and Social Practices," *Improvement Era* 20 (Dec. 1916): 172.

56. Ibid., 172–73.

57. The most complete discussion of the Social Advisory Committee appears in Thomas G. Alexander, "Between Revivalism and the Social Gospel: The Latter-day Saint Social Advisory Committee, 1916–1922," *BYU Studies* 23 (Winter 1983): 19–39.

58. "Teacher-Training and Social Work," *Improvement Era* 23 (June 1920): 746.

59. "Synopsis of Course in Social and Recreational Leadership, 1920," 1. A copy of the synopsis can be found in the LDS Church Historical Department, Salt Lake City.

60. For more on the life of Charlotte Stewart, see Robert C. Lally, "The Life and Educational Contributions of Charlotte Stewart" (Master's thesis, University of Utah, 1950).

61. For the titles, though not the texts, of the "Special Lectures," see "Synopsis of Course in Social and Recreational Leadership, 1920," 2–3.

62. See David O. McKay, "Religious Instruction in Relation to Recreation," in ibid., 26.

63. *Social Advisory Committee News Letter,* no. 3, 12 July 1920: 3–4.

64. Ibid., 4.

65. Lowry Nelson, "The University a Workshop for Leaders," *Improvement Era* 26 (Mar. 1923): 450.

66. "Passing Events," *Improvement Era* 26 (Apr. 1923): 585.

67. Elmer G. Peterson, "Utah Invites the Nation: A National Summer School at Logan," *Improvement Era* 27 (Mar. 1924): 445. During the UAC summer session of 1924, Frederick Jackson Turner, the "Prince of American Historians" (445–46), taught a course on the Utah, California, and Oregon pioneer movements.

68. See advertisement for "National Summer School," *Improvement Era* 30 (Apr. 1927): back page.

69. "Mutual Work—Appreciation for the M.I.A. Handbook," *Improvement Era* 29 (Oct. 1926): 1199.

70. "Mutual Work—Leadership Schools for Recreation," *Improvement Era* 27 (Feb. 1924): 389.

71. "Mutual Work—Recreation Leadership Institutes," *Improvement Era* 28 (May 1925): 703.

72. "Mutual Work—Preaching the Gospel of Better Recreation," *Improvement Era* 27 (May 1924): 696. For further information on church recreation institutes,

see W. O. Robinson, *The Church and Recreation: A Resumé of the LDS Recreation Program as Directed by the Mutual Improvement Association* (N.p., n.d.).

73. "Editor's Table—The June M.I.A. Conference," *Improvement Era* 26 (July 1923): 843.

74. "Timely Thoughts from the June Conference," *Improvement Era* 26 (Aug. 1923): 924.

75. Ibid. See E. E. Ericksen, *Memories and Reflections: The Autobiography of E. E. Ericksen,* ed. Scott G. Kenney (Salt Lake City: Signature Books, 1987); and Scott Kenney, "E. E. Ericksen—Loyal Heretic," *Sunstone* 3 (July–Aug. 1978): 16–27.

76. "Timely Thoughts from the June Conference," 924. On the dissolution of the Social Advisory Committee, see Alexander, "Between Revivalism and the Social Gospel," 35–39. For another perspective, see Kenney, "E. E. Ericksen—Loyal Heretic."

77. "Timely Thoughts from the June Conference," 930.

78. *MIA Recreation Bulletin No. 5* (Salt Lake City: General Boards of MIA, 1925).

79. *MIA Handbook* (Salt Lake City: General Board of MIA, 1928), 342.

80. For a full list of prescribed activities for each age group, see *MIA Recreation Bulletin No. 5,* 29–30.

81. *MIA Handbook,* 369.

82. See Davis Bitton, "These Licentious Days: Dancing among the Mormons," *Sunstone* 2 (Spring 1977): 16–27; Karl E. Wesson, "Dance in the Church of Jesus Christ of Latter-day Saints, 1830–1940" (Master's thesis, Brigham Young University, 1975); Leona Holbrook, "Dancing as an Aspect of Early Mormon and Utah Culture," *BYU Studies* 16 (1975): 117–38; Michael Hicks, *Mormonism and Music: A History* (Urbana: University of Illinois Press, 1989), esp. chap. 5.

83. *MIA Handbook,* 369.

84. Ibid., 370, 371.

85. Ibid., 403.

86. Ibid., 434. Though the reading lists played a major role in the MIA's educational and literary programs, they were not entirely successful in reaching young church members. For example, only 4 percent of the active membership read the assigned books in 1907. The next year only 7 percent participated in the program. See Thomas G. Alexander, *Mormonism in Transition: A History of the Latter-day Saints, 1890–1930* (Urbana: University of Illinois Press, 1986), 142.

87. *MIA Handbook,* 440.

88. Ibid., 442–43.

89. For more on the attitudes of reformers about athletics and female reproductive health, see Susan K. Cahn, *Coming on Strong: Gender and Sexuality in Twentieth-Century Women's Sport* (1994; rpt., Cambridge, Mass.: Harvard University Press, 1995), esp. chap. 1 and pp. 165–68.

90. *MIA Handbook,* 446. See also chap. 4 in this book.

91. Ibid., 451.

CHAPTER TWO

"A Strong Arm to the Church"

Recreation Building Boom

> "We are very anxious to make this institution a real blessing to
> the men and women of this community, and at the same time to
> make it a strong arm to the church."
> —Letter to bishops promoting the newly built Deseret Gymnasium
> (about 1912)

After the construction of the Deseret Gymnasium in Salt Lake City in 1910,
gym executives sought a creative method to advertise the athletic training
facility. Deciding that the developing technology of motion pictures was
optimal for their needs—viewers would actually get to see the action in the
gym—they solicited several scripts for short film advertisements. Each film
had a different theme and highlighted a unique offering of the urban gymnasium before referring pointedly to the Deseret Gymnasium as the "Temple
of Health." One short film entitled "The Champion," for example, showed
a "little comic man" getting thrown in the air for an extended period (with
the help of "trick photography") and then landing on a larger man and
pinning his shoulders to the ground. The suggested wording to accompany
the film advised not only wrestlers but residents of Salt Lake interested in
recreation: "If you want to wrestle / Light in the right place / The Deseret
Gym / The Temple of Health." The Deseret Gym was designed as the "right
place" for Mormon adults and adolescents to land.

Taken together, the films showcased the main reasons for gym attendance.
One comical short was directed at businessmen and stressed the relationship between physical fitness and business efficiency. In "The Submarine,"
a swimmer—mistaken for a submarine—gets knocked askance by a water
ball thrown by an onlooker. Busy businessmen beset by economic torpedoes
at the workplace might have been comforted by the film's words: "Sometimes there's a feeling of sadness / At the end of a long busy day / Why not
convert it to gladness / By joining the Gym while you may / Special class
for business men." As always, the text was followed by, "Deseret Gym, the

Temple of Health." To assist the growing numbers of white-collar workers in the early twentieth century, the gym was offered as a place where a businessman could increase his bottom-line efficiency by improving his physical stamina. As another film advised, "When business disregards the body, the body will disregard business." A film showing the athletic achievements of young men was designed to "cause every boy who sees it to keep after his parents until he joins the gym." The words accompanying that film recognized that the street was a dangerous place and advertised that young men would be safeguarded in the Temple of Health, where a year's fee cost less than a week's doctor bill.[1]

Whether it was boys or businessmen, girls or their mothers, leaders of the LDS Church believed that the Deseret Gym could provide Mormons with a "right place" to land. The construction of the gym—the largest church-sponsored effort at creating supervised recreation space—highlights a recreational building boom that changed the face of LDS architecture and rearticulated the LDS concepts of sacred and secular space. The programs that were designed to complement the newly constructed play spaces also offer unique insight into LDS gender roles during the early twentieth century.

Early Organization of Recreation Space

Gymnasiums—organized spaces for play, exercise, and recreation—were not unknown to the Mormon community in the nineteenth century. Families or community groups sensed the need for supervised exercise and equipped rooms in homes or rented space where a variety of physical activities could take place. The Lion House, built by Brigham Young in central Salt Lake City in 1856, included a gymnasium among its accoutrements. Equipped with horizontal and straight ladders, horizontal bars, back boards, jumping ropes, wands, roller skates, and hoops, the Lion House gym must have been a beehive of activity with children drawing wooden swords to do mock battle while balls flew overhead and intrepid gymnasts rolled on exercise mats. To ensure that the play remained wholesome and constructive, an expert was hired to teach the children the rudiments of gymnastics, fencing, and dancing.[2] In 1896, the recently organized Mutual Improvement League emphasized "physical culture" and opened a gymnasium. Housed in the old Social Hall building in downtown Salt Lake City, the "first class" gymnasium contained "all the necessary apparatus designed for the perfect development of the human body." Besides baths, bathtubs, and showers, the building contained a library and reading room that were open to the public six days a week.[3]

Civic officials, who were often leading members of the church, also sensed the need to provide recreational facilities and wholesome leisure-time activities. In 1909 the Utah legislature created a state library-gymnasium commission to oversee the construction and day-to-day activities of gymnasium complexes throughout the state. State officers, like the president of the State Library-Gymnasium Committee, Howard R. Driggs, saw the same social problems that concerned Mormon leaders and likewise pinned their hopes on rational recreation. In describing the need for library-gymnasiums—"a new center of culture for the community"[4]—Driggs first turned to the perceived problems: "A mighty demand is being made today to do something to turn our misguided youth from the baneful influences of street loafing and the saloon." Concern about juvenile misbehavior had boiled over into "righteous wrath" that would not dissipate until "that pernicious institution [the saloon] has been swept forever from our midst." Echoing the ideas of Progressive reformers like Jane Addams, Driggs argued that merely removing the saloon was not enough. In its place, state leaders needed to plant "another institution that will cultivate manliness in the thousands of schoolless [sic], careless, but not necessarily bad boys." That institution was the library-gymnasium, which offered an amalgam of educational and physical pursuits for the potential delinquent. Driggs described the facilities in bucolic terms: "Every city should establish a public home for its street-boys— a place where they can go of an evening to mingle freely in manly sports— to swim, to play wholesome games, to read good books and magazines; a place where they can have well-directed physical play and enjoyment free from the vice and vulgarity of the saloon."[5]

Driggs argued that the library-gym played an important educational role as well. For the athletically inclined boy who had shown little interest in education, the path to the sports facilities led him through "a cheery room where good books and magazines invite[d] [him]" to read. Once intrigued by the book, the boy will "discover that mental enjoyment is just as entrancing as physical sport." That intellectual transformation accomplished, the boy's mind will be turned from "cigarettes, smutty yarns, and worse sins" toward intellectual development.[6] Supported by a small tax—enough to pay for expenses, including a play director and a librarian—these leisure-time complexes would become integral to Utah's communities. By inviting loafers into the library, the positive social power of recreation could save youthful miscreants from the evils of the saloon and street.

Local units of the church likewise recognized the need to create a space where Mormons could pursue recreational activities under the watchful eye of church leaders. In the last three decades of the nineteenth century—following the reorganization of the Relief Society (1867), the formation of teenage-centered Retrenchment Societies (1869), and the organization of the youth-oriented Primary (1876)—many wards erected recreation halls and Relief Society halls. Built to house auxiliary programs and social activities, the buildings were simple vernacular structures built near the local meetinghouse.

By the turn of the twentieth century, however, according to the architectural historian Martha Sonntag Bradley, LDS Church buildings commonly housed the worship area and the recreational space under the same roof. Evincing a "flexible attitude toward the secular v. sacred nature of the chapel space" that had long been an LDS tradition, Mormons in the twentieth century worshiped in one area of the meetinghouse on Sunday and pursued amusement and recreation in another part of the building during the week.[7] In a typical articulation of church space, the Granite Stake Tabernacle placed worship services on the main floor and recreation space in the basement. Completed in November 1903, the Tabernacle's basement floor contained a sizeable assembly room (64 x 64 ft.) with a large stage. The available open space hosted a variety of amusements, including sports, games, and dances.[8] Housed under the same roof, the chapel and the amusement hall remained segregated, though both were designed to inculcate the principles of proper LDS behavior.

The rationale behind the allocation of resources for church-sponsored gymnasiums appeared in a May 1911 *Improvement Era* editorial. President Joseph F. Smith made it clear that church-controlled gymnasiums had become an indispensable weapon in the organization's arsenal against improper amusement. In the months immediately following the opening of the Deseret Gym, Smith contended that the establishment of the centralized gym was not enough. Local wards and stakes must likewise provide for their members' recreational needs. The church leader advised: "Gymnasiums have become apparently a very urgent necessity of late, also places of amusement. We must not only provide places of worship for the youth of Zion, as well as for their fathers and mothers, but also find places for the rational amusement of our children, in order that they may be kept under proper influences, away from the contaminating, degrading practices too common in the world with reference to and in connection with the amusement of the people."[9]

Though many wards had the necessary space for a gymnasium in their amusement halls, most did not know what equipment was required to establish a working facility. Reacting to "numerous inquiries sent me from the country districts of Utah, and the general interest being taken by the Church, from Canada to Mexico, in adopting a course in physical education or athletics," E. J. Milne, the physical director at the University of Utah, published an article in the *Era* showing that a "crude though decidedly attractive room may be equipped where basket ball, hand ball and gymnastic work, can be given in every ward, at a comparatively small cost." Milne first described how to set up a basketball court. Devised in 1891 by James Naismith, basketball was only a decade or so old when Milne put it within reach of most Mormons. Contending that it already was one of the greatest indoor games in the country ("especially in the state of Utah"), Milne explained the need for a large room (35 x 70 ft.) with screened windows and lights. Strips of hard wood placed six inches apart would protect the windows, while a wire wastebasket worked nicely to shield the lights from errant balls. The dimensions of the court were illustrated in any basketball rule book, Milne noted, but the rims required specific instruction. The two rims should be made of iron about eighteen inches in diameter and placed ten feet above the ground on opposite ends of the court. Aware of his audience, Milne prescribed that if regular goals cannot be secured, "an old hay rake tooth will do nicely." Nets, though not required, could be made from mason's twine or small window-cord rope. An inflated rubber bladder with a leather cover served as a ball. In Utah, as was the case in most areas, Spalding's rules were to be observed.[10]

After creating the playing surface, basketball players also had to ready themselves, according to Milne. He dictated that each individual's equipment should include "rubber-soled shoes (high tops preferred), long stockings, knee pants, jock straup [*sic*], and a one-quarter sleeve jersey."

Basketball was not the only physical activity that ward amusement halls should prepare for, however. Milne recommended a "few Indian clubs and dumb bells" as well as the procurement of a pair of flying rings ("one of the most attractive features of a gymnasium") to round out the gymnasium's offerings. Finally, if water systems were installed, each ward should create facilities for a shower bath. Not only hygienic, a bath after exercise was a "great preventive of colds after a vigorous hour or so in the gymnasium."[11] Joseph F. Smith had provided the "why" behind the creation of local gymnasiums, and E. J. Milne then provided the "how." Together, they set off a boom in the construction of LDS amusement halls and gymnasiums. The Mormon landscape—religiously and geographically—would never be the same.

In northern Utah, the Cache Stake, under the direction of the superintendent of the YMMIA, A. E. Cranney, made plans for a reading room and gymnasium in Logan. To acquire an appropriate site, Cranney contacted the General Board of the YMMIA in Salt Lake City, which arranged to have the Preston Block donated for the purposes of creating a community recreation center. The YMMIA outfitted three rooms in the centrally located building—reading room, game room, and gymnasium. The goal in creating the center, according to Cranney, was to provide "an attractive rendez-vous for the boys, especially those who are attracted from home influences to the alluring downtown districts." He continued, "In our rooms we offer them not only good reading, clean and attractive games, associations un-der more favorable environment, but we endeavor in this way to encour-age and help them to more fully understand that, for a 'wise and glorious purpose we have been placed here on earth,' and that 'The man who wins is the man who does.'" Though young men were their primary concern, Logan's leaders considered finishing another room for the exclusive use of the sister Saints. In the meantime, women were permitted to use the exist-ing rooms, and rightly they should have been. It was largely through ba-zaars and entertainments sponsored by the women's auxiliaries that over a thousand dollars was raised for the outfitting of the reading room.[12]

In Hyrum, Utah, the members of the Second Ward followed a similar pro-cess in constructing a $12,500 recreation hall. Financed by volunteer con-tributions—including five thousand dollars in donated labor and $1,080 raised in a three-day "round-up"—the project "foster[ed] a spirit of unity" in the community. Other social and spiritual ends were served as well. Ac-cording to one participant, the people of Hyrum "now have a modern rec-reation hall where they can have dramas, dances, and other socials, free from the evils of privately conducted halls."[13] A more striking example came from Panaca, Nevada, where, under the leadership of Brother J. R. Smith, the young men created a gymnasium out of a former saloon building by equip-ping it with wrestling mats, a punching bag, and boxing gloves. Reporting this success story, the editors of the *Era* gushed with pride: "Where men once let whiskey rob them of their better selves, the young men are now rallying for healthful exercise and wholesome amusement."[14] The transformation of a whiskey den into a gymnasium in Panaca symbolized the hope that church-sponsored recreation areas would replace illicit activities with wholesome amusements and exercise. By the mid-1920s, Salt Lake City alone boasted more than sixty recreation halls in conjunction to LDS meetinghouses.

The local ward meetinghouse/amusement hall was the center of LDS spiri-tual and social life. Regarding the social phenomenon, Levi Edgar Young, a professor of western history at the University of Utah and one of the First Seven Presidents of the Quorum of Seventy, noted that Mormons placed a value on leisure-time pursuits second only to spiritual prerogatives. "Inter-esting above all," wrote Young, "is the manner in which the 'Mormon' people make of their ward recreation houses [and] social centers. Young and old seek amusements, and what amusements should be encouraged is a vi-tal question for all people interested in the uplift of the youth of our land.

Today, the Church is erecting beautiful places of worship all over the West. . . . These church buildings have their hall for divine service, but under the same roof is an amusement hall, where the boys and girls hold their dances, and give their dramatic performances." Describing the multifunctional meetinghouse/amusement hall at the hub of LDS society, Young concluded: "One passing a meetinghouse almost any night or afternoon, will find there either divine service or some stimulating social activity."[15]

The activities that occurred in Mormon amusement halls, while not accorded the status of worship services, were acknowledged as a primary contributor to the physical, social, and spiritual welfare of church members. With that in mind, the General Boards of the MIA directed that after April 1924 all "amusement halls" should be referred to as "recreation halls," since the latter term was "more appropriate . . . to the educational purpose of the Committees on Recreation throughout the Church."[16] Though the name change might seem insignificant, it reflects an allegiance to the tenets of "rational recreation." The use of the term "amusement" denoted purposeless uses of leisure time; "recreation" implied a more concerted, directed effort at using free time in wholesome, constructive ways under the leadership of trained church members. Amusements wasted free time; recreation had an important "educational purpose." The name change was symbolic of a change in attitude and approach.

The growing importance of LDS recreation halls is evident in a brochure to raise funds for the new recreation facility adjacent to the Twenty-Seventh Ward chapel in Salt Lake City. Situated on the corner of Fourth Avenue and P Street, the proposed sixty-thousand-dollar hall was advertised as an up-to-date community center that would house the most important social activities of men, women, and children. Fund-raisers hoped that this magnificent structure would become the heart of the community.

The advertising brochure claimed that the new recreation hall would provide for the social, physical, and spiritual needs of community members. First, and perhaps most importantly, the hall offered a "modern, elegant, and attractive place for dances, parties, games, and other forms of recreation," where all activities were "conducted under proper supervision." Moreover, a "Little Theatre" for plays, moving picture shows, debates, and oratorical contests would be open to all members of the community. A Boy Scout area—complete with trophy room, athletic space, and showers—meant a new home for scouts in Troop 39. The potential pitfalls that awaited boys on the streets provided a major impetus in the push for the new building: "What is it worth to you to have the lives of your sons or grandsons, or the boys of the community generally, filled, through their critical years, with these wholesome activities? The beauty and dignity of the building will add to the value of all property in this part of the city. To have available a high-class place of amusement, a wholesome social center will help young folks to keep off the streets. Do we not owe it to the youth of our neighborhood to provide for them this community recreation center?"[17] The prospect of adolescent misbehavior, however, was not the only reason for constructing the recreation complex. The adjacent chapel, as always, was available for funerals at no charge, regardless of religious affiliation. The recreation center thus provided a place of gathering for all members of the community in all seasons of life. This expansive and expensive social hall represented a significant departure in form (if not in function) from the auxiliary halls built fifty years earlier. Recreation had been exalted as the church's premiere social program; new social halls and gymnasiums throughout the church provided a fitting throne.

Although recreation halls were designed to be locations where leisure activities could uplift and train young people under the watchful eyes of church leaders, it was not always possible for Mormon officials to control what occurred inside the centers. In some cases, competition for control of the church hall came from outside commercial interests vying with church programs for members' attention. Despite prescription and proscription from church leaders, recreational activities often took on a trajectory of their own.

Traveling shows in particular interfered with recreational activities in the first decade of the twentieth century. The YMMIA General Board reported that it was becoming commonplace for ward MIA activities to adjourn so that the amusement hall might be leased to traveling theatrical companies. In order to create revenue to meet ward expenses, the local leaders preferred the rental income from the hall to the spiritual and social impact of the weekly MIA meeting. Amusement halls, in keeping with the LDS tradition of multifunctional space, could improve financial bottom lines, too. General church leaders, however, found this a "very poor excuse." Instead, the leaders instructed, "the ward organizations should come first, when it is the question between the appearance of a transient show company, or even a local show company, and a religious meeting." Nevertheless, arrangements were permitted that allowed MIA members to attend both weekly religious meetings and theatrical shows. For example, associations could hold their MIA meetings early enough in the evening to allow participants the opportunity to attend the theater. Local leaders were likewise instructed to make arrangements with the "show people" to begin their programs after the weekly church gatherings adjourned. In no case, warned the General Board, should the religious meetings be abandoned.[18] Experience had shown LDS leaders that the various forms of commercial and church recreation could not be contained strictly by general pronouncements. Local arrangements had to fit local needs—within certain parameters. Ward organizations could not do as they wished, but they were given enough freedom to construct programs that had the best chance of success under local circumstances.

The articulation of interior space that placed Mormon recreational and religious activities in close quarters reached a crescendo between 1949 and 1955, when the architect Theodore Pope's designs came into widespread use. Among the approximately three hundred buildings designed by Pope, Martha Sonntag Bradley notes "the first use of the juxtaposition of the recreation hall area to the rear of the chapel in order to achieve a more flexible expansion of the assembly space for large gatherings." Bradley argues that the creation of a continuous flow between chapel and recreation area accelerated the secularization of wardhouse space. "Many wards opened the doors between cultural hall and the chapel," Bradley writes, "joining them together and creating an easy flow from formal sacred space to informal secular space and in this way inevitably changed the relationship of each member to the space in which he worshipped."[19] There is an alternative way to view the changing spacial orientation of LDS meetinghouses. Rather than segregate church structures into "formal sacred space" and "informal secular space"—the chapel versus the gymnasium—it is more fruitful to discern the evolving definition of recreational activities from nonsacred toward sacred. If "sacred" activities are defined as any that bridge the gap between humanity and divinity, then early twentieth-century Mormons could argue that properly directed recreational activities qualify as sacred. Though organizational and spiritual power still separated the bishop from the basketball coach, it was commonly agreed that they were waging the same war. If spiritual and social evil was the ever-present enemy, then sacred activities could range from sacraments to shuffleboard, from sermons to Scout meetings. The curtain that separated the chapel from the recreation hall did not create a barrier between sacred and nonsacred space in LDS chapels; it merely separated sacred worship space from sacred play space.

On the local Mormon landscape, the addition of separate amusement halls alongside meetinghouses and the eventual inclusion of recreational space within church buildings meant that recreation was accorded official status within the religious organization. Church-sponsored recreation, as evidenced by the building boom that constructed recreational buildings throughout the intermountain West, changed the very shape of LDS meetingplaces. The advent of rational recreation also changed the definition of sacred and secular activities for many church leaders and members.

The Temple of Health

Looming over the LDS recreation landscape was the church-sponsored Deseret Gymnasium in Salt Lake City. By understanding the rationale that led to the gym's construction and analyzing the various social and athletic programs sponsored by the institution, we can gain a deeper appreciation of how integral recreational activities were to Mormon society in the early twentieth century. Furthermore, a close examination of Deseret Gym programs reveals in sharp relief the prescribed gender roles of Mormon men and women in the early twentieth century.

In February 1907, the church president, Joseph F. Smith, attended the celebration of Domestic Arts Day at the Latter Day Saints University (LDSU) in Salt Lake City, where he announced that the church had finally extricated itself from debt. Following the Edmunds-Tucker Act of 1887, which forbade the church from owning any property over fifty thousand dollars, the church had been forced to borrow money to maintain its organizational infrastructure. That debt had placed a heavy burden on the Saints for several decades, forcing church leaders to forestall expansion in favor of paring down the principal owed to creditors.[20] Now that the church was completely out of debt, according to Smith, it was time to use the income that had been earmarked for debt service for other purposes. After describing the annual savings of thirty to sixty thousand dollars that had previously been made in interest payments, Smith announced to the LDSU audience that he would "'like to see a part of this means expended for the building of a gymnasium for the University.'"[21] At a later date, he expanded on the reasons for building the gymnasium as part of the church school system:

> "Physical education" as a part of school training in the latter part of the nineteenth century had become an integral and indispensable part of education, and before the end of the first decade of the twentieth century had become, in many colleges, the dominant factor. In our Mutual Improvement organizations and Church schools, athletics and physical training were also features of considerable importance, and many of the brethren felt that through such activities the youth of the Church could be controlled and trained in proper habits and sportsmanship as well as receiving the exercise needed for the proper care of the physical man.[22]

The problems inherent in city life also propelled the construction of the new gym. Underscoring the concept that "it is a part of [the Mormon] creed that the most efficient Latter-day Saint is the one who is well balanced mentally, morally, and physically," one article noted that urban residents lacked opportunities for physical development. Rather than growing up healthy and strong—in contrast to the robust youth of agricultural areas—youth in the city had a tendency to "grow up hollow-chested and weak-eyed." There-fore, church authorities provided a site where young Mormons could im-prove their physical stamina through exercise and athletics under the "di-rection of our own people."[23] The need for physical exercise under LDS supervision may have seemed particularly pressing after the construction of a new YMCA building in downtown Salt Lake City in 1904. Situated on the corner of First South and First East, the centrally located facility drew its share of Mormon customers. Until the construction of the Deseret Gym, LDS Church leaders could offer no realistic alternative to the comprehen-sive programs at the Y.[24]

Great social, spiritual, and physical results were expected to flow from the new Deseret Gymnasium. Those employed by the gym spoke in rever-ential tones about the aims of the institution. A letter from the chairman of the gymnasium, LDS Apostle Hyrum M. Smith, and the gym secretary, Bryant S. Hinckley, informed LDS bishops of the great potential of the facility's activities. The letter promised that the gym leaders were "very anxious to make this institution a real blessing to the men and women of this community, and at the same time to make it a strong arm to the church." The letter asked bishops to explain the advantages of the gymnasium to their ward members at a suitable time.[25] On another occasion, Hinckley reminded "friends" of the gymnasium that the ultimate aim of the recreational com-plex was to help young Mormons live "nobler and better lives."[26] In the words of the leaflet newspaper published by the institution—the *Deseret Gymlet*—physical development had a "serious purpose."[27] More than eight decades after the organization of the church, there was finally a permanent facility dedicated to the physical well-being of the Saints. Though amuse-ment halls had long been familiar sites in Mormon communities, the con-struction of the Deseret Gym affirmed the religious organization's interest in physical fitness. By constructing a "Temple of Health," Mormon leaders supplied a suitable location for LDS members to care for their physical bodies. If, as Paul described, the body was a temple, Mormons worshiped at the Deseret Gym.

Opened on 20 September 1910, the gym was hailed as "the largest and best equipped institution in the intermountain district." Before finishing their plans, the designers of the building—the architects Lewis Telle Cannon and Ramm Hanson and the engineer A. P. Merrill—traveled the country and vis-ited the newest and best gymnasiums. The final product represented a com-posite of the structures they encountered in their travels.[28] Ninety feet wide, 150 feet long, and three stories high, the gym cast an imposing shadow on the block just east of Temple Square. An immense ground floor housed offices for the director and instruction staff, a barber shop, six standard bowling alleys, a handball room, a private exercise room, two rooms for visiting teams, twenty-three private dressing rooms, a locker room complete with thirteen hundred steel lockers, and a private locker room. Special accommodations were made for a "ladies' hair-drying room."[29] The swimming pool was flanked by twelve showers and a washroom with toilets. Shower baths were required of all swimmers. The 30–by-60–foot pool's depth ranged from four and one-half feet on one end to eight feet at the other; slate steps and brass ladders led into the water, and a springboard was attached at the edge of the deep end. Bowing to the demands of modesty, a unique floor plan isolated the pool and the two female locker rooms from the rest of the building. The pool was reserved for women at regular intervals, which allowed for private swimming while activities continued in the rest of the building.[30]

The stairs on either side of the entrance hallway led to the main gymnasium, the wrestling room, and the physical examiner's office. The large gymnasium—or Main Hall—was the central feature of the building. A "splendid room," the gym measured seventy-one by 146 feet with a thirty-two-foot-high ceiling.[31] Indian clubs, dumbbells, and chest weights lined the perimeter of the room, and ladders were attached to the walls. Gymnastic devices included jumping and vaulting standards, parallel bars, horizontal bars, horses, and mats. The middle portion of the room was taken up by four basketball courts, flying rings, traveling rings, trapezes, and rope ladders. Medicine balls, a rowing machine, neck, wrist, and leg machines, and other apparatuses filled the room's ample space. With a polished maple floor, the hall could quickly be transformed from a gymnasium into a dance hall. A large skylight crowned the structure and made the interior pleasant and inviting. A third-floor spectator gallery surrounded the main room and accommodated crowds of more than one thousand for games and exhibitions. Suspended above the gallery was a cork running track (fourteen and one-half laps to the mile) wide enough for two runners. In two corners of the room, athletes could slide down to the main floor via brass rods. The Salt Lake Temple may have been the most prominent structure on the city's skyline, but the Deseret Gym was the area's most up-to-date facility.

Though monumental in size, the popularity of the gymnasium prompted regular additions to the physical plant. In 1913, three handball courts and a spectator's gallery were added to meet the demand for that sport. The cost of six thousand dollars was offset primarily by public subscription. Five years later, at a cost of thirty thousand dollars, a women's gymnasium opened with a separate locker room, showers, a steam room, and hair dryers. Additional sports were added to the gymnasium's offering when the gym took over control of Wandamere Park and built the Wandamere Golf Course. The golf course was subsequently sold to Charles W. Nibley. In 1926 a fifty-thousand-dollar construction project added seven handball courts, a visitors' gallery, wrestling room, shop, and an additional entrance for boys. By 1928, the athletic institution had been enlarged to over fifty-one thousand square feet.[32]

The gymnasium's proximity to the Salt Lake Temple and the advertising films depicting the athletic complex as the Temple of Health spoke to the growing importance of religious recreation in the Mormon church. When guided into proper channels, recreation assumed religious significance; athletics, socials, and even Scouting activities took on a holy tenor. Elder Brigham H. Roberts, a Mormon theologian and longtime member of the First Seven Presidents of the Seventy, enunciated the place of athletics in LDS theology. In an address delivered at the Salt Lake Tabernacle in October 1912, Roberts built an ideological bridge across Main Street connecting the Temple of the Lord and the Temple of Health:

> I do not wish to appear over-bold and certainly not sacrilegious, in any respect— but I do venture this assertion, that after this six-spired building [the Salt Lake Temple] here, on this square, and the other temples of God builded [sic] by Latter-day Saints, which for us are the holy of holies, the temples of God, but after the temples of God, I say there is no holier building erected by our hands than this other temple within shouting distance of us, which is devoted to the physical training and development of our youth, the gymnasium that the Church has established under the guiding vision and by the aid of the presidency of the Church.[33]

He also proclaimed that the gymnasium symbolized the Mormon belief in the sacredness of the human body. The sports and games that went on in the gymnasium could, according to Roberts, help young men maintain clean hands and a pure heart. Keeping in mind the common wisdom early in the century that masturbation caused men and boys to lose their physical vitality,[34] Roberts's thinly veiled message seems clear: "Pride in manly strength leads the boy to despise and turn away from the things which in his adolescent age would undermine his strength, bow his head and compel him, shame-faced and eyes cast down to the ground to move among his fellows a conscious weakling and a coward!" Roberts found the solution in physical exertion. "Through outdoor sports, through inviting to contests of strength and of skill," the general authority argued, "we hope to infuse into the youth of Zion this pride in manly strength, physical strength, which shall feel [sic] courage and enable a man to face the duties and the responsibilities of life with his forces unimpaired, including—pardon me for saying it— no, you need not pardon me, I ask no pardon, it is proper to say it—including his duty, not only as a citizen, but his duties and responsibilities as husband and father; the most solemn duties that a man can face."[35] Just as attendance at the Temple of God promised spiritual blessings and renewal, participating in games at the Temple of Health brought physical renewal. One temple cared for the spirit, the other tended the body. Both were necessary appendages to a Mormon theology concerned with the spiritual, physical, and social welfare of humankind.

From the beginning, the Deseret Gym offered an ambitious physical exercise program for members. The first major advertising campaign for the institution—a pamphlet entitled *The Wise—For Health on Exercise Depend*—outlined the facility's programs and the rules that governed member participation. The main attraction for gymgoers (and the major initiative for gym workers), as the title of the pamphlet indicated, was increased health. And finding health was no narrow labor focused solely on building strong muscles and healthy appetites. Rather, borrowing a quote from J. J. Pope, "health" was defined as widely as possible. According to Pope, health was "not mere freedom from pain or sickness" but encompassed "an entire soundness—a wholeness or holiness—an integrity of every structure, embracing in its true extent both mind and body, and demanding, therefore, a perfect harmony in the play of every function of the living organism."[36] As both an ideological statement and advertising technique, a crusade for holiness (stemming from the interconnection of body and spirit) played a central role in LDS hopes for the Deseret Gym.

The athletic complex bustled with activity. Based on a foundation of strict rules that ensured social order within its ladder-laden walls, the gym offered a variety of programs to meet the range of physical needs. Opening each year on 1 September, the gymnasium's season of organized activities ran throughout the winter and closed the first of May. For the 1911–12 season, annual fees varied from seven dollars (including a one-dollar locker fee) for boys and girls (ages twelve through fourteen), twelve dollars for students attending Salt Lake High School, fifteen dollars for intermediate men and women (ages sixteen through eighteen), and eighteen dollars for men and women over age eighteen. Businessmen paid twenty-five dollars for full gym privileges. The youngest boys were admitted to the gym only two afternoons a week, while the intermediate boys could participate any afternoon until six P.M. Senior men could use the facilities at any time except when it was occupied by women. Women controlled the gym each morning (except Saturday) and on Monday and Thursday evenings. The gym reserved Thursday afternoon for women as well.[37] A 50 percent discount applied to young men and women who were "faithful in attendance in Sunday School and either Primary, Religion Class, or Young Ladies' Mutual Improvement Association."[38] Thus the Deseret Gym sought to insure that the physical development of Zion's youth would not outpace their spiritual growth.

Each individual who applied for membership underwent two examinations: a "physical examination" to determine bodily needs so that a proper exercise regimen could be devised "to remedy any physical or organic defect" in the applicant, and a medical examination to test the heart and organs of the applicant to make sure he or she could withstand violent and strenuous exercise.[39] Prospective members could either present a certificate from a reputable physician or receive a complete physical examination by gymnasium officials, free of charge.

Once the battery of physical tests had been satisfied, gym members had to follow specific behavioral guidelines while using the facility. For example, clothing regulations kept members in clean, functional garb. Whether this represented a democratic leveling of gymnasium apparel or an authoritarian grab for clothing control, the Deseret Gym was no place for the display of sartorial splendor. The "regulation suit" prescribed for men included a white sleeveless shirt, rubber-soled shoes, a leather belt, and "Turner" trousers; black socks and knee pants differentiated the men from the boys. Girls and women received fewer guidelines—they were instructed merely to wear "regular gymnasium suits."[40] Appropriate gym apparel was available through the gymnasium at a discount. With rules governing what went on the body firmly in place, gym officials turned to controlling unruly mouths. Two of the myriad gymnasium rules specifically proscribed language that came out of members' mouths and intoxicants that went into them. Rule 13 advised, "PROFANE OR INDECENT LANGUAGE, LOUD TALKING, WHISTLING OR UNNECESSARY NOISE WILL NOT BE TOLERATED. Quiet and orderly behavior will always be expected from members and visitors." Loud, raucous, gymnasium-type antics would not be tolerated. Rather, an attitude of reverence—befitting a Temple of Health—should prevail. The next rule declared, "Smoking or the use of tobacco or intoxicants in any form is strictly forbidden in any part of the Gymnasium."[41] From the LDS perspective, good health and the Word of Wisdom required such a rule. But respect for the physical body was not the only reason to prohibit tobacco use. The gym was, in essence, a holy building that would be defiled by the use of worldly intoxicants. The regulation of everything from footwear to foul language promised to keep the gymnasium and its users clean.

Following a demanding physical workout—or perhaps in place of traditional exercise—gymgoers could receive treatment from a "first class masseur and medical gymnast," Erland Druselius, late of the Stockholm Royal

Medical Institute. Druselius came to the gymnasium with impeccable credentials. A graduate of the school of Massage and Medical Gymnastics at Upsala Medico-Mechanical Institute in Sweden, Druselius had worked as an assistant in histological anatomy at the medical department of Upsala University and in various hospitals in Brussels. A former masseur at the Battle Creek Sanitarium, he came to the Deseret Gym from Augustana Hospital in Chicago.[42] Interestingly, the techniques of "scientific massage" were offered not only as a recuperative therapy but as a "curative treatment." "If scientifically given," read an advertisement, "the massage alone is a highly valuable means of maintaining a good healthy, physical condition, and of restoring health, either as a direct curative, or as an adjunct and auxiliary to the physician's special treatment. No claim is made for massage as a 'cure all,' but when applied by a scientific masseur will not only relieve and cure a number of physical ailments but prevent them also."[43] Treatment would only be applied after consultation with the patient's physician. Massage was particularly well suited to the physically disabled or those disinclined to physical activity.

Validation of the gym's approach appeared in a series of letters published in an advertising pamphlet. Extolling the success of the businessmen's activities sponsored by the gymnasium, each letter emphasized the healthful benefits of exercise. One participant reported, "Since joining the gym my health has improved wonderfully; have increased in weight; reduced my waist measurement; and am entirely free from occasional headaches and dull sensations which gripped me occasionally in previous years." Another asserted that he felt happier, looked better, weighed less, and had more friends since joining the gym; his waistline was smaller by four inches. The praises of the gym were sung by another participant who advised readers: "All who want to enjoy life, to eat well and sleep like a child, join the Gym . . . have a game of volley, basket or baseball with a jolly lot of boys, then a shower bath, and a plunge and swim in the pool, a rub-down and you will say with me, 'I feel like a new man.'"[44] During the early twentieth century—when a premium was placed on professionalization—testimonials from businessmen must have carried particular weight as an advertising tool.[45] Judging from these experiences, the church had succeeded in helping members to live "nobler and better lives" through gymnasium work.

Gender Roles and the Deseret Gym

Sports skills and exercise plans were not the only subjects taught at the Temple of Health in downtown Salt Lake City. In the process of learning about medical gymnastics or the rules of handball, gymnasium members were also schooled in the expectations surrounding gender roles in the Mormon community. Because little has been written on the historical process that created gender expectations among the Saints—or about the relationship between leisure-time activities and gender-role prescription—the activities at the Deseret Gym and the gender-laden messages that they transmitted to generations of Mormons help us understand how Mormon gender roles were propagated.

The Deseret Gymnasium float entered in the Pioneer Day parade in 1941 reflected the gendered messages that the gym had been teaching for decades. Aboard the gaudily decorated float as it cruised down Main Street stood three prominent groups: muscled male bodybuilders posing in trunks; stately women modeling swimming suits; and young boys wearing track singlets.[46] However unrepresentative of LDS society they might have been, in many ways the groups on the float symbolized the gender-role lessons that gym members could logically take away from the courses offered by the gym. Gym activities taught men to be strong (in the physical "waistline" as well as the fiscal "bottom line"), women to be smooth and svelte of figure, and boys to be constructively engaged in physical activity rather than the destructive behavior of the streets. Young women—taught largely along the same lines as their mothers—seem to be subsumed in the floating category of bathing beauty.

As far as the Deseret Gym was concerned (at least as it appears in various forms of advertising), all men were businessmen—chained to a desk, chasing the next dollar. Progressive-Era "men on the make" comprised the main target audience for the gym. In an effort to attract the business of businessmen, the gymnasium's advertising and exercise programs centered on the concept that physical fitness contributed to business efficiency. One advertising booklet sold businessmen on the physical-fiscal connection. "Are you all tired out," asked the pamphlet, "ready to drop at the end of the day's work, or do you walk along the street with your head up and chest out, as if you owned the town? The Deseret Gymnasium offers to every business man in Salt Lake City, thru their business men's classes, the opportunity of putting himself in that superb physical condition that is evidenced by a good carriage of the body (head held high and chest out), and which will make him feel like doing a full day's work every working day in the year." Increased efficiency, bolstered bottom lines, and an improved appearance all resulted from the "hygienic exercises, recreation and relaxation" available to the city's business professionals. Over 550 men had enrolled in the previous year, and, according to the booklet, the consensus of the group was that participation *"pays."*[47] No greater inducement could have pried busy men away from ledgers and contracts to pick up dumbbells and medicine balls. Physical health and business health went hand in hand. A poem directed to the "Busy Man" advised:

> Now wipe your pen
> And close your desk
> 'Tis time to go to Gym.
> 'Twill rest your brain
> Improve your health
> Increase your business vim.[48]

In many respects, to paraphrase a well-known refrain from the 1920s, the business of the Deseret Gym was business.[49]

Businessmen were invited to take advantage of their "Business Partner, Gym." In a booklet by that title, written by Samuel Hopkins Adams for *Collier's Weekly* and reprinted by the Deseret Gym, a fictional businessman becomes involved with his local YMCA gymnasium to improve his health. Owing to his newfound energy and clarity of thought, the man's business prospers. With "new vitality," problems are more easily solved and business efficiency soars.[50] Salt Lake businessmen merely had to substitute the Deseret Gym for the YMCA.

The stock of homilies connecting physical performance with business success seemed without end. A pamphlet entitled *Dividends,* probably produced in the early 1930s, contained a plethora of pithy quotes extolling exercise to urban professionals. Consider a few:

> The man who has not cultivated two habits—that of saving and investing—will not only miss many of the best things in life, but will finally be overtaken with bankruptcy. There is no form of bankruptcy more serious than physical bankruptcy; no failure more tragic than health failure.
>
> The man to be envied is the man who has upon his cheek that proof of a sound digestion.
>
> Proper exercise not only adds to one's efficiency but to the sweetness and satisfaction of living.
>
> There are better ways of keeping fit than the ways of the teaspoon.
>
> You can't be right on the job unless you are on the job right.[51]

The terms employed clearly appealed to the sensibilities of businessmen. Saving, investing, bankruptcy, soundness (whether in digestion or currency), and efficiency all speak directly to the business experience. It was as though the scientific management of the body (recall the "scientific massage" techniques of Erland Druselius) had been combined with the managerial techniques that brought efficiency to industrial production. As one gymnasium director told the members of the Salt Lake Executive Club in 1938, "Sound health is sound business."[52]

To meet the needs of modern businessmen, myriad programs were instituted during the first decades of the century. Initially, the gym fashioned itself as a "well-equipped resort" for urban men who could not make it to the seashore or mountains. "After the hot, hard hours of work" at stores, offices, and factories, businessmen were invited to the "unbounded pleasure" of the gym's athletic fields and tennis courts.[53] The game of handball was likewise trumpeted as an easy exercise option for "Busy Business Men." One gym advertisement called attention to the fact that "any business man in Salt Lake City can leave his office, play a lively game of hand ball, have a shower, swim, dress and return to his office within an hour. Four courts means no waiting."[54] The gym's highly advantageous location in the middle of the city's business district meant that businessmen did not have to wait until the shop was closed to visit the gym.

The opportunity to sunbathe on the Deseret Gym's roof lured many businessmen from their windowless offices. One newspaper article, illustrated with an aerial view of sunbathers on the roof of the gymnasium, praised the virtues of sun seeking with a special appeal to businessmen: "Sun bathing promotes health in young or old. Every man can now take his daily sun bath and swim or shower without going to the beaches. On the roof of the Deseret Gymnasium . . . right in the heart of town . . . just one-half block from Main and South Temple Streets. . . . Facilities have been provided for business and professional men to relax with a sun bath, shower and swim in an hour's time, or less, for only a few cents a day. No need to go to the beaches for such a luxury. Where else can you find such an opportunity?"[55] The variety of activities available at the gym—handball, volleyball, swimming, weightlifting, calisthenics, and sunbathing, to name a few—made it easy for businessmen to pursue physical fitness. Moreover, the gym promised that physical fitness led to fiscal fitness in the workplace; bodily and business health closely correlated. The answer was clear to purveyors of physical exercise. If a businessman had become "sluggish from too much swivel chair duty" or if he "lack[ed] confidence, [was] easily bluffed, or [was] not sure of [him]self," there was "only one worth while remedy—exercise."[56]

The model for Mormon men promulgated by the Deseret Gym's advertising is clear. Mormon men were businessmen—pursuing profits during the day and chasing a handball during their leisure hours. At a time when

Americans were beginning to regain respect for the titans of industry (after many had fallen out of favor in the "trust-busting" fervor at the turn of the century) and when urban professionals were laying the foundation for a "new middle class," the Deseret Gym sought to enshrine the gendered standard of the LDS businessman and to attract customers by portraying the gymnasium in business-friendly terms.[57]

Mormon women, by contrast, were presented with a traditional model of feminine activity that prescribed physical fitness primarily to enhance physical beauty. Although some consideration was given to the "New Women" of the 1920s—working women with an aroused feminist consciousness—the general trend was toward maintaining a "trim figure"; any muscles developed at the Deseret Gym were to be used only within the traditional confines of the domestic sphere. One of the earliest attempts to motivate women to attend the gymnasium made it clear that "mothers and housewives" were "women who have watched over and taken care of others at the expense of their own health and beauty." "Corrective work" available in the "Matron class" included floor gymnastics, swimming, and a weekly "demonstration on some practical vital household subject" like cooking, sewing, or personal hygiene.[58] By the 1920s, the virtual motto of the gymnasium combined fitness and feminine physical appearance; the gym promised women and girls "to preserve health and beauty to those who already possess it" and "to give health and beauty to those who seek it."[59]

The message sent out by the Deseret Gym stressed that health and beauty (with some housework thrown in) formed the core identity of most Mormon women. A poem from the mid-1930s elaborates on the gymnasium's appeal to female participants:

> You gotta bend down, Sister, bend down, Sister
>   If you want to keep thin.
> No more messing with French dressing,
>   Sister, bear it and grin!
> You can flirt with noodle soup,
>   Sniff, but don't give in. . . .
> Throw your strudels to the poodles,
>   Sister, bear it and grin!
> Ev'ry mouthful that you eat,
>   Adds another chin!
> You gotta bend down, sister, bend down, sister,
>   If you want to keep thin.[60]

On other occasions, women's exercise classes were touted for their contribution to feminine beauty. "Try this one, some of you plump girls," ran the caption to a photo spread in the *Deseret News*, "it is highly recommended as a flesh reducer."[61] Both examples are far removed from the testimonials of businessmen extolling the virtues of the gymnasium that had helped them to *gain* weight! Viewed not as a method to increase business efficiency, exercise for women was marketed as a way to maintain physical attractiveness—presumably as a lure to attract or keep male suitors interested. This campaign, then, reworked a biblical injunction by teaching women to reduce and multiply. Helping women increase their sexual attractiveness to men was the keystone in the gym's effort to attract women.

Female beauty may have been the main selling point, but the Deseret Gymnasium also offered women an opportunity to improve their overall quality of life through exercise and athletic participation. There was some suggestion that female beauty went deeper than tight skin and trim waistlines. For example, a twenty-lesson course in dancing demonstrated that "dancing is for the purpose of beautifying the soul."[62]

Physical beauty, at times allied with more meaningful issues, remained central among the myriad virtues available to gymgoing women. An advertising letter sent out by the gym manager, H. C. Mortensen, in 1940 detailed the variety of reasons for women to attend the gym. "How would you like to have overflowing health, keen enthusiasm, vivid life? How would you like to keep that lovely figure? How would you like to be thoroughly well, youthful in looks and activity, physically perfect, mentally keen?" Prospective clients who answered any of these questions affirmatively were invited to the gym for "wholesome, exhilarating exercise," including floor classes, swimming, tennis, and badminton.[63] Women workers in the Relief Society—presumably suffering from the stresses of motherhood and church service—received a poetic invitation to "Park Your Worries at the Deseret Gymnasium":

> Got any aches, got any pains?
> Fallen arches, varicose veins?
> Muscles relaxed until they sag
> Legs can't hurry, seem to drag?
> Pep you used to have all gone
> Hardly strength to carry on?
> We have a cure for all such ills,
> Better than tonic, powders, or pills—
> Try exercise and learn to swim
> Park your worries at the Deseret Gym.

Offering more than "relief" to workers in the Relief Society, the gym promised

> health and happiness
> Relief from mental strain
> We offer joy of living
> Offer youth again.[64]

While health and beauty remained the premium feminine virtues advertised by the Deseret Gym, the 1920s saw a concerted effort to reach out to the growing community of working women. Learning lessons from World War I—that women could "do their share of the world's work" and that "the promise of an intellectually, physically fit, democratic people" rested with American men and women—gymnasium advertising targeted the New Women of the postwar decade. This new generation had a new attitude about their societal roles and were less likely to succumb to the marketing ploys centered on domestic activities.[65] "The women who picked up the commercial gauntlet laid down by the men when war called them," one gymnasium pamphlet advised, "will not silently slop back into the old domestic condition." Rather, bolstered by their success in dealing with the industrial problem during the war, these women looked to futures in business and industry; lessons in home economics no longer satisfied them. The future, according to gymnasium literature, would see women marching "shoulder to shoulder with their men . . . into the new world of Democracy—into their Land of Promise."

To succeed in this much wider field of activity, women needed to cultivate physical fitness. Women were warned to "resist against being weighed down with an unsightly burden of degenerating fat; refuse to be a flat-chested, stooping, puny apology for a woman—refuse to carry a handicap of bodily feebleness; resist against your languidness, against being stiff in muscles, short of breath, easily tired; against being considered anything else than a real live, vital, worthwhile woman if you wish to hold your place in the sun."[66] Women in this industrial age had a new role to play, and like their male business counterparts, they needed to stay in shape to fight the economic battles they faced. Unlike the gym's appeal to businessmen, however, a fixation on feminine beauty remained. Whereas men were instructed that tight muscles led to sharp minds, women were reminded that "degenerating fat" was unsightly and that a small chest measurement made females an "apology for a woman." The message was largely the same for both genders—physical fitness results in industrial success—but the messages directed toward women continued to connect physical health and feminine beauty.[67]

Though charged with the important task of improving the physical fitness of Mormon women, Deseret Gym advertising writers maintained a sense of humor. They realized that while exercise brought beauty, the rough-and-tumble world of the gymnasium did not always immediately improve appearance. Rather than emphasizing improvements in strength and stamina provided by gym attendance, one anonymous writer catalogued the various "changes" of another sort experienced by regular gymgoers:

It's time for you to graduate
So—this is your "degree"—
A charley-horse, a broken nose
A crippled shin and knee.

A nice sprained tendon, one black eye
Some knuckles minus skin,
Your fingers with the joints all out,
My—what a shape you're in!

I'm sure that just to glance at you,
Most anyone would say—
"I wonder where these girls all go
To get to look this way?"

The Deseret Gymnasium
Has kept its word to you—
No matter how the job was done,
It's made a *change* in you![68]

Perhaps in the long term physical beauty was enhanced, as the gym promoted; however, the short term was often a much different story, complete with bruises, broken bones, and loosened teeth. Such irony surely was not lost on the women who frequented the gym's courts.

The Deseret Gymnasium was a place where men learned to be men and women how to be women. As shown through their advertising campaigns and exercise programs, LDS gender expectations more or less mirrored the "cult of domesticity" that flowered in the nineteenth century, separating the world into a feminine domestic sphere and a masculine work world.[69] Though this bifurcation applied to any American social group in only the most limited fashion, as an ideology it continued well into the twentieth century. Proponents of the gym, however, were not slavishly tied to an antiquated definition of gender roles. When women entered the workforce in greater numbers during the First World War, gym advertising reflected the emerging attitudes of America's New Woman without completely celebrating her role outside of the home. Even though some new attitudes were forming in the early twentieth century, the overwhelming message emanating from the Deseret Gym was that men were supposed to work outside of the home (and exercise in the gym to increase their business efficiency). Women were primarily to remain in the domestic sphere as mothers and wives and exercise in the gym to maintain their sexual attractiveness.

Men and women were not the only ones who learned proper behavior from gymnasium programs. Adolescent boys—whose free time might otherwise have been spent loafing on street corners or in other delinquent activities—prompted great concern among Mormon recreational leaders who saw the Deseret Gym as a haven where misguided boys could be given lessons in wholesome leisure-time activities. Much like settlement houses in other urban areas, the gym would fill the boys' time with meaningful and uplifting activities.[70] Summer courses, vocational training, and myriad recreational options existed to occupy the spare hours in any young man's life. The gym's appeal to parents and other social and religious leaders emerges in a letter written just after the athletic facility opened. "Experience shows that a gymnasium can do more to help a boy at a certain age than any other institution can," argued the letter. "Its purpose is to take boys from the streets and give them something to do which is both recreative and educational, to establish them in habits of cleanliness and self respect, and thus to start them on the royal road of life." If used properly, as the early experience of gymgoers had proven, the gym was of "inestimable value" to a young man's life and future. "Physical training increases the boy's efficiency. It adds years to his life and life to his years."[71] In a letter to "Parents of Real Boys," the gymnasium secretary Bryant S. Hinckley proposed that membership in the Deseret Gym would provide boys with specific lessons and opportunities. Hinckley's list included furnishing the boy "with the best of associations," cultivating his "play instinct," and "teach[ing] him to play on the square and to work on the same plan." In general, the gym provided a boy with a "sound body, a clean mind and a clear head."[72] To worried parents and church leaders, this represented a new approach to keeping wayward youths in line—send them to the gymnasium, where physical defects would be corrected and social dysfunction avoided.

The gym took its calling to aid the youth seriously. If there was a program that might interest young men and direct their energy in a wholesome direction, the institution sponsored it. For example, in February 1912, the gymnasium organized a band and orchestra for boys and young men. Classes in violin, trombone, clarinet, cornet, and other band instruments were taught by Clarence J. Hawkins, a graduate of the New England Conservatory of

Music. Gymnasium members paid fifty cents per month, while nonmembers paid one dollar.[73] For those more interested in outdoor activities, the gym hosted a nine-day summer excursion to Camp Saratoga in 1912. Nestled along Utah Lake, the camp contained an athletic field, baseball diamond, grandstand, and open-air mess hall. Fine fishing, beautiful lawns, beach facilities, and a large swimming pool of hot sulphur water rounded out the area's attractions. Moreover, the camp offered "manly supervision" and the knowledge that the young man was "in a much safer place than if he were on the streets of his own city." Gymnasium members paid five dollars for the camp; the six-dollar fee charged to nonmembers needed to be accompanied by a recommendation from "some reliable person."[74]

In addition to providing for a summer camp far from the mean streets of the city, the Deseret Gymnasium held annual summer courses to "help boys who have nothing to do during their vacation." Founded on the concept that "there is nothing so detrimental to a boy's welfare as idleness, and one of the serious problems which confronts parents in the city is to find a suitable employment for their boys during summer," the gym offered a woodworking course for boys aged ten and above. Meeting for three hours each morning, the course not only kept boys from the street corners but taught them a useful skill as well.[75] The annual summer program began in 1912 and continued for several decades. In 1914, the Vacation School was part of a cooperative effort between the gymnasium and the Young Men's Christian Association.[76] One summer, the Manual Training Department of LDSU sponsored a summer course at the gym that focused on manual training in the morning followed by an hour of exercise, a shower bath, and a plunge in the swimming pool. Hands and minds—the "open doors through which flows the evils and follies of boyhood"—were kept busy as boys learned how to work and how to play.[77] Future summer courses, such as the school held in July 1922, furthered the trend toward "recreation of a highly practical character."[78] That summer, boys were trained in cabinet work, lathe turning, radio construction, auto mechanics, and home electricity. Through programs such as these, the Deseret Gym turned summer from a season of idleness into a time of "pleasure and profit" for the young man.

Though proportionally fewer programs were created to meet the needs of young women, a variety of activities was available. Like their male counterparts, girls could participate in summer courses designed to teach practical skills. While boys were learning the rudiments of woodworking, girls received instruction in dressmaking and millinery. If interested, younger girls could enroll in courses teaching first aid, tennis, swimming, and dancing.[79] In the summer of 1935, the gym and the Lion House cooperatively taught girls the practical household arts and the basics of dancing and swimming. What girl could resist the siren song of the course's advertising flyer?

> Come girls let's go to the Lion House
> And learn to sew or knit a blouse—
> And then we'll run into the gym
> And learn to dance and have a swim.

Not only would each girl make something useful and beautiful, she would "work and play with the finest and best companions."[80] At times the male bias of the gymnasium was unmistakable. According to Elsie Ellen Hogan Van Noy, general secretary of the YLMIA, groups of LDS girls had to use the swimming pool at the YWCA because "it seemed the Deseret Gymnasium was so busy with the Boy Scouts that we had a difficult time working in swimming classes at the Gym for our Bee-Hive girls."[81] Other courses—including an amazing array of dance programs—brought together boys and girls on the floors of the gymnasium.

In addition to special programs that appealed to young men and women, the Deseret Gym was the mainspring of recreational instruction and athletic exhibition in Salt Lake City during the first half of the century. Free dancing lessons for area bishops, regional meetings of the National Recreation Association, indoor golf school, and fencing lessons made up only the smallest fraction of what went on in the gym. Exhibitions of world-famous sports teams and athletes brought hundreds of thousands of visitors to the gym each year. The Harlem Globetrotters, championship rounds of church athletic tournaments, and tennis exhibitions that included Fred Perry were among the regular attractions at the gym in the middle decades of the twentieth century. Some lesser-known acts also found their way to the Deseret Gym. In 1940, the five-year-old muscle marvel Billy Withers bent steel bars across his throat and lifted fifty pounds with his baby teeth for an audience at the gymnasium. Two years earlier, a crowd had gathered to watch the champion boxer Gene Tunney get in shape on the gym's squash court.

Over the years, the Deseret Gymnasium expanded to meet the increasing needs of church members and Salt Lake City residents. By the 1950s, however, it became clear that the original gym had outlived its usefulness. In 1963, the church constructed a new facility one block to the north and razed the old Deseret Gym to make way for a new church administration building. An important chapter in Mormon social history was ended. The new gym would have its own stories to tell. The second Deseret Gymnasium was torn down in 1997 to make way for the LDS Conference Center.

The Deseret Gym, like the recreation halls that dotted the Mormon landscape, evidenced the growing importance accorded recreation and athletics within the LDS Church. The redefinition of recreational activities as sacred culminated with the construction of the Temple of Health in 1910. Within its hallowed walls, Mormons learned not only the rudiments of wholesome recreation but also the gendered expectations of life in LDS society. In the early twentieth century, holy spaces occupied both sides of Main Street in downtown Salt Lake City.

Notes

1. The scripts for each of the films are located in Deseret Gym Records, LDS Church Historical Department, Salt Lake City (hereafter Deseret Gym Records), 17. No author or date appears on the scripts.

2. See James B. Allen, *The Man—Brigham Young* (Provo, Utah: Brigham Young University Press, 1968), 42.

3. "The Mutual Improvement League," *Contributor* 11 (Sept. 1896): 691–92.

4. Howard R. Driggs, "The Library-Gymnasium Movement: Elements of Success in the Work," *Improvement Era* 13 (Mar. 1910): 442.

5. Howard R. Driggs, "The Utah Library-Gymnasium Movement," *Improvement Era* 12 (May 1909): 510, 511.

6. Ibid., 512.

7. Martha Sonntag Bradley, "'The Church and Colonel Saunders': Mormon Standard Plan Architecture" (Master's thesis, Brigham Young University, 1981), 33.

8. "Events of the Month," *Improvement Era* 7 (Jan. 1904): 233. One of the first sermons in the new building was delivered by the church president Joseph F. Smith, who spoke to a large gathering of young people on the subject of "Conduct and Amusements."

9. "Editor's Table—Amusements," *Improvement Era* 14 (May 1911): 638–39.

10. E. J. Milne, "Ward and Gymnasium Hall," *Improvement Era* 12 (Dec. 1908): 162.

11. Ibid., 163.

12. "Mutual Work—M.I.A. Reading Room and Gymnasium in Logan," *Improvement Era* 13 (Mar. 1910): 469–70.

13. Melvin Lemon, "How Hyrum Second Ward Built Its Recreation Hall," *Improvement Era* 28 (Aug. 1925): 976. In many cases, the money for constructing new recreation halls was raised in raffles or at church fairs. This form of fund-raising came under attack from the University of Utah philosophy professor Milton Bennion in 1907. Bennion, who later became president of the LDS General Sunday School, decried those who focused on the ends without considering the means: "The money may come from the saloon or the gambling den, but it is thought to be all right, so long as this money is used to build or furnish a church. The aim of the church, to save and exalt the souls of men, is forgotten in the mad rush to excel in church build-

ings and furnishings, or other material ways." Rather than using raffles or other gambling games to raise money, Bennion countered, "Why not give these people a chance to contribute in a way that would eliminate all possibility of selfish motives, and by so doing also refrain from appealing to avarice and fostering evil habits in the morally weak?" See Milton Bennion, "The Ethics of Church Fairs," *Improvement Era* 10 (Oct. 1907): 959.

14. "Mutual Work—Saloon Becomes Gymnasium," *Improvement Era* 9 (Apr. 1916): 568.

15. Levi Edgar Young, "Sociological Aspects of Mormonism," *Improvement Era* 23 (July 1920): 828–29.

16. "Recreation Halls," *Improvement Era* 27 (Apr. 1924): 576.

17. "The New Recreation Hall in Connection with the Twenty-seventh Ward Chapel" (ca. 1927), 1–2. Located in the LDS Church Historical Department, Salt Lake City.

18. "Mutual Work—M.I.A. Meetings and Theatrical Shows," *Improvement Era* 11 (Jan. 1908): 229–30.

19. Bradley, "'Church and Colonel Saunders,'" 53, 136. Though Bradley contends that Pope introduced the "juxtaposition of the recreation hall area to the rear of the chapel," it appears that a connection between the chapel and the recreation hall had been created by 1922. In an Ocean Park, California, chapel completed in September 1922, the amusement hall was separated from the main auditorium (chapel) by built-in sliding doors. See Rulon H. Cheney, "Chapel in Ocean Park Dedicated," *Improvement Era* 26 (Nov. 1922): 46.

20. For more on the church debt, see Leonard J. Arrington, *Great Basin Kingdom: An Economic History of the Latter-day Saints, 1830–1900* (1958; rpt., Salt Lake City: University of Utah Press, 1993), 400–403.

21. As reported in Edward H. Anderson, "Events and Comments," *Improvement Era* 10 (Feb. 1907): 316.

22. Joseph Fielding Smith, *Life of Joseph F. Smith* (Salt Lake City: Deseret Book, 1969), 425.

23. "The Deseret Gymnasium," *Improvement Era* 13 (Sept. 1910): 1048.

24. The ground breaking for the new building was announced in "Events of the Month," *Improvement Era* 7 (June 1904): 634–35.

25. Letter from Chairman Hyrum M. Smith and Secretary Bryant S. Hinckley to Bishops (undated), Deseret Gym Records, 11.

26. Letter from Bryant S. Hinckley to "Friend" (undated), Deseret Gym Records, 10.

27. *The Deseret Gymlet* 1 (17 Apr. 1912): 1.

28. "Mutual Work—The Deseret Gymnasium," *Improvement Era* 13 (Feb. 1910): 381.

29. Ibid., 379.

30. For information on the amenities of the gym, see "The Deseret Gymnasium" and "Mutual Work—The Deseret Gymnasium."

31. "Mutual Work—The Deseret Gymnasium," 380.

32. For a short but useful history of the Deseret Gymnasium written by one of the main proponents of physical fitness in the church, see Bryant S. Hinckley, "History of Deseret Gymnasium" (12 Jan. 1928), Deseret Gym Records.

33. B. H. Roberts, "Sphere of Y.M.M.I.A. Activities," *Improvement Era* 16 (Jan. 1913): 191–92.

34. One account of nineteenth-century fears of masturbation can be found in G. J. Barker-Benfield, *The Horrors of the Half-Known Life* (New York: Harper and Row, 1976), esp. 175–88 ("The Spermatic Economy and Proto-Sublimation").

35. Roberts, "Sphere of Y.M.M.I.A. Activities," 191, 193.

36. *The Wise—For Health on Exercise Depend* (Salt Lake City: Deseret Gym), 21. This pamphlet contains an extensive outline of the gym's programs for 1911–12; L. Tom Perry Special Collections, Harold B. Lee Library, Brigham Young University, Provo, Utah.

37. For scheduling information, see "The Deseret Gymnasium," 1050.

38. *The Wise,* 11.

39. "The Deseret Gymnasium," 1050.

40. *The Wise,* 6.

41. Both rules appear in ibid., 18.

42. For more information on Druselius, see the pamphlet *Medical Gymnastics and Scientific Massage,* Deseret Gym Records, 113.

43. *The Wise,* 13.

44. Ibid., 8.

45. On the Progressive push for professionalization, see Robert H. Wiebe's discussion of the "new middle class" in *The Search for Order, 1877–1920* (New York: Hill and Wang, 1967), 111–32.

46. This picture can be seen in Deseret Gym Records.

47. Untitled pamphlet, Deseret Gym Records, 5.

48. Advertisement for Deseret Gym, Deseret Gym Records, 61.

49. In the records of the Deseret Gymnasium, only a handful of references to men other than business professionals appear. The most notable instance—though the original source is unclear—appears in an advertisement for the gym that might have run in a local Jewish newspaper. The ad claimed, "The privileges of the Deseret Gym are within the reach of the Laboring man. The facilities are the best, the program is delightful and health building and the terms are easy. Why not ENJOY LIFE through HEALTH and EXERCISE?" Deseret Gym Records.

50. Samuel Hopkins Adams, *My Business Partner,* "Gym," 39 (LDS Church Historical Department, Salt Lake City).

51. *Dividends,* Deseret Gym Records.

52. "Health Value Explained by Gymnasium Head," 17 Jan. 1939 newspaper clipping in Deseret Gym Records.

53. *Summer Days and Nights in Salt Lake City, Utah: Where and How to Spend Them,* Deseret Gym Records, 39.

54. *Handball, a Game for Men: A Lively Pastime Full of Brief Breezy Bits for Busy Business Men,* Deseret Gym Records, 39.

55. *Deseret News,* 1936, Deseret Gym Records.

56. *Deseret Gym Digest: Promoted in the Interest of Health, Happiness, and Humor* 1 (26 Apr. 1950): 1, Deseret Gym Records.

57. Interestingly, at the same time that the gym was combining business acumen and physical fitness, leadership in the church was placed in the hands of Heber J. Grant, a man who had found success both as a businessman and athlete. Though Grant does not appear to have influenced the gym's advertising campaigns or business-oriented activities, he certainly created a cultural standard for Mormon men to emulate. On the life of Grant, see Ronald W. Walker, "Heber J. Grant," in *The Presidents of the Church,* ed. Leonard J. Arrington (Salt Lake City: Deseret Book, 1986), 211–48.

58. "Deseret Gymnasium Season 1912–1913," 13, Deseret Gym Records, 114.

59. "What the Gymnasium Means to Women and Girls," 3, Deseret Gym Records.

60. Untitled poem, dating from approximately 1934, Deseret Gym Records.

61. *Deseret News,* Rotary Gravure Section, 16 Apr. 1921.

62. "Dancing for Middle Aged Women," Deseret Gym Records, 217.

63. Letter from H. C. Mortensen to "Friend" (ca. 1940), Deseret Gym Records.

64. "Park Your Worries at the Deseret Gymnasium," advertisement, Deseret Gym Records.

65. On the emergence of the "New Woman," see Lois W. Banner, *American Beauty* (New York: Alfred A. Knopf, 1983), 187–89.

66. *What This Gymnasium Means to Women and Girls,* 3–4. A few years earlier, the gym began a special class for "business girls" on Thursday evenings. Worried that "thumping typewriters, keeping books, clerking and like occupations [did] not provide opportunities for physical diversion," the gym was made available to working women on a regular basis. The women were promised a "jolly affair," emphasizing dancing and swimming. See letter, 3 Apr. 1916, Deseret Gym Records.

67. For additional background on the changing definitions of female beauty, consult Banner, *American Beauty.*

68. Untitled Poem (May 1935), Deseret Gym Records.

69. On the "cult of domesticity," see Barbara Welter's groundbreaking article "The Cult of True Womanhood, 1820–1860," *American Quarterly* 18 (Summer 1966): 151–74. On Mormon women in the nineteenth century, see Jill Mulvay Derr, Janath R. Cannon, and Maureen Ursenbach Beecher, *Women of Covenant: The Story of Relief Society* (Salt Lake City: Deseret Book, 1992); Chris Rigby Arrington, "The Finest of Fabrics: Mormon Women and the Silk Industry in Early Utah," *Utah Historical Quarterly* 46 (Fall 1978): 376–96; Jill Mulvay Derr and Ann Vest Lobb, "Women in Early Utah," in *Utah's History,* ed. Richard D. Poll et al. (Provo, Utah: Brigham Young University Press, 1978), 337–56; Carol Cornwall Madsen and Susan Staker Oman, *Sisters and Little Saints: One Hundred Years of Primary* (Salt Lake City: Deseret Book, 1979); Carol Cornwall Madsen, "Mormon Women and the

Struggle for Definition: The Nineteenth-Century Church," *Sunstone* 6 (Nov.–Dec. 1981): 7–11, rpt. in *Dialogue: A Journal of Mormon Thought* 14 (Winter 1981): 40–47; Maureen Ursenbach Beecher, "The 'Leading Sisters': A Female Hierarchy in Nineteenth-Century Mormon Society," *Journal of Mormon History* 9 (1982): 25–39; Jill Mulvay Derr, "'Strength in Our Union': The Making of Mormon Sisterhood," in *Sisters in the Spirit: Mormon Women in Historical and Cultural Perspectives*, ed. Maureen Ursenbach Beecher and Lavina Fielding Anderson (Urbana: University of Illinois Press, 1987), 153–207; Jessie L. Embry, *Mormon Polygamous Families: Life in the Principle* (Salt Lake City: University of Utah Press, 1987).

70. For activities at Chicago's Hull-House, see Jane Addams's firsthand account in *Twenty Years at Hull-House* (1910; rpt., Urbana: University of Illinois Press, 1990) and Addams's *The Spirit of Youth and the City Streets* (1926; rpt., Urbana: University of Illinois Press, 2001). On the settlement-house movement generally, see Allen F. Davis, *Spearheads for Reform: The Social Settlements and the Progressive Movement, 1890–1914*, 2d ed. (New Brunswick, N.J.: Rutgers University Press, 1984).

71. Unsigned, undated (ca. 1912) letter, Deseret Gym Records, 7.

72. Letter from Bryant S. Hinckley to "Parents of Real Boys" (ca. 1912), Deseret Gym Records, 16.

73. Letter from Bryant S. Hinckley to "Brother," 7 Feb. 1912, Deseret Gym Records, 16.

74. *Camp Saratoga: Deseret Gymnasium Boys' Camp*, June 1912, Deseret Gym Records, 26.

75. Letter from Parents' Department (Deseret Gym) to Parents, 14 June 1912, Deseret Gym Records, 31.

76. *Vacation School, Young Men's Christian Association*, 1914, Deseret Gym Records, 52.

77. *An Ideal Summer Course for Boys: He Goes Home Clean and Contented*, Deseret Gym Records, 78.

78. "A Vacation with Pleasure and Profit—The Deseret Gymnasium Summer School," 1922, Deseret Gym Records.

79. Ibid.

80. "1935 Summer Activities Deseret Gym and Lion House," Deseret Gym Records.

81. Elsie Ellen Hogan Van Noy, "Young Ladies' Mutual Improvement Association from April 1927 to December 1937" (ca. 1957), 12, located in the LDS Church Historical Department, Salt Lake City.

CHAPTER THREE

"FOR THE UPLIFTING AND THE BETTERMENT OF THE YOUTH OF ISRAEL"

Athletics, Socialization, and the "Selling of the Word of Wisdom"

> I suppose I played tennis on almost every public and private court in town, and I know I hiked over every golf course. For three or four winters, with a club basketball team, I ran myself ragged in the frigid amusement halls of a hundred Mormon ward houses and took icy showers and went home blown and rubber-legged late at night. With a team in the commercial league, or with the freshman squad at the university, I hit all the high school gyms, as well as the old rickety Deseret Gymnasium next door to the Utah Hotel, where cockroaches as big and dangerous as roller skates might be stepped on behind the dark lockers. From games and parties I ran home under dark trees, imagining myself as swift and tireless as Paavo Nurmi, and the smell and taste of that cold, smoky, autumnal air and the way the arc lights blurred in rounded golden blobs at the corners is with me yet.
>
> —WALLACE STEGNER, "At Home in the Fields of the Lord"

While the Deseret Gymnasium offered urban Mormons a grand Temple of Health dedicated to physical fitness and well-being, the gymnasium was merely the centerpiece of a large church-sponsored athletic program designed to serve a myriad of social and spiritual ends. From Salt Lake City to Samoa, young men and women participated in an array of athletic and recreational activities that maintained adolescent involvement in the church and ensured that commercial amusements were not the only leisure-time activities available.

The onus of putting LDS recreational philosophies into practice fell largely on the church's youth auxiliary organizations—the Young Men's and Young

Ladies' (later Young Women's) Mutual Improvement Associations (YMMIA and YLMIA). In organizing the YLMIA in 1869, Brigham Young had instructed: "There is need for the young daughters of Israel to get a living testimony of the truth. Young men obtain this while on missions, but this way is not opened to the girls. More testimonies are obtained on the feet than on the knees. I wish our girls to obtain a knowledge of the Gospel for themselves. For this purpose I desire to establish this organization." The cultivation of spiritual gifts and the creation of "testimon[ies] of the truth" likewise played a central role in the founding of the Young Men's auxiliary in 1875. In that year, Young charged Young Men and their leaders to "let the key-note of your work be the establishment in the youth of individual testimony of the truth and magnitude of the great latter-day work; the development of the gifts within them that have been bestowed upon them by the laying on of hands of the servants of God; cultivating a knowledge and an application of the eternal principles of the great science of life."[1] Though testimony building lay at the heart of the youth organizations, the major focus of the groups, as Brigham Young had advised, quickly became activities that kept adolescent feet busy. Spiritual awakening may have remained the auxiliary's ultimate goal, but physical activities comprised the bulk of day-to-day programs. Where the previous generation had found salvation on their knees by learning to pray, young Mormons in the early twentieth century were taught to find God on their feet by learning to play.

As recreational activities moved to the center stage of Mormon adolescent social life, no single auxiliary had been appointed to provide leadership. Previously, each auxiliary (Sunday School, the Relief Society, priesthood quorums, children's Primary, and the youth MIAs) had organized parties, get-togethers, and excursions for its members. Because the church had no overall organizing plan for recreation before the early 1900s, each group was left mostly on its own to devise social activities. Though each auxiliary continued to provide social and recreational activities, by the dawn of the twentieth century the burden of promoting church-sponsored activities had fallen to the youth organizations. In part, this was due to the belief that adolescents were more likely to have the time and inclination to support games, sports, and other recreations. Likewise, church leaders recognized that young persons needed special attention if they were to remain allied with the church.

As early as 1903, the YMMIA and YLMIA formulated guidelines for directing proper "amusements and entertainments." As a bedrock principle guiding LDS recreation, the General Board of the YMMIA declared that Latter-day Saints had recognized the need for amusements "from the beginning." More importantly for the youth auxiliary, however, the General Board argued that in LDS circles "the older people fully recognize the fact that amusements are necessary for the young folks" and that "recreation and rest are not useless; nor a necessary evil." Amusements for young people, then, were "not a luxury but a positive necessity, and the efforts of our officers should be not to suppress, but to control them." As part of the effort to control amusements, the board called for the organization of local committees to regulate the recreational offerings of wards and stakes. In keeping with the fluid nature of recreational management, the bishop (or stake president) would supervise a committee composed of at least one representative from each auxiliary organization. This committee, in turn, made sure that all local activities adhered to the standards established by the General Boards.[2]

The board furnished guidelines for the local committees to follow. All amusements were to be educational—not necessarily boring or of a serious nature but "of a high class." In fact, the board confessed, "merriment and wit are not only allowable but advisable." The General Board recommended literary entertainments but advised local leaders to "avoid all objectionable methods of dancing, late hours, and card-playing." Dancing, amateur theatricals, picnics, concerts, and home socials qualified, while "brain-taxing games" were not encouraged in areas where young people worked "in occupations requiring the exercise of the brain more than the muscles." Late hours were to be avoided everywhere, but especially in country districts, where late-night travel was likely to prove physically and morally injurious. Other forms of amusement—billiards, commercial dance halls, and late-night buggy riding—received similar discouragement. Although complete leadership of LDS recreation programs had yet to be assigned to the YMMIA and YLMIA, their leadership on issues concerning the recreation of adolescents was already evident just after the turn of the twentieth century.[3]

Writing a year after the formation of the stake and ward committees on amusements and entertainments, the YMMIA board member Willard Done argued in 1904 that the organization had drifted away from its original calling, which included the "development of religious faith" and the "development of proper social intercourse and recreation," to a focus narrowly confined to theological issues alone. Theology, Done concluded, was only one part of the MIA's program. If the organizations were to keep young people within the church, they needed to emphasize debate, music, science, and history. Therefore, the YMMIA "desire[d] to depart from this exclusive work, and make our work a little more general, and begin again to occupy the field we practically abandoned a few years ago, viz., the field of general culture and social enjoyment."[4]

In 1909 the General Board of the YMMIA passed a resolution calculated to secure control of church recreation and to ensure the future viability of the auxiliary. "Owing to the fact that the priesthood quorums have formally taken up the study of theology," YMMIA leaders resolved to provide "educational, literary, and recreative studies, permeated by religious thought." The organization would support music and art programs, and leaders stressed that "social culture and refinement of manners constitute an important part of our endeavor." Athletic programs were likewise encouraged, and the resolution called for manuals to be written that reflected the organization's shift in emphasis.[5] These were not wholly new ideas in a church that had long stressed the positive nature of wholesome recreation. By staking claim to recreational leadership, however, the YMMIA created a new niche for itself in the church's organizational scheme. Now that the priesthood quorums had assumed control of theological instruction, the MIAs needed to legitimize their existence. By providing recreational leadership, the MIAs could serve the youth of the church as well as the institution. Over the next two decades, the organizations honed their approach toward recreation and ensured that the youth auxiliaries would continue to play an integral role in the church.

From nearly all quarters, great results were expected from the leisure-time leadership of the MIA. Perhaps the most wide-ranging expectations for the MIA's new role came from Apostle Heber J. Grant. Describing the "Place of the YMMIA in the Church," Elder Grant joined Willard Done's call for an inclusive MIA program that extended beyond theology. The youth organizations, Grant wrote, "give opportunity for study along religious, social, scientific, intellectual and physical lines." Just as importantly, the apostle argued that church youth activities kept young Mormons within the fold and away from social clubs and select educational societies. Church influence and direction were needed in all areas, particularly recreation. "If we fail to provide our young men with the opportunity of [wholesome church recreation]," Grant warned, "they will go outside of Church influences to indulge in these things." Later in his address, he described the variety of church recreational options and detailed why the programs were so important:

> Do away with our associations and you reduce the young ladies' opportunities to capture good husbands. As a social center in which public and private amusements may be carried on, and proper conduct inculcated and made popular, our organizations are useful and beneficial. Here the young may engage in musical, dramatic, and other like entertainments and festivities. Scouting, field sports, athletic tournaments, excursions, dances, and other social gatherings are here encouraged, giving the young people an opening under proper tutelage and supervision

for their pent-up energy that might otherwise display itself in wrong actions. . . . The [recreation] field, if not occupied by this Church organization, will be occupied by private companies and associations, not always desirable and clean, but formed for money-making. How many crimes are committed for money! We want these amusements, not for the dollars, but for the uplifting and the betterment of the youth of Israel.[6]

No single statement better captures the expectations for and the philosophy behind the MIA's recreation program in the Progressive Era and beyond. Providing an appropriate gathering place for young men and women, teaching proper conduct, developing personal talents, and keeping Mormon youth away from the perverting influences of commercial recreation comprised the hopes and the challenges facing the youth-directed recreation programs. These ideals found poetic expression in Jane McJackson's poem, "The M.I.A." (1921):

> Strong's our organization of the M.I.A.;
> It stands for our improvement all along the way.
> It gives us high ideals, helps us reach our aim;
> It keeps us up and doing in a worth-while game.
> For we've no time for loafing, or for idle play,
> If we are earnest workers in the M.I.A.[7]

The high ideals of earnest MIA workers often translated into worthwhile games that aimed for personal improvement and kept youngsters off the streets.

While most church leaders supported the new recreational aims of the MIA organizations, a handful of prominent Mormons questioned whether recreational programs were best suited to teach their youth the physical and spiritual skills needed to survive. In September 1911, the Salt Lake physician Charles L. Olsen penned a letter to the editor of the *Improvement Era* offering an alternative to the recreation-based youth programs. "If but a fraction of the time, talent, and energy now spent in exploiting amusement for our young people were utilized in devising means of *useful employment* for this same class of individuals," Dr. Olsen wrote, "I do not hesitate to assert that we should have better, nobler, more useful and positively more valuable young people than at present. As it is we rear a lot of assuming, expectant, demanding, dependent leaners. Where are the lifters among our young people? There are some, but they are very few."[8] Unlike most LDS recreation theorists, Olsen complained that structured leisure-time activities were turning out lazy, sniveling "leaners"—not the hardy "lifters" who would lead society down the proper paths. Play had little currency in Olsen's scheme; "useful employment" provided the answer.

Recreation's ability to develop spiritual skills was assailed by Edward P. Kimball, a member of the church's music committee. Though Kimball believed that religious ideals should be applied in practical ways, including amusement and recreation, he reminded church members "to see to it that [recreation and amusement programs] fulfill constantly [their] highest service, and [do] not become perverted to such an extent that real improvement and culture can not follow in [their] wake." Kimball feared that youth recreational activities had overstepped their bounds and become an end unto themselves. Speaking particularly of the field of recreation, Kimball argued that since recreation "touches more easily the profaner things in our nature, there is danger of some things connected with it, which originally were intended to be merely incidental to the program, becoming from choice and practice the principal features in the program—not of course, in the minds of the officers, but in the conception of the work by the membership." Perhaps Kimball was only protecting his turf as a member of the music committee, or as an intellectual he may have carried a bias against physical forms of recreation. Whatever the reasons, his message was clear—too much recreation shifted the focus of young church members away from the higher pursuits that led to "real improvement and culture."[9]

Kimball and Olsen were joined by others who discerned a misplaced emphasis on youth recreation. In 1915 the editors of the *Improvement Era* related the story of a General Board member invited to speak to a local association. In preparing his address, he was informed that any topic was acceptable except for "religion and vocations." Incensed, the editors shot back a sharp reminder to local MIAs: "It must be remembered that the main purpose of our organization is to impress the membership with a testimony of the gospel, and its restoration in the latter days through the Prophet Joseph Smith." Building on that foundation, the editors turned their attention to secondary issues in the youth groups. "All other work and activities and studies that we engage in are merely means to this great end. How, then, can the membership of an association justify themselves in asking merely for entertainment? And how can they consistently request that a speaker shall not discuss religion before them?"[10] The inculcation of religious values was the goal of the organization, and recreation provided merely one means. An overreliance on leisure-time activities, according to the editors and others, was not merely an oversight but a repudiation of the basic tenets of the youth organizations.

Calls for reining in the church's recreational activities remained in the minority for most of the early twentieth century, however. In fact, the horse was already out of the stable, as ward-sponsored recreation programs had become the center of social life for adolescent Mormons. Instead of fighting against the program, most ward leaders focused their efforts on providing wholesome and proper recreational outlets for their young members and hoped that activities at the meetinghouse would lead to lifelong activity in the church.

Not to Make Records, but to Make Men

Without question, the linchpin of the church recreation program was the organization of a variety of competitive and cooperative athletic events. By 1909, when the MIA General Board resolved that "athletic work be encouraged and established wherever practicable," athletic activities had already become a major aspect of local MIA efforts.[11] The movement toward establishing athletics within the church was founded on what MIA leaders considered to be firm philosophical and theological ground.

In employing athletics as an arena for social and moral instruction, Mormon leaders placed themselves in the mainstream of Progressive social thought. Progressive playground theorists, according to the historian Dominick Cavallo, linked "muscular coordination and 'efficiency' acquired through careful physical conditioning to moral development and control. In fact, they argued that it was possible to determine both the content and strength of the child's moral faculty by means of prescribed, and repetitive, physical drills." Though LDS thinkers never made explicit the connection between strength and spirituality, most LDS writings on the subject accepted some correlation between flabby muscles and flabby morals. Mormon leaders were more likely to echo the accepted sociological dictum that sports, and particularly team sports, developed a social sense among participants. Striving for a common goal (in the case of some sports, quite literally), players fostered a sense of community where team success outweighed individual accomplishment. As Cavallo describes the ideas of the respected play theorist James Mark Baldwin, "The primary value of team games . . . was their role in teaching the child that he must conform to the values and aspirations of his social group. . . . For instance, baseball engendered a 'spirit of union' among the players, a desire for each to be like all. If the youngster wanted to be accepted as a valued member of the team, he had to acquire 'the habit of suspension of private utilities for the larger social good.' In sports, society's values, mores, and techniques of social competence were 'projected' into the child. The individual learned that his abilities and desires were meaningless outside the context of communal approval."[12] Like Progressive theorists who primarily concentrated their efforts on "Americanizing" immigrant children in urban areas,[13] Mormon leaders socialized youngsters through sports; they merely changed the primary social allegiance from nation to church. The same principles applied whether reformers wanted young persons to assimilate into a national community or into a religious group.

Team sports played a central role for Progressive playground planners and for Mormon play organizers. In fact, the same theories energized both efforts. Describing the philosophy that led play leaders toward team competition, Cavallo writes: "The team as 'one great community' shaped and legitimized the player's behavior and values. It also placed specific limits upon his right to behave in a 'competitive' or 'individualistic' manner. The rhythmic, synchronized movement of a basketball team as it roamed up and down the court forced players to see, feel, think, and act as a unit rather than as individuals. . . . Because the team experience forged social unity out of individuals from diverse ethnic, class, and religious backgrounds, play organizers viewed it as an antidote to the alienation, violence, and loneliness seemingly inherent in urban society." The team aspect of games promoted a "corporate conscience" in individuals who realized that membership in a larger social group or organization synergistically affected personal worth. As part of a team, youngsters learned that community responsibility outweighed individual needs. Individuality was transcended through the team experience; personal identity became a function of membership in a social group. Cavallo characterizes the lessons that Progressives found in team play: "The player should obey the rules, but he must also be loyal to teammates, willingly sacrifice personal glory to the common cause, graciously accept defeat, perceive victory as a group rather than an individual achievement, and obey the team captain. . . . The team experience was an attempt to create an equilibrium, a creative balance, between individuality and group direction."[14]

At times, Mormon athletic philosophy conformed almost perfectly with certain strands of Progressive playground thought. Though written slightly after the heyday of most playground theorists, the *Handbook of the YLMIA and YMMIA,* published in 1931, taught two of the central concepts of Progressive thought—the correspondence between muscles and morals and the potential of team sports to socialize adolescents. According to the handbook, "at no time has there been such a need for clean athletics as there is in America today." Urban children, especially boys, were growing "pretty soft" from a constant diet of commercial entertainment, riding in "fine automobiles," and eating rich food. Citified urban boys had missed out on the rugged experiences from which the "early American pioneers derived so much good in the moulding of their characters." With little hope of future frontiers to tame, Mormon leaders turned to athletics as a form of vicarious pioneering. Because hard work no longer led to hard muscles, hard play would have to suffice. A young man would learn physical and moral lessons by participating in athletics. Though the wording is somewhat ambiguous, it is easy to see the moral underpinnings that formed the philosophical foundation of the athletic program. The lessons appeared everywhere to athletic enthusiasts. "First the boy is taught that to sweat is not vulgar and that a young body will function better if the blood is forced to circulate a little faster occasionally. He is taught to take care of his body," the manual advised. Remembering that the dietary Word of Wisdom contains both physical and moral components, the handbook emphasized the link between team sports and moral behavior. "If he is to compete on an athletic team there are some things he cannot do. He is taught to say 'no' to excesses in eating. He knows he cannot smoke, and that he cannot drink. He knows he cannot stay out late at night, and that his body will not function at its best if he abuses it. The self-denial, which is one of the greatest developers of character, is very good for him." For the individual player, the development of muscular strength and moral fortitude seemed to go hand in glove, or perhaps hand in mitt.

Participation in team sports, especially under the watchful eye of a moral coach, also taught social skills in a powerful way. Again, speaking of the sporting young man,

> His athletic coach can exact more self-denial from him than can his own parents. He is taught there are rules in the game. Again there are things he can do and things he cannot do. This respect for law, if early inculcated in the lives of our young boys, would do much toward the remedy for the neglect of law that is now prevalent in America. He is taught to be loyal to himself, and loyal to his team, and loyal to his school, and loyal to his Church. This will carry over into his life and inspire loyalty to his home, his wife, his family and his country. He is taught never to quit. To be called "yellow" is the worst name one can call an athlete. This test of character he will carry on into the battle of life. He is taught "team play" or cooperation—a wonderful trait to develop.[15]

This statement represents the Progressive playground code translated to fit the Mormon experience. Team sports not only had the power to "Americanize," they also carried the potential to "Mormonize" urban adolescents.

It would be nearly impossible to catalog the variety of sporting events sponsored on the ward, stake, and general levels of the LDS Church. Tens of thousands of basketball games, thousands of baseball games, hundreds of track and field meets, and countless field days could be accounted for by naming the victorious squads or recounting final scores. It is more important to examine why church leaders turned to athletics and what they expected competitive athletics to mean in the lives of young church members, especially boys.

An analysis of LDS athletic programs lays bare the male-centered nature of Mormon recreation. Although it is clear that young women participated in athletic events, they were not the primary focus of recreation leaders. Sports helped to resolve the "boy problem." If girls received positive socialization through athletic events, all the better. But boys were the main target.[16]

In athletics, church play leaders found a flexible social device that could be shaped to address an assortment of problems within the church and in Mormon society. Athletic involvement spurred male adolescent activity within the church and promoted adherence to church principles. Moreover, participation in sports filled a need for physical training among the young as well. By modeling a sense of order, team sports gave young men the skills to cope with the temptations of urban life. Furthermore, church leaders noted that athletics provided a ready-made tool for proselyting missionaries throughout the world. More than anything else, however, church leaders hoped that athletic participation in a wholesome atmosphere would shepherd the adolescent male along the path toward moral maturity.

Noting the variety of social and personal problems afflicting adolescent males, the YMMIA General Board member Lyman R. Martineau preached about the social and moral lessons found in athletics. In an October 1912 *Improvement Era* article, Martineau wasted little time addressing the needs of young men: "Some say they do not need athletics. It seems to me that all young men need them. Where is there a ward without the idler, the 'kicker,' the tempter, who especially need them? There is a crisis in the adolescent period of every boy." From Martineau's perspective, a major component of the adolescent crisis was biological—sexual stirrings that once lay deep beneath the surface were beginning to bubble over. Social problems only added to the explosive biological mix. "The change from boy to man is a physical change," Martineau asserted. "New ideas come to him, and he obtains a broader view of things, and a thrill of conscious power and self-reliance stirs the blood that hitherto has readily yielded to parental rule. The anxious parent needs help under these conditions. There is need to give direction to the hot blood and enthusiasm of youth, rather than to allow it to be wasted in the mania for speed, or lost in the stagnant stupidity that comes from idleness and bad company." Besieged by both sex drive and social stresses, young men needed all the help they could get. Athletics offered the answer. "The boy needs constructive discipline, and he needs someone to associate with, who has a purpose in life and who, understanding the boy-spirit, may teach him that organized play is better than destructive deviltry or stupid idleness." Athletics, then, provided the means to inculcate proper social behavior and high morals. In Martineau's words, "Athletics in the

M.I.A. has a higher purpose than mere recreation. Our track meets are not primarily to make records, but are a part in the program to make men. The mission of the [ward] Mutual Improvement Associations is to save and develop our boys and young men, and an important element in their development is giving them such physical, mental, and moral vigor as shall place them in the highest standards of efficiency."[17] The goal in this athletic program was not winning gold medals but teaching youngsters to live the golden rule. By creating a structure to contain the "hot blood" of youth, church athletics put the lid on simmering sexuality and changed misdirected boys into moral men.

To create an organizational structure that used sports to influence young men, the YMMIA in the urban Ensign Stake began serious gymnasium work in 1908. Under the careful supervision of E. J. Milne, then a member of the stake board and the physical director of LDSU, and Dr. E. G. Gowans, a member of the stake board, boys gathered at the LDSU gymnasium twice a month for a theological lesson and an hour of physical sports, including basketball and foot races. On one occasion, the church president Joseph F. Smith and many members of the General Board watched 127 young men go through their paces and were "delighted with the exercises." Smith's visit provided official approbation for MIA-sponsored athletic programs. As the *Era* recorded, "In our large cities, physical training in connection with the Mutuals is a crying need, and doubtless more will soon be said and done in this matter."[18] Physical training for the young men was considered so valuable (particularly in keeping youth from "downtown places") that exercise was permitted to infringe on the time normally devoted to theological training. "'Even if the regular lessons should be curtailed by these exercises,'" the *Era* directed, "'it is believed that no harm will result, for many of the boys and young men are doing fairly good work in the quorums of the priesthood, where they are taught theological subjects, and their religious duties.'"[19] Physical exercise programs were never intended to replace theological training for young men in the church, but by 1908 the emphasis of the YMMIA was beginning to tilt toward athletics as the most valuable aspect of the youth organization.

Church-sponsored athletic programs meant that boys were not only improving their physical stamina, they were playing under the direct supervision of church officials. In other words, by getting a boy to participate in LDS sports, leaders ensured that at least the boy was spending some time at the church. Athletic programs kept young men from the vagaries of street life and also created a positive church-related experience for many. At the annual MIA conference in 1910, Lyman Martineau promised that "if our organizations would take up athletics and make it one of the prominent features of their work, and invite the boys that were inclined to be wayward, that in due course of time these very boys would become enrolled members in the organizations." Striking two of the major chords accompanying athletic work among LDS youth, Martineau concluded, "Athletics, carried on in a proper manner, will do much to increase our attendance and bring about a general moral uplift."[20] Other YMMIA leaders, like the General Board member and Deseret Gym architect Lewis Telle Cannon, reiterated the attraction that athletics offered to boys who might otherwise avoid the meetinghouse. "Already some of the stakes have demonstrated the power of [athletics] properly managed to increase the interest and attendance at Mutual meetings," Cannon related. "There is chance here for all possible diversity. Get organized for it and try it out and you will recognize its value in adding interest to your work and in enabling you to reach some who might be otherwise unapproachable."[21]

Success seemed to follow the athletic programs. Hailed as a motivating factor for many young men, athletic participation increased attendance at meetings and adherence to church principles (primarily the Word of Wisdom). As early as 1902, the organization of an athletic club had helped the Colonia Juarez (Mexico) Ward "suppress blasphemy" among the young men. As sponsor of an athletic club, the ward proscribed profanity among club members; offending members were subject to expulsion. Their efforts found success as young men who had been "addicted to small swearing, quit, and assisted in the labor of suppressing the evil."[22] In Duchesne, Utah, the YMMIA superintendent Edwin L. Murphy reported that the formation of an MIA basketball league "proved of great interest in bringing the boys to the Mutual and in doing away with tobacco." For the following summer, Duchesne Stake planned to arrange interward athletic contests to maintain the momentum created by the interest in the winter sports.[23] E. W. Watkins, the athletic director of the stake board, reported that the participants in the Box Elder program learned impressive sports skills and stayed out of trouble. "The type of baseball played by these young men was equal in many cases to some of the professional games," Watkins claimed. "It has the tendency to encourage parents to take greater interest in their young sons and assist materially in solving some of the social problems of the day."[24] Box Elder's investment in physical programs had paid immeasurable dividends: athletic excellence, family unity, and social peace. No sociological study was needed to convince Watkins of the impact that MIA sports had on his local community. In Salt Lake City, it was reported that Sabbath attendance at pleasure resorts had dropped primarily because athletics and other activities kept young men "so occupied, so interested, so wrought up with the splendid things they have to do" that they soon learned that "they will have greater joy in performing this work than in seeking pleasure in an illegitimate way."[25] As these cases indicate—at least in anecdotal form—the athletic programs of the LDS Church often lived up to the high expectations of Progressive and Mormon play theorists.

LDS recreation programs also helped Mormons export their doctrines throughout the world. Church leaders quickly learned that athletic participation by LDS proselyting missionaries often made inroads with potential converts that otherwise would have been impossible. This strategy was widely advertised by reports in the *Improvement Era*. Readers of the magazine could not avoid the message that sports and proselyting created a potent combination. The first account linking missionaries to sports came from Japan where, in 1911, American missionaries working in Tokyo joined the "Tokyo-American Baseball Team." Composed of about thirty expatriate Americans, the team played once a week against Japanese student or club teams and other American teams, including a group of sailors visiting Yokohama. An eighteen-game season allowed the missionaries to rub shoulders with teammates from throughout the United States and Canada. Most importantly, as Elbert D. Thomas, president of the Japanese Mission, reported, the eclectic group crossed denominational lines. "For instance," wrote Thomas, "there were a Baptist, an Episcopalian, a Presbyterian, a Quaker, a Methodist, and a 'Mormon' missionary; a United States army officer, an attache of the American embassy, a secretary of the American embassy, and an American electrical engineer." Thomas concluded that "all were the best of fellows." The accompanying pictures showed Rev. E. C. Lloyd, a missionary-teacher for the American Episcopal church and captain of the 1911 squad, standing with Elder H. Grant Ivins, an LDS missionary and captain of the 1912 team. No baptisms were reported by Thomas, but the feelings of good will proved the proselyting potential of "a phase of missionary experience that [was] a little out of the ordinary."[26]

The novelty of the American national pastime likewise brought attention to missionaries working in Samoa. On New Year's Day 1924, a missionary team played a game against a team of experienced baseball players from American and British Samoa. Though the missionaries won the game (they had lost to the same team several days earlier), the more important victory was the increasing rapport between the Mormon elders and community members. According to Melvin G. Wagstaff, the secretary of the Samoan Mission, "Our games were marked by good sportsmanship and clean playing, and they have been the means of disposing of much of that lack of understanding which formerly existed between us and our good neighbors. We hope that this play may be the means of more friendly relations and better understanding between us 'Mormon' missionaries and the local people in charge here."[27] Whether in Utah or far-off Samoa, Mormons in the early twentieth century were playing with a purpose. Using athletics as a tool to break down barriers between themselves and non-Mormons, missionaries believed they were truly at play in the fields of the Lord.

Although athletics played a central role in the church's efforts to keep young men within the fold, leaders cautioned against an excessive emphasis on sports. The degree of involvement in athletic activities was to be determined by the interest level in local areas. As Lyman R. Martineau lectured to stake YMMIA superintendents, "It is not our desire to force scout work nor any form of athletics upon any ward or stake, but we are ready and anxious to aid in organizing when and where a local demand for it is manifested. It is our aim and desire that the Y.M.M.I.A. shall organize, direct and control these activities along wholesome and uplifting lines as fast as wards and stakes can get ready."[28] The infrastructure to organize athletic programs had been created and awaited implementation; it was up to local units, however, to pick up the ball and run with it. And it did not take long for many wards and stakes to rush headlong into athletics.

Field Days

Annual track meets or field days, when members from wards or stakes competed against each other in a variety of athletic and oratorical events, were among the earliest manifestations of the church's athletic program. Though the general MIA did not hold its first official field day until 1911, sports and games had become a major attraction of the annual MIA conference several years earlier. In 1906, for example, one afternoon and evening of the eleventh annual MIA conference was completely dedicated to sports and "field day exercises" at Calder's Park in Salt Lake City. After attending theological and spiritual meetings earlier in the day, MIA workers watched a baseball game between the Box Elder and Weber Stakes, which lasted twelve innings and ended in a 4-4 deadlock. Basketball and foot races offered competitive outlets for others, while some joined boating excursions or played on the park's amusements—all free of charge to MIA visitors. An informal reception and an evening of dancing rounded out the day's events. More than three thousand free tickets had been distributed to MIA officers and workers for the event.[29] By 1911, the number of entries in the field day portion of MIA conference had grown so large that two theological training sessions were rescheduled so that an entire day could be devoted to the MIA athletic meet at Wandamere Park.[30]

The annual MIA field days were designed to showcase sporting skills and to instill sportsmanship. At the 1912 convention, a baseball team from Box Elder Stake beat a select team from Salt Lake and in the process received "many compliments on their nobby [stylish] suits." The compliments extended beyond stylish playing duds. Regarding the athletic contests held at the June conference, Lyman R. Martineau congratulated all participants: "The proper athletic spirit led several of the contesting stakes to enter the meet with less expectation to win than for the effort to secure clean, fair sport and training for sports' sake; after all, 'it is more important to play than to win.' While to win is of course desirable, it is not paramount." By extolling the virtues of clean play at the conference, Martineau established the standard for all church athletes: winning was not everything; participation counted most. To paraphrase Shakespeare, play was the thing.

Although platitudes about clean play were well intentioned, it was soon apparent that not all athletes played for sports' sake. Participation may have been the primary virtue, but winning, as Martineau mentioned, was nevertheless desirable. Some competitors undoubtedly grumbled that lopsided contests were neither fair nor fun. Because sports were supposed to produce social cohesion, the program was modified to equalize the skill level of competitors. MIA leaders created skill- and age-level classifications to ensure that athletes not only had an opportunity to compete but to win as well. "It is the intention to develop in the Y.M.M.I.A. the best talent in the Church, in athletic efficiency, regardless of whether college or high school athletes enter or not," Martineau explained. "There is much interest in these wholesome sports, among those who do not attend college or who have left school. At the next annual meet it is the intention to classify events so as to provide fair contests. . . . This will give the meet a much wider scope and invite more numerous participants in wards and stakes, resulting in bringing together at the June meet the very best men in our organization."[31] In calling for "athletic efficiency," Martineau understood that participation in sports not only taught athletic skill and grace but moreover fostered group socialization through cooperative teamwork. Martineau's efficient athletes were not only good sports but good citizens and church members. The athletic leader had surely remembered his own advice that church athletics were not instituted to make records but to make men.

At the same time that sporting events and other competitions began to dominate the MIA's June conference, athletic programs in wards and stakes experienced a similar rise to prominence. Judging from the reports that local units periodically provided to the *Improvement Era,* sports programs—especially competitions between wards and stakes—were the hub around which YMMIA programs revolved. Believing that athletic participation could teach moral and physical lessons and knowing that competitions motivated many boys toward church activity, local MIA groups turned to athletics with unparalleled enthusiasm. The importance of regular athletic participation to the success of their program was captured in a resolution passed by the Preston, Idaho, YMMIA:

> Whereas, every young man needs some wholesome recreation, which he cannot obtain unless means are provided, and
>
> Whereas, the time so devoted should be made interesting and profitable, and
>
> Whereas, Athletic sports cannot be successfully promoted unless a uniform time is devoted to them, be it resolved that,
>
> As stake and ward officers we earnestly urge the setting aside of Saturday afternoon throughout the stake for this purpose, and pledge ourselves to work to this end in our respective wards. It being understood that this resolution does not apply where young men or young ladies are engaged during the week in school work where the needed recreation is obtained.[32]

The time had come to regularize athletic work within the church. Weekly, seasonal, and annual events soon dominated MIA calendars throughout the church.

Reports flowed into Salt Lake City from wards and stakes holding regular athletic meets. The Millard, Utah, Stake YMMIA and YLMIA hosted a stake track meet at Holden, Utah, in April 1910. For three days, more than one hundred contestants from eight wards (out of eleven in the stake) competed in athletic events and oratory competitions. Though details are scarce, the young women of the stake competed in a basketball tournament won by the women of Oasis Ward. This example clearly shows female athletic participation, but the lack of detail downplays the importance of sports in the socialization of young Mormon women.[33] The following year, Millard's MIA day included oratorical contests, music, storytelling, basketball, track and field events, debate, and a grand ball. Of that event, one participant wrote, "some fifteen hundred people from different parts of the stake attended the gathering, and it was pronounced one of the most entertaining and instructive social and literary affairs and athletic meets ever held" in that stake.[34] The experiences in Millard seemed to validate the place of athletics as the main source of both entertainment and instruction in the church.

In American Fork, Utah, the Alpine Stake sponsored their second annual MIA athletic contest in June 1910. As reported by the stake secretary, John

E. Standing, a "large and enthusiastic crowd was present, every ward being represented, which speaks volumes for the interest taken in, and the popularity of, the meet." For those less interested in athletics, the Lehi Silver Band provided entertainment beyond the sporting spectacle.[35] In Salt Lake City, four urban stakes created the YMMIA Athletic League, which oversaw competitions in running, jumping, and basketball. In the first year of the annual competition held at the Deseret Gym, the Salt Lake Stake won the "silver loving cup" known as the Daynes Trophy, named after the jewelry company that had donated the prize.[36]

Other stakes used athletic competitions not only to reward victors but to earn money as well. North Weber Stake, for example, held a field day to raise funds to offset the travel expenses of stake officers visiting the far-flung wards. Various races, a high jump, pole vault, ball games, and boxing contests were augmented by a dance, picture shows, and refreshments for sale.[37] It did not take long for stakes and wards along the Wasatch Mountains and throughout the intermountain West to utilize athletic meets to entertain as well as instruct participants and spectators in the lessons of competition—namely, teamwork and cooperation. Along the way, other needs—like raising funds—could be met by the widespread popularity of stake and ward field days.

While track and field events drew thousands of participants and spectators on an annual basis, unquestionably the most popular sport among Progressive-Era Mormon adolescent males was basketball. The push to build and equip church gymnasiums stemmed largely from the desire to make basketball available for young men and women. Introduced to LDS youth soon after its invention in 1891, basketball provided an opportunity for physical exercise, while the team aspect of the game promoted proper socialization. As early as 1903, the *Improvement Era* noted that an LDS basketball team had defeated a team from Colorado.[38] By 1908, a competitive league had been organized in Salt Lake's Ensign Stake. In annex halls located near meetinghouses (the Deseret Gymnasium would not be built until 1910), wards battled it out for hoop supremacy in front of audiences often containing several hundred spectators. In several of the Ensign Stake's wards, the sport was popular enough that two teams were created; in essence, wards organized a "varsity" team containing the premiere players and a "junior varsity" (or "second team") squad made up of less talented players. In both categories, teams from the Twentieth Ward were recognized as the champions that first season.[39]

Although team-oriented sports had been hailed as a Progressive method to socialize urban populations, the popularity of LDS basketball quickly extended beyond the city limits. In rural areas, where distant neighbors and arduous travel made regular visits difficult, basketball games proved reason enough for far-off Saints to gather. When travel required overnight stays, the game itself became only one activity in a day full of socializing. One particular contest—pitting the young men from Almo and Malta, Idaho, against a team from Grouse Creek, Utah—details the commitment to basketball and fellowship that energized LDS congregations early in the twentieth century. In March 1923, the young men from Almo and Malta began the forty-mile journey by crossing snowy mountain passes under circumstances "calculated to test the genuine sport spirit, and make character." At 8:30 A.M. on 14 March, the boys and their leaders left town in a blizzard and hiked toward the mountains that divided the competing wards. Arriving at the foot of the mountains near the home of Bishop Ernest Simpers, the bishop's wife insisted that the group have dinner with her family. Tired and hungry, the traveling party "readily abided by her counsel." After the meal, the bishop loaded his bobsleigh and the group continued their journey under the power of the four horses in the lead. When the horses gave out halfway up the summit, the boys and leaders marched in single file along the ridge following each other's footsteps as best they could. Upon reaching the other side of the mountain, they met Bishop W. F. Richens of Grouse Creek and his four-horse bobsleigh. "How we did appreciate rolling into that sleigh, tired and leg weary!" wrote one of the adult leaders. The visiting team received dinner at the Grouse Creek chapel immediately preceding the game.[40]

The game itself—played in the basement amusement hall of the chapel—presented the visiting team with a distinct handicap. Although the hall was equipped with electric lights, the hoops were only two feet from the ceiling. In the words of Superintendent J. Henry Thompson, the visitors "had a poor show for scoring," while the Grouse Creek team was "used to the peculiar situation of the baskets" and found scoring much easier. Quite a home-court advantage! After losing both games, the good-natured visitors promised the Grouse Creek boys a "hot contest" when they played the return games on the Malta side of the mountain.[41] Traveling during four days of storm and sunshine, socializing with other LDS members, and playing competitive sports transformed such trips from athletic contests to sites of socialization. Sports provided the excuse; socialization was the result. Along the mountains of Malta and in the gymnasium at Grouse Creek, Mormon males were made.

Basketball—and the use of recreation facilities—often provoked "hot contests" of a different variety among members of the same ward. In Salt Lake Stake's Fifteenth Ward, for example, a number of interorganizational disputes erupted when the M-Men (auxiliary for males aged seventeen to twenty-three) expressed the desire to take up basketball. The minutes of the Ward Recreation Committee for 25 November 1925 record that the "M men signify intention of attending M.I.A. and participating in Stake contests in basketball, etc., and request regular nights for practice if possible, also that said basketball be in their possession and control during the MIA season." In this case, it appears that scarce resources (only one amusement hall and one basketball had to be split among the various auxiliary groups) led to conflict. By decision of the bishop, the M-Men were allowed to use the gymnasium on Monday and Wednesday evenings after nine P.M.; they were also put in charge of the basketball. Though no overt conflict appears in the committee minutes, it is not difficult to decipher a stinging rebuke in the committee's instruction to the M-men: "We suggest that in a co-operative manner the M men continue to grant the other MIA classes the use of the ball, as at present, when proper authority requests the ball, and when the ball is returned to the M men by one party who should be responsible for the care of the ball, when in the hands of the class borrowing it. At some time it is the purpose of the Recreation Comm[ittee] to provide Ward properties of this nature for the use of the Ward, and until such time we respectfully ask the M Men to co-operate with us in this matter."[42] Perhaps a failure to cooperate had marred interauxiliary relations in the past, or maybe the M-Men were unwilling to share the valued basketball. Whatever the reason, church-sponsored basketball seemed to be driving ward members apart. Team spirit and cooperation may have thrived on the court, but it did not seem to translate from the M-Men to the rest of the congregation.

The following autumn, when basketball season was scheduled to begin, another unexplained controversy divided ward leaders. This time the conflict was more serious. On 14 December 1926, the Recreation Committee minutes recorded that "with regards to basketball, quite a dispute has come up." Committee members then voted "with regard to having basketball in the Ward," and all members were undecided.[43] Basketball continued that season, but by the next year its prospects again seemed dim. In December 1927, the recreation committee debated whether to leave up the decorations for the bishop's party or remove them to allow basketball. While M-Men representatives "insisted on basketball," others on the committee suggested fixing up the amusement hall, sanding the floor, and putting curtains on the windows. If such renovations had been made, basketball would have been discontinued. The committee considered boxing and wrestling to be legitimate alternatives.[44] The following week, the recreation committee chose to continue basketball but to rein in the M-Men with rigid rules. Each player must have gym shoes, and seventy-five cents "must be presented to chairman of recreation committee before they can enter hall." After three violations of this rule, basketball privileges would be revoked. Further, the committee required M-Men to replace amusement hall decorations before all special events; one breach of this rule would mean the end of basketball in the hall.[45] Three years in the making, a modus operandi emerged among competing interests in the Fifteenth Ward—adherence to strict rules and the fear of prompt punishments opened the gymnasium doors for the young men. The Fifteenth Ward experience offers an apt reminder: though an athletic program played a major role in the young men's auxiliary, it was not the only program that vied for church recreation space. With limited resources, ward recreation leaders had to juggle competing demands to ensure that all groups had the time and space to play.

Throughout the first third of the twentieth century (and continuing today), competitive basketball was the main athletic activity of young men in the LDS Church. By one estimate, in 1928 between eight and ten thousand young men took part in Mormon hoop games. As with other recreational and athletic activities, however, the final score was not tallied in baskets, rebounds, and steals. To LDS leaders, the lessons learned on the basketball court had much larger, even eternal, ramifications. The key to Mormon athletics lay not in the athletic heights reached but in the moral and spiritual standards required before young men could participate. Just like the requirements to join the athletic club at Colonia Juarez, to be a Mormon athlete you had to act "Mormon." Members of other faiths participated, but usually only after accepting the standards of the LDS Church, including the Word of Wisdom. Players did not have to be baptized Mormons, but they had to be "Mormon" in their behavior. This requirement brought many new members into the church and also brought many wayward Saints back to the fold. As one report observed, "A set of rules was carefully formulated to govern these various events [basketball games]; and many inspirational stories have come to us of young men who reformed their lives in order to live up to the ideals and standards of their associates who were participating."[46] Such was the goal of LDS athletics—inspiration, not perspiration; moral men, not athletic achievement.

Athletics and the "Selling of the Word of Wisdom"

Though athletic programs socialized a generation of Progressive-Era Mormon adolescents, the most enduring legacy of LDS sports was the rhetorical construction of a connection between athletic excellence and the Word of Wisdom, the LDS dietary code. To this day, stories of athletes refusing to smoke or drink and then excelling in a sporting event are legion throughout the LDS Church among believers of all ages. In fact, a mythology has been carefully constructed explicitly linking dietary obedience and sporting success. As a buttress to a new interpretation of the Word of Wisdom emerging in the early twentieth century, narratives of successful teetotaling athletes helped church leaders commit young Mormons to a life of abstinence and obedience. The evolution of the Word of Wisdom has been clearly laid out by able historians; the prominent role played by athletics has yet to be discussed in any depth.

Revealed to the Prophet Joseph Smith in February 1833, the Word of Wisdom proscribed the use of alcohol, tobacco, and "hot drinks" (interpreted a decade later to be tea and coffee). Furthermore, the revelation instructed the Saints to avoid excessive meat eating and encouraged the use of herbs, fruits, and grains. If members abided this counsel, they were promised "health in their navel and marrow to their bones; And [they] shall find wisdom and great treasures of knowledge, even hidden treasures; And [they] shall run and not be weary, and shall walk and not faint."[47] Throughout the nineteenth century, adherence to the dietary regulations was sporadic. In the years immediately following the Civil War, obedience to the principle increased, while at other times more important issues pushed the dietary strictures aside. The most astute historian of the Word of Wisdom, Thomas G. Alexander, has observed: "We find then a diffuse pattern in observing and teaching the Word of Wisdom in 1900. Some general authorities preached quite consistently against the use of tea, coffee, liquor, tobacco, and meat. None supported drunkenness, and no one insisted on the necessity of vegetarianism. In practice, however, they and other members also occasionally drank the beverages which current interpretation would prohibit." The first quarter of the twentieth century, however, witnessed the transformation of the dietary code from a "principle with promise" (as the original revelation records) to a central tenet of LDS orthodoxy. By 1921, obedience to the Word of Wisdom was required for admission to the Temple. Alexander notes that Mormon leaders, including most prominently the church presidents Joseph F. Smith and Heber J. Grant, pushed for strict prohibition of alcohol and tobacco not only to inspire moral uplift among church members but to win Protestant evangelical acceptance as well.

To ease the transition to strict Word of Wisdom adherence, church leaders turned to scientific evidence, pronouncements from the pulpit, and a gradual easing in of substance abstinence as a requirement for holding church positions and performing church ordinances. Though not noted by

Alexander, a tremendous effort involving abstaining athletes and their accomplishments helped smooth the bumpy transition to the new interpretation of the Word of Wisdom. The transition was eventually successful since, according to Alexander, "nothing, with the possible exception of the wearing of the temple garment, serves to distinguish Latter-day Saints and thus set them apart from the larger community more than does observance of the Word of Wisdom."[48] Sports were central in the conversion of the Word of Wisdom from "principle" to "commandment"—from *a* word of wisdom to *the* Word of Wisdom.

Stories of athletic prowess and clean living did not cause the twentieth-century emphasis on substance abstinence. Prayerful consideration and the context of tradition plus political, social, and economic conditions prompted the change.[49] But when it became necessary to "sell" the new interpretation to church members, athletic success through abstinence became a major part of the campaign. Second only to admonition from church leaders, narratives linking sports and the Word of Wisdom carried the load in convincing young Mormons to abstain. Drawing from the examples of prominent abstaining athletes, church leaders and the *Improvement Era* taught adolescent Mormons that the scriptural promise that adherents would "run and not be weary, and shall walk and not faint" translated directly to success on the athletic field.

As the Word of Wisdom gained adherents in the early part of the century, the *Improvement Era* regularly showcased the athletic success of young Mormons who abstained. Reports abounded about the championships and winning form of MIA teams and school teams made up of abstaining Mormons. One report from Colonia Juarez—where the MIA team placed second in the basketball championship of the Southwest—placed obedience to the Word of Wisdom at the heart of their successful training regimen. With only five players (their one substitute was "out of commission"), the young men from Colonia Juarez reached the championship final, where they were defeated by Bisbee High School. More importantly, however, the MIA team proved to other contestants the virtues of clean living. "The grit of the M.I.A. boys was the general topic of conversation," reported the *Era,* "and it was said, by an observer, that he had never seen such endurance in young men. Their friends attributed it to the exercise which they obtained on the farms, but their parents believe that it is due to their clean lives and the observance of the Word of Wisdom."[50] Though obedience to the Word of Wisdom had yet to be established as a requirement for LDS membership, the link between observance and physical endurance had already been forged on the basketball courts of the Southwest.

In New Zealand, the rugby team from the Maori Agricultural College (MAC), established by the church in 1913, won the Hawk's Bay Union Football Cup three successive years. Because they were "strict observers of the word of wisdom," they not only garnered championships but accomplished "considerable in putting before the people of this locality one great principle of our gospel."[51] The MAC team might have taught New Zealanders the upside of substance abstinence, but the report in the *Improvement Era* carried the message to Mormons throughout the world. Cardston High School—with a team composed of "M Men who attend M.I.A. and who keep the Word of Wisdom"—won the Alberta, Canada, basketball championship in 1924 and 1925 and received accolades from the church magazine.[52] In Laie, Hawaii, when a church-sponsored basketball squad won the Rural Oahu championship, the reason for their triumph was apparent to many. "The 'Mormon' school teams are praiseworthy for their fine spirit and clean sportsmanship," read the report from the Islands, "and the practice of the Word of Wisdom has had much to do with their success. Some people say our boys are 'different'—they are. Why? We know."[53] The Word of Wisdom made the difference; in effect, substance abstinence led to the team's fine spirit, clean sportsmanship, and many victories.

Closer to home, the geography was different, but the story remained the same. Young men living the Word of Wisdom and excelling in athletics continued to be extolled by the *Era*. An article entitled "Good Team; Noble Work" commended the M-Men baseball team from Winder Ward, winners of the Cottonwood (Salt Lake) Stake pennant, who "made it a rule of their organization that all members of the team should observe the word of wisdom, and that there should be no swearing or vulgar language during any of their games. They were able to keep their pledge."[54] The "noble work" of this "good team" included not championships alone but strict conformity to church principles. The championship basketball team representing Stone Ward (Curlew Stake) received accolades from one church official because they were "clean sports, [and] not a member of the team uses tobacco, or dissipates otherwise."[55] From the islands of the sea to the amusement hall of Winder Ward, LDS athletic champions received approbation not only for winning but for clean living.

Mormon editors and leaders were not alone in praising LDS athletes. The *Arizona Gazette,* not a Mormon paper, picked up where the *Era* left off. After predominantly LDS basketball teams—a high school team from Safford and the Gila College squad—both won their respective state tournaments, the paper came to the conclusion that the LDS lifestyle led directly to athletic accomplishment. "If there is anyone left who wonders just how much help right-living is to an athlete," the paper noted, "cite him to Arizona's 'Mormon' schoolboys." The Mormon boys from Safford had defeated "bigger, faster, better-drilled team[s] by the sheer pluck and stamina that come from right-living." The Gila College team, drawn from the second smallest student body in the conference, went through the entire twenty-four-game season without defeat. In a passage that must have thrilled LDS leaders faced with converting adolescents to a strict view of the Word of Wisdom, the newspaper continued: "Mesa, predominantly a 'Mormon' community, has a record of athletic achievements that would compare favorably with that of any other town of its size in the country. The tenets of the 'Mormon' Church demand temperate habits and abstention from those vices which, it so happens, are most likely to undermine athletic stamina. 'Mormon' athletes seldom break training." The *Era* editors concluded, "These STANDARDS [keeping the Word of Wisdom] comprise a safe recipe for SUCCESS."[56] Standards and athletic success became the key concepts for "selling" the Word of Wisdom. Abstinence led to athletic success, which promoted more abstinence. In Arizona, at least, people outside of the church even bought into the union of substance abstinence and athletic excellence.

Church leaders fortified the relationship between substance abstinence and athletic accomplishment by linking them in clear public statements. At times, church leaders focused on the positive physical effects stemming from abstinence. President Heber J. Grant's address at the General Conference of April 1926 used non-Mormon examples to hammer the message home. "The trained athletes of the nation are pretty good authorities on the harm to the physical body," argued Grant, "and they are practically a unit that tobacco and liquor do harm the body. Some of the great baseball clubs of America, who have won championships won't allow liquor or tobacco to be used by their men. The head of the New York Athletic Club, one of the greatest in the country, announces that there is no prospect of success in the athletic line to the man who uses tobacco and liquor."[57] Promises of health had been associated with observing the dietary regulations since the revelation itself promised the obedient "health in their navel and marrow to their bones" in 1833.[58] By linking the promises specifically to "success in the athletic line," Grant publicized a new rationale for adherence to the code.

Ott Romney, the football coach at Brigham Young University, made a less eloquent but still powerful statement that athletic success follows in the wake of righteous living. After BYU's most productive football season (which included only one loss and one tie) in decades, Romney declared that "'clean living, serious endeavor, dedication to a cause are all second nature to "Mormon" boys, and . . . athletic supremacy will follow.'"[59]

Mormon boys, however, did not have to be fans of BYU football or listen to the radio coverage of General Conference to learn about the athletic-abstinence connection at the heart of the selling of the new interpretation of the Word of Wisdom. *The Log of the Vanguard Trail,* an MIA lesson manual for boys aged fifteen to sixteen, contained the following information to be included in the MIA lesson for the third week of March 1931. In LDS churches throughout the world, the young men were instructed that "any boy who hopes to excel at athletics must observe the Word of Wisdom. It is the most scientific system of diet ever given to mankind. Its promises are marvelous, but they are all dependent upon strict observance of its teachings."[60] By 1931 the "marvelous promises" of the Word of Wisdom included athletic excellence. The scriptural assurance of running without weariness found a real-world application on track ovals and basketball courts.

Other church leaders went beyond physical blessings and argued that success in most endeavors (though still heavily weighted toward athletics) hinged on substance abstinence. In a "Message to the Youth of the Land" in 1920, Apostle David O. McKay (who had played football at the University of Utah during the 1890s) advised young men "that if they want to live physically, if they want to be men strong in body, vigorous in mind, if they want to be good sports, enter the basket ball game, enter the football game, enter the contest in running and jumping, if they want to be good scouts, if they want to be good citizens, in business, anywhere, avoid tobacco and live strictly the religious life."[61] It could certainly be argued that abstaining from tobacco and other substances prohibited in the Word of Wisdom might have a direct impact on physical health and perhaps lead to success on the athletic field. To link substance abstinence with good citizenship and business acumen, however, signals that the rewards for obedience to the LDS dietary code were more than physical.

The beneficiaries of abstinence-induced excellence need not even be Mormon. According to some church officials, the promises of physical fitness found in the Word of Wisdom crossed denominational lines to include all who obeyed the guidelines. One month after Charles A. Lindbergh completed the first solo nonstop flight from New York to Paris, Apostle Richard R. Lyman hailed not only that historic accomplishment but the physical preparation that led to Lindbergh's much-celebrated stamina. Speaking at the YMMIA conference in June 1927, Lyman pressed Lindbergh into the fold of abstainers who had excelled in feats of physical skill and strength. "This American, Col. Charles A. Lindbergh, in whose honor the world celebrates today," Lyman asserted, "has been devoted to things worthwhile. He has lived strictly in accordance with the ideals of our Church, the ideals of all churches, the ideals of all philosophers." Lest his listeners become too ecumenical in their appreciation of Lucky Lindy, Lyman then rooted his praise not in the principles of Christianity or philosophy but in the Word of Wisdom. Lindbergh, he noted, "began his tour without liquor, without tobacco, without tea, without coffee. His life has been such that he has made of himself a man thoroughly efficient, seemingly, in all respects."[62] This "man among men" may not have been a Mormon, but he acted like one. By living according to LDS standards, Lindbergh enjoyed increased physical efficiency—an up-to-date rendering of the scriptural promise of "health in the navel" to all Word of Wisdom adherents.

During the first decades of the twentieth century, members and leaders of the LDS Church were not alone in their concern about the detrimental physical effects of liquor and tobacco use. Willing to enlist allies from virtually any field, the *Improvement Era* introduced well-known athletes and coaches who spoke out against the consumption of tobacco and alcohol. One of the earliest examples of securing non-LDS support in the battle against illicit substances appeared in June 1913. Writing about "The Physical Square Deal and the Cigarette Habit among Boys," Samuel Hamilton of Allegheny, Pennsylvania, borrowed terms from Theodore Roosevelt in preaching to boys about athletics and substance abstinence. Though Hamilton likely did not have the Word of Wisdom in mind, the editors of the *Era* knew a friendly voice when they heard it. Arguing that the "foul habit" of cigarette smoking virtually barred access to professional athletics, Hamilton related the story of a "great ball pitcher with a national reputation" who failed to live up to his potential due to cigarette smoking. Once the pitcher quit smoking, he "recovered his old form, became a star again, and the coming season will earn possibl[y] $20,000." Other examples of athletic redemption following a commitment to substance abstinence would become a staple of the narratives that LDS leaders used to motivate young men to observe the Word of Wisdom. Hamilton's diatribe extended well beyond the pitcher's story, however. Using phrases that combined the verbal acuity of Roosevelt and Knute Rockne, Hamilton declared that smokers faced a bleak athletic future. "No physical director in this country will place a cigarette-smoking boy on any crack athletic team," advised Hamilton. Then, reaching his full Rooseveltian posture, the author insisted that coaches wanted "men with vigor and endurance; men with courage in their hearts, iron in their blood, and with grit that will cut down the grindstones of opposition to the last point. Directors know that the only place in all athletics for the milk-fed, nicotine-bleeched [sic], devitalized mollycoddle is on the bleachers. There neither brains nor effort are necessary; only mouth and lungs are required."[63]

Readers of the *Era* learned that the football coach of Vanderbilt University, Dan McGugin, believed that cigarettes "retard or stunt the physical growth of a boy" and "make boys stupid." Moreover, in the coach's fifty years of athletic experience, he claimed to have "never known of a boy who became a confirmed cigarette smoker when young who ever really amounted to anything very much in his life later on."[64] Other coaches weighed in on the subject of tobacco use. Walter Christie, the longtime coach at the University of California, warned prospective athletes that "tobacco is the greatest curse in America today, doing far more harm than liquor has ever done." Apostle Heber J. Grant, in a 1915 address, turned not only to the scriptures in his call for substance abstinence but to the major-league manager Connie Mack, "a name familiar to all baseball people." Mack's ideas, of course, paralleled those of the church leader. "It is my candid opinion that boys of the age of ten to fifteen, who have contracted the habit of smoking cigarettes, do not as a rule amount to anything. They are enfeebled in every way for any kind of work where brains are needed. No boy or man can expect to succeed in this world to a high position who contracts the use of cigarettes."[65] And from the Midwest, Mormons discovered that three state high school athletic associations—those of Minnesota, Kansas, and North Dakota—had prohibited smokers from participating in school athletics. Not only were the athletes in better physical shape, their examples helped other students "to whom many of the athletes are heroes."[66] The evidence of substance abstinence leading to athletic achievement abounded in the pages of the *Improvement Era*. Far from the borders of Mormon Utah, winning coaches and athletes subscribed to the core concepts found in the Word of Wisdom and succeeded in athletic contests. The Word of Wisdom offered a blueprint of substance abstinence from which all athletes, Mormon or not, could benefit.

Anecdotal evidence from well-known athletes was only one strategy used by the church to sell the new interpretation of the Word of Wisdom. "Scientific" evidence—collected using the emerging technique of the sociological survey as well as physiological data—also helped church leaders connect substance abstinence and athletics. Dr. Frederick J. Pack, a professor of history and sociology at the University of Utah and later a member of the Deseret Sunday School Union General Board, published an article on "Smoking and Foot-ball Men" in the October 1912 issue of *Popular Science Monthly*. After interviewing coaches and athletic directors from fourteen colleges and universities, Pack concluded that only half as many smokers as nonsmokers made their respective football teams. Furthermore, in the "able-bodied men" he studied, smoking was associated with a loss in lung capacity approaching 10 percent. Finally, Pack noted that smoking was "invariably associated with low scholarship."[67] Republished by the *Era* on several occasions, this study provided "scientific" backing for the assertion that substance abstinence improved physical health and enhanced athletic performance. In a 1921 article for the church magazine, Pack reiterated the results of his study and offered a telling interpretation of the information. "When it is kept in mind that this investigation had to do only with *physically perfect men*," wrote Pack, "the indictment is seen to be an unusually strong and sweeping one, for certainly no one will disagree with the conclusion that *if tobacco is bad for this type of men, then it must be even worse for all others*."[68] Although athletes were the subject of Pack's study, all Mormons could understand the consequences of trespassing the Word of Wisdom. If athletes, even "physically perfect men," could be brought down by smoking, little argument could be made with Pack's conclusions about the physical effects on average Mormons. Pack's articles added "scientific" sinew to the connection between Word of Wisdom adherence, physical health, and athletic prowess.

Advice from non-Mormon athletes, pronouncements from church leaders, and scientific evidence all played a role in constructing an athletic myth to accompany the Word of Wisdom. The legacy of this effort, however, was not statistics from social scientists or scoldings from church leaders; rather, what is most remembered is a series of narratives in which Mormon athletes adhered to the LDS dietary code, overcame great odds, and triumphed on various athletic fields. The names of Mormon champions who abstained during this period—Alma Richards, Creed Haymond, and others—continue to resonate with LDS members today.[69] Offering concrete examples of Mormons who first abstained and then overcame athletic obstacles, the connection between the Word of Wisdom and champion athletes was complete.

From time to time in the early years of the century, the *Era* reported extraordinary athletic or team achievements by Mormons. In many of these articles, adherence to the Word of Wisdom was listed as one reason behind the success. By the 1920s—when many Americans became obsessed with professional and collegiate sports—a more vigorous effort was made to link specific athletes with substance abstinence. Essentially, the church was enlisting celebrity endorsements to entice young Mormons to stay away from alcohol and tobacco. One 1924 article announced the athletic and intellectual achievements of LDS young men throughout the country: Earl Merrill won the high school oratory state tournament in Arizona; Melvin Tolman Burke (from Honeyville, Utah) was crowned as the national champion high school mile runner; and the Pennsylvanian Harry Glancey made the U.S. Olympic swim team. To explain their various successes, the *Era* did not need

to look far. "We are simple enough to believe," announced the self-depre-
cating editors, "that the clean life which the young people of the Latter-day
Saints are enjoined to live has much to do with the success they gain in the
various lines of accomplishment." More specifically, "the Word of Wisdom
gives all who abide by its counsels, chance for both physical and intellectual progress. The promises of the Lord to those who live right and conform to its requirements are always fully verified."[70] Though the style of this
story seems strikingly similar to the type of athletic reporting earlier in the
century, it marks a subtle but important change. Rather than report on teams
that succeeded on local levels or in church competition, reports now centered on *individual accomplishments* in more significant state or national
meets. The Word of Wisdom was leading to success in major athletic events,
and it was hoped that high-level success would translate into an increased
awareness of the potential of abstinence to unlock athletic greatness.

By 1928, the use of sporting superstars to market the new interpretation
of the Word of Wisdom had reached full stride. In August, the Brigham Young
University journalism professor Harrison R. Merrill recounted the success
of various Mormon athletes and explained the integral role played by the
athletes' adherence to the Word of Wisdom. Many of these sports stars were
destined to become household names among Mormons; they became the
"folk heroes" who laid the foundations for Word of Wisdom obedience.

Setting the scene, Merrill summarized what each LDS athlete had accomplished. To pragmatic twentieth-century American Mormons, these athletic
feats proved the promise of substance abstinence. Alma W. Richards, Merrill's
first example, set an Olympic record in the high jump at the 1912 Olympic
Games in Stockholm, Sweden. Other Mormon athletes reached similar if less
spectacular heights in athletic competition. Clinton Larson won the high jump
at an inter-Allied meet held at Paris in 1919 in addition to holding the world
indoor record in the same event. The national broad jump champion, Clinton
Luke, and the high school mile record holder, Melvin Burke, both hailed from
Utah and belonged to the church. The swimmer Alma Budd Shields, representing Brigham Young University, singlehandedly (he was the school's lone
representative) won third place in one meet by winning the 220- and 440-
yard races. Likewise, Creed Haymond, a track star at the University of Pennsylvania, made his mark setting a world record in the 220-yard dash as well
as belonging to a relay team that broke world records in the 400-meter, 800-
meter, and half-mile relays. And the list went on.[71]

It was not unusual for the *Era* to laud outstanding Mormon athletic
achievements. But this article was not merely congratulatory; it was written to teach a message. Immediately following the laundry list of athletic

accomplishments, Merrill made his case. "It is interesting to note," he explained, "that every one of these unusual men is not only a member of the Latter-day Church, but each one has been a more or less rigid observer of the Word of Wisdom. Not a man among those who have won national honors has ever used regularly tea, coffee, tobacco, or strong drink." Though Merrill employed some measure of sophistry in describing the athletes' adherence patterns, the message clearly promoted the rigid observance of the dietary directions.

Merrill drew at length from the abstaining athletes' testimonials. Melvin Burke's comments fit Merrill's argument perfectly: "'I have not used regularly tea, coffee, tobacco, or liquor in any form. I am a firm believer in the Word of Wisdom. It is a great feeling to come to the end of a hard contest and still have a reserve for the sprint. I had considerable sickness when a child, but proper living helped me to overcome it.'" Likewise, Owen Rowe named abstention as a key to his success. "'I never have used coffee, tea, tobacco, or liquor in any form. I am a firm believer in the Word of Wisdom and adhere to its teachings rigidly. I know it pays.'" To guarantee that his point was not lost in the glorification of these LDS athletes, Merrill quickly returned the spotlight to the Word of Wisdom. "'It may be regarded as significant that from a state possessing less that one two-hundred-seventy-fifth of the population of the United States there should come so many athletes of national renown and that of that number every one was, is, and expects to continue to be a strict observer of the Word of Wisdom. . . . Of course, the testimonies of these young men do not prove conclusively that the Word of Wisdom is an aid to athletes, but their testimony, since every national character has agreed, is significant, to say the least.'"[72] Regardless of the spiritual or physical benefits of abstention, the success of Mormon athletes forged a connection between athletic performance and substance abstinence that made a powerful argument for obedience to the Word of Wisdom.

The crescendo of the connection between abstinence and athletic victory occurred in the narrative of Creed Haymond, the University of Pennsylvania track star who refused to violate the Word of Wisdom and was rewarded with world-record speed. Long before 1928, church members had been aware of Haymond's track exploits. It was not until Joseph J. Cannon's article "Speed and the Spirit" appeared, however, that most Mormons learned the story behind the story. Once Haymond's narrative was publicized, it quickly became a staple of church folklore. Haymond and the new abstemious interpretation of the Word of Wisdom were forever linked.

Born on 2 December 1893 in Springville, Utah, Haymond was educated in local schools and then attended the Universities of Utah and Pennsylvania, where he studied dentistry. Reflecting on his early commitment to abide by the Word of Wisdom, Haymond recalled:

"I have never tasted tea, coffee, tobacco, or liquor in any form. I promised my mother when I was eight years old, I would never break the Word of Wisdom. I was with her in the Utah Stake Tabernacle at the time and Senator Reed Smoot was speaking on that subject. That was twenty-five years ago, and I have kept my promise and expect to the rest of my life. My coaches at Pennsylvania thought it peculiar that I would never take tea during the season or wine before a meet, but told me later that it was that perhaps which kept me up (they guessed), because I never had time to train, but was always in condition."[73]

It was at the University of Pennsylvania that Haymond permanently linked abstention and athletic success for generations of LDS faithful. The time was May 1919, the place was Harvard Stadium, and the occasion was the annual meet of the Inter-Collegiate Association of Amateur Athletes of America (ICAAAA). Over fifteen hundred competitors represented the nation's finest colleges and universities. Creed Haymond, captain of the Pennsylvania team, expected to lead his top-ranked squad to the tournament title.

On the night before the meet, Penn's coach, Lawson Robertson (who went on to coach the U.S. Olympic teams in 1920, 1924, and 1928), asked each of his team members to take a little sherry wine to blunt the edge of their nervousness. When Lawson got to Haymond's room, the star athlete replied, according to Joseph J. Cannon's account, "'I won't do it, Coach.'" Taken aback, Lawson countered, "'But, Creed, I'm not trying to get you to drink. I know what you "Mormons" believe. I'm giving you this as a tonic, just to put you all on your metal.'" Unwilling to take the coach's tonic, Creed set himself apart from other team members and set himself up as the scapegoat if Penn were to lose the meet. In his room that night, Haymond questioned his actions. Later, he related his doubts to Cannon: "What right had he to disobey? Only one right, one reason, this thing he had been following and believing all his life—this Word of Wisdom. But what is it anyway, something Joseph Smith thought up or really a revealed message to us from God? It was a critical hour of the young man's life and, with all the spiritual forces of his nature suffusing him, he kneeled down and earnestly, very earnestly, asked the Lord to give him a testimony as to the source of the revelation he had believed and obeyed. Then he went to bed and slept the sound slumber of healthy youth."[74]

The rest of the heroic narrative is familiar to many Mormons. The spiritual manifestation that Haymond sought would come clearly to him during the races the next day. When he awoke, he was greeted with the news that his teammates were vomiting, sick from the coach's tonic. Haymond, however, felt fine as he lined up in the hundred-yard dash. Poised in lane two, he crashed to the ground as the gun sounded. Apparently, a taller athlete had used the second lane in the semifinals and kicked a hole for his toes an inch or two behind Haymond's fresh marks. The great thrust at the start of the race had broken through the dirt between the marks and sent Haymond to his knees. Undaunted, he hopped to his feet and pursued the others. Cannon described Haymond's first heroic feat as a Word of Wisdom warrior thus:

> No coach or crowd would expect a man to get up and make a pitiful spectacle of himself running behind. . . . [Haymond] got up and ran behind, but, man, how he did run! His brain on fire—the school—the team—Robby [Coach Robertson]—desperate, but not hopeless—at sixty yards, the last in the race—then seeming to fly—passing the fifth man—the fourth—the third—the second—only the tall Johnson ahead—and close to the tape—lips away from teeth—face drawn in agony—heart bursting with the strain—sweeping in that climax of whirlwind swiftness past Johnson to victory. The timers caught the flash as he crossed the tape and called it ten seconds flat;—but no man could know the actual speed of that running.

But Haymond's heroics did not end there. Later, in the 220-yard dash, he raced in the last qualifying heat and then in the finals only five minutes later. Though exhausted from the preliminary, Haymond had no trouble running away from the competition and winning the race eight yards ahead of his nearest rival. "The Mormon speed demon" had swept his events that day; moreover, he had proven to himself the value of keeping the Word of Wisdom.[75]

At Harvard Stadium in May 1919, a Mormon hero was introduced to his church and to the world. In retelling the story ten years later—and fitting it in the framework of an heroic struggle against insurmountable odds—Joseph Cannon created a Mormon icon worthy of the new interpretation of the Word of Wisdom.[76] In their own right, Haymond's athletic achievements would have garnered him fame and respect throughout the church. When Cannon connected that success with adherence to the Word of Wisdom, Haymond's experience became a proof-text of the power of abstinence. From Cannon's poetic phrasing, the moral of the story was clear:

> At the end of that strange day, as Creed Haymond was going to bed, there suddenly came to memory his question of the night before regarding the divinity of the Word of Wisdom. The procession of that peculiar series of events then passed before his mind—his team-mates taking the wine and failing—his own abstinence and victories, victories that were amazing to himself. Had Daniel and his three

continent companions as startling reason for testimony? He had asked the favor of some witnesses from the Lord. What relation did all those things have to his prayer? In the sports of track and field, does God teach his purposes?[77]

As Haymond concluded and Cannon recorded, God's purposes could be revealed through sporting success if athletes followed the divine advice given in the Word of Wisdom.

During the initial decades of the twentieth century, leaders of the LDS Church relied on athletic events to help members learn the purposes of God. Whether it was the social cooperation and teamwork skills inculcated by team sports or increased loyalty to the church, young Mormons were provided myriad opportunities to participate in sports in the hopes that their experiences would transform wayward youths into responsible adults. The use of abstaining athletic heroes to sell the emerging interpretation of the Word of Wisdom capped the flurry of athletic activities during the period. The massive athletic programs sponsored by the church did not focus on play for play's sake—there was purpose behind each activity, a point to every game. LDS athletics did not exist to make records but to make moral men.

Notes

1. Both quotes appear in Scott Kenney, *The Mutual Improvement Associations: A Preliminary History, 1900–1950* (Salt Lake City: Historical Department of the Church of Jesus Christ of Latter-day Saints, 1976), 2.

2. "Our Work—Amusements and Entertainments," *Improvement Era* 7 (Dec. 1903): 146–47.

3. Ibid., 146–48.

4. Willard Done, "Our Work—Preliminary Programs," *Improvement Era* 7 (Mar. 1904): 390.

5. "Mutual Work—The Policy of the Y.M.M.I.A.," *Improvement Era* 12 (Jan. 1909): 247.

6. Heber J. Grant, "The Place of the Y.M.M.I.A. in the Church," *Improvement Era* 15 (Aug. 1912): 873, 875–76.

7. Jane McJackson, "The M.I.A.," *Improvement Era* 24 (Mar. 1921): 406.

8. "Editor's Table—Hints to the Editors," *Improvement Era* 14 (Sept. 1911): 1038.

9. Edward P. Kimball, "Character of Music Programs for Joint M.I.A. Meetings," *Improvement Era* 25 (Jan. 1922): 274–75.

10. "Editors' Table—On Who Can Entertain," *Improvement Era* 8 (June 1915): 736.

11. "Mutual Work—The Policy of the Y.M.M.I.A.," 247.

12. Dominick Cavallo, *Muscles and Morals: Organized Playground and Urban Reform, 1880–1920* (Philadelphia: University of Pennsylvania Press, 1981), 50, 64–65.

13. On the "Americanization" of immigrants during the Progressive Era, see John Higham, *Strangers in the Land: Patterns of American Nativism, 1860–1925,* 2d ed. (New Brunswick, N.J.: Rutgers University Press, 1988), 234–63; John D. Buenker, *Urban Liberalism and Progressive Reform* (New York: Charles Scribner's Sons, 1973), 198–239; Alan M. Kraut, *The Huddled Masses: The Immigrant in American Society, 1880–1921* (Arlington Heights, Ill.: Harlan Davidson, 1982), 111–47; Gerd Korman, *Industrialization, Immigrants, and Americanizers* (Madison: State Historical Society of Wisconsin, 1967), 136–66.

14. Cavallo, *Muscles and Morals,* 99, 92–93.

15. *Handbook of the YLMIA and YMMIA* (Salt Lake City: General Boards of MIA, 1931), 88–89.

16. For a discussion of the "boy problem," see the introduction.

17. L. R. Martineau, "Some Problems in Athletics," *Improvement Era* 15 (Oct. 1912): 1139, 1137.

18. "Editor's Table—Physical Exercise and the M.I.A.," *Improvement Era* 11 (Feb. 1908): 305.

19. Quoted in Kenney, *Mutual Improvement Associations,* 9.

20. "Mutual Work—Annual Conference," *Improvement Era* 13 (July 1910): 858.

21. Lewis Telle Cannon, "Increasing Enrollment and Interest in the Mutuals," *Improvement Era* 16 (Oct. 1913): 1223.

22. "Our Work—Seventh Annual Conference of Mutual Improvement Associations," *Improvement Era* 5 (July 1902): 727.

23. "Mutual Work—Basket Ball League," *Improvement Era* 24 (Apr. 1921): 662.

24. "Mutual Work—Winning Ball Teams, Box Elder Stake," *Improvement Era* 25 (Dec. 1921): 178.

25. Thomas Hull, "Study Period and Activities," *Improvement Era* 25 (Aug. 1922): 920.

26. "Mutual Work—The Tokyo-American Baseball Team," *Improvement Era* 15 (May 1912): 664, 663. On the introduction of baseball to Japan, see Allen Guttmann and Lee Thompson, "Educators, Imitators, Modernizers: The Arrival and Spread of Modern Sport in Japan," *European Sports History Review* 3 (2001): 23–48; Donald Roden, "Baseball and the Quest for National Dignity in Meiji Japan," *American Historical Review* 85 (June 1980): 511–34.

27. "Messages from the Missions—Playing Ball," *Improvement Era* 27 (Mar. 1924): 457.

28. "Mutual Work—M.I.A. Scouts," *Improvement Era* 15 (June 1912): 755.

29. "Our Work—Eleventh Annual M.I.A. Conference," *Improvement Era* 9 (July 1906): 738. The following year, the field day was held at Wandamere Park in Salt Lake City. Participants played in the park, danced, and took boat rides. There was no mention of any athletic competition. See "Our Work—General M.I.A. Conference," *Improvement Era* 10 (July 1907): 761.

30. "Mutual Work—General M.I.A. Conference," *Improvement Era* 14 (Aug. 1911): 943.

31. L. R. Martineau, "Second Annual M.I.A. Field Day," *Improvement Era* 15 (July 1912): 860, 859.

32. "Mutual Work—A Day for Recreation," *Improvement Era* 14 (Dec. 1910): 183. This call for weekly recreation coincided with a call for a Saturday half-holiday by the MIA General Boards. In 1914–15, the theme of the auxiliary organizations was, "We stand for a sacred Sabbath, and a weekly half-holiday." Part of the reasoning behind the weekly holiday was to end participation in athletic events on Sunday. See "Mutual Work—Resolutions Respecting Weekly Half-Holiday," *Improvement Era* 15 (Aug. 1912): 860–61, for a resolution adopted by the MIA calling for a weekly half-holiday dedicated to recreational and athletic pursuits.

33. "Mutual Work—M.I.A. Track Meet," *Improvement Era* 13 (July 1910): 851–54.

34. "Mutual Work," *Improvement Era* 14 (July 1911): 844. In July 1911, the *Era* reported on athletic meets held in the Wasatch, Millard, Uintah, and Alpine Stakes in addition to the First Annual Field Day sponsored by the general MIA.

35. "Mutual Work—Alpine Stake Athletic Contest," *Improvement Era* 13 (Aug. 1910): 952–53.

36. "Mutual Work—The Daynes Trophy," *Improvement Era* 14 (July 1911): 848.

37. "Raising Funds by Recreation," *Improvement Era* 23 (Sept. 1920): 1036. Interestingly, one of the boxing matches pitted two eight-year-old twin brothers, Lee and Dee Brown, against each other.

38. Thomas Hull, "Events of the Month," *Improvement Era* 6 (May 1903): 558.

39. "Mutual Work—Basket Ball," *Improvement Era* 7 (May 1908): 562–63.

40. "Mutual Work—The Genuine Sport Spirit," *Improvement Era* 26 (May 1923): 668.

41. Ibid., 668–69.

42. Both quotes appear in Fifteenth Ward, Salt Lake Stake, "Recreation Committee Minutes, 1925–1928," LDS Historical Department (hereafter Fifteenth Ward Recreation Committee), 25 Nov. 1925, 1.

43. Fifteenth Ward Recreation Committee, 14 Dec. 1926, 1.

44. Fifteenth Ward Recreation Committee, 6 Dec. 1927, 1.

45. Fifteenth Ward Recreation Committee, 13 Dec. 1927, 1–2.

46. "Mutual Work—Basketball Leads in M-Men Activities," *Improvement Era* (May 1928): 621.

47. Doctrine and Covenants 89:18–20.

48. Thomas G. Alexander, *Mormonism in Transition: A History of the Latter-day Saints, 1890–1930* (Urbana: University of Illinois Press, 1996), 260.

49. These represent Alexander's conclusions regarding the doctrinal development of the Word of Wisdom. See ibid., 270–71.

50. "Mutual Work—Juarez M.I.A. in Championship Contest," *Improvement Era* 13 (June 1910): 762–63. Other participants in the tournament included the El Paso YMCA, El Paso Military Institute, and New Mexico College.

51. "Editors' Table—Maori Agricultural College Team Again Champions," *Improvement Era* 21 (June 1918): 740.

52. "Mutual Work—Cardston High School Basket Ball Team," *Improvement Era* 28 (June 1925): 793.

53. "Mutual Work—A 'Mormon' School in Hawaii," *Improvement Era* 28 (Sept. 1925): 1101.

54. "Good Team; Noble Work," *Improvement Era* 27 (May 1924): 695–96.

55. "Mutual Work—Curlew Stake Champions," *Improvement Era* 29 (July 1926): 901.

56. "'Mormon' Standards Approved," *Improvement Era* 30 (Apr. 1927): 564–65. Another prominent voice from outside the Mormon community concluded LDS athletic success stemmed not from adherence to the dietary code but from superior genetic stock. Knute Rockne, the football coach at the University of Notre Dame and a regular participant in summer coaching schools at Utah Agricultural College, expressed his view in the *Milwaukee Sentinel:* "The reason for these [Mormon] men is not because the distance between water holes is great, nor that one had to jump high to be able to pick the berries. They are the result of heredity. The people who pioneered this state [Utah], were, absolutely, of the best American stock." See "A Good Word for Utah Athletes," *Improvement Era* 31 (Dec. 1927): 173.

57. "Editors' Table—President Heber J. Grant's Conference Message," *Improvement Era* 29 (May 1926): 679.

58. Doctrine and Covenants 89:18.

59. Quoted in Harrison R. Merrill, "Playing the Great Collegiate Game Football," *Improvement Era* 34 (Jan. 1931): 147.

60. *The Log of the Vanguard Trail* (Salt Lake City: Mutual Improvement Associations, 1931), 163. The previous week's lesson called for the telling of the Mormon athlete and abstainer Creed Haymond's well-known success in track and how Paul Kimball had employed the principles of the Word of Wisdom to help an Oxford crew team to victory.

61. David O. McKay, "A Message to the Youth of the Land," *Improvement Era* 24 (Jan. 1921): 191.

62. Richard R. Lyman, "A Man among Men," *Improvement Era* 30 (Aug. 1927): 872.

63. Samuel Hamilton, "The Physical Square Deal and the Cigarette Habit among Boys," *Improvement Era* 16 (June 1913): 817.

64. "The Effect of Tobacco on the Boy," *Improvement Era* 21 (Nov. 1917): 11.

65. Heber J. Grant, "Testimony—The Little White Slaver," *Improvement Era* 18 (Aug. 1915): 912–13.

66. "Passing Events," *Improvement Era* 28 (Apr. 1925): 616.

67. "On Smoking," *Improvement Era* 16 (Nov. 1912): 90.

68. Frederick J. Pack, "How the Impending Tobacco Crusade Can Be Avoided," *Improvement Era* 24 (Jan. 1921): 223.

69. The Creed Haymond story is regularly retold by church leaders to teach the benefits of adherence to the Word of Wisdom. In the church's General Conference of October 1996, Elder L. Tom Perry, one of the church's twelve apostles, retold Haymond's story. Four years later, President James E. Faust repeated the story during the priesthood session of General Conference. See L. Tom Perry, "Run and Not Be Weary," *Ensign* 26 (Nov. 1996): 37–38; James E. Faust, "The Enemy Within," *Ensign* 30 (Nov. 2000): 44–46.

70. "Y.M.M.I.A. Champions," *Improvement Era* 27 (Aug. 1924): 1004. Another article in the same issue described the swimmer Harry Glancey as having a "wonderful physique obtained from clean living and from a life that our Latter-day Saint boys lead." See "Mutual Work—Member of American Olympic Swimming Team," 1011.

71. For more details about each of these athletic achievements, see Harrison R. Merrill, "Utah Athletes Coming to Their Own," *Improvement Era* 31 (Aug. 1928): 820–25. Additional biographical information appears in William T. Black, *Mormon Athletes* (Salt Lake City: Deseret Book, 1980), 6–10 (Richards), 109–12 (Larson), 11–16 (Shields), 1–5 (Haymond).

72. Quoted in Merrill, "Utah Athletes," 824–25.

73. Quoted in ibid., 824.

74. Joseph J. Cannon, "Speed and the Spirit," *Improvement Era* 31 (Oct. 1928): 1003–4.

75. Ibid., 1005. Cannon's retelling has become the classic Mormon version of the story. The *Era* editors noted that "this story was read to Dr. Haymond in order to assure accuracy of details. He objected to the suggestion of the heroic, but we agree with the author that as long as he refrained from the slightest exaggeration, adhering strictly to the facts, the story should stand as it is." See ibid., 1001. Though the details of Haymond's personal experiences at the ICAAAA meet cannot be verified in separate sources, it is clear that his performances during the meet comport with Cannon's description. The *New York Times* reported that "Haymond got away badly in the hundred, and with 60 yards covered, he was in fourth position, with Johnson of Michigan leading. The Pennsylvanian sprinted past the field and won by inches." The newspaper recorded Haymond's times as 21.8 seconds in the 220-yard dash and 10 seconds in the 100-yard dash. See *New York Times,* 1 June 1919, 21.

76. The *Improvement Era* also used the heroic formula to sell the Word of Wisdom through fictional sports stories. Typical examples showed star athletes refusing to consume alcohol and overcoming long athletic odds. See Harrison R. Merrill, "Speck's Faith," *Improvement Era* 19 (Feb. 1916): 345–49; Carter E. Grant, "Double Victory," *Improvement Era* 31 (Aug. 1931): 874–76.

77. Cannon, "Speed and the Spirit," 1007.

LDS College Field Day, 1892.

A dance hall, located in Canyon Creek, around the turn of the twentieth century.

Lehi, Utah, Ward basketball team, 1912.

A Boy Scout band on the steps of the LDS Church Administration Building.

The well-appointed lodge at Brighton Girls' Camp in July 1924.

A group of girls cleaning the trail outside of Brighton Girls' Camp, 1924.

Brigham Young Academy women's basketball team, about 1900.

A noontime class at Deseret Gymnasium, about 1913. Standing in the third row are Heber J. Grant (4), Bryant S. Hinckley (10), and Joseph Fielding Smith (17).

The LDS Church hoped that participation in Boy Scout programs would teach good citizenship and promote church attendance. Troop 6, Santa Monica, Calif., 1938.

Australian Mission basketball team, 1938. Missionaries throughout the world used sports to meet potential converts in nonconfrontational settings.

CHAPTER FOUR

"A Means of Preserving the Memory of the Mormon Pioneers"
LDS Recreation in the Great Outdoors

> It's the wonder program of the century,
> Hi Ho for Scouting, O she's good enough for me.
> Here's a song for Scouting, let's sing it merrily;
> Hi Ho for Scouting, O she's good enough for me.
> Just like a good Scout we are growing,
> We've started something and we'll keep it going;
> Half a million Boy Scouts,
> A million more you'll see—
> Hi Ho for Scouting, O she's good enough for me.
> Then may all our Boy Scouts strong men grow to be,
> Hi Ho for Scouting, O she's good enough for me.
> Full of zeal and honor and personality—
> Hi Ho for Scouting, O she's good enough for me.
> And may our hearts thrill with elation
> For scouting's gift to the next generation;
> Then let's cheer old Scouting—
> Cheer it lustily,
> Hi Ho for Scouting, O she's good enough for me.
> SOME MEN HAVE THEIR MILLIONS (spoken),
> SOME OWN LAND and SEA,
> But give us good old scouting for (sing)
> She's good enough for me.
> —*Fathers and Sons Annual Outing, Summer of 1927*
>   (sung to the tune of "Hi Ho the Merrio")

Since American urbanization proceeded apace in the nineteenth century, the city had been the locus of fears regarding the loss of community and individuality. As early as the 1830s, urban dwellers (and critics of the rising cities) sensed that urban life rent the fabric of social deference that had once knit-

ted colonial towns and villages into a unified whole. In urban areas populated by unknown neighbors and untrustworthy reputations, moral and
financial exploitation were too common. Cities became, at least to some
observers, centers of social anomie where young men faced difficulty in
forming an identity and acquiring moral bearings because they were so far
away from the reach (quite literally) of village elders who had once determined appropriate social behavior. Elites in the burgeoning American cities struggled to create avenues of reform that would not only socialize young
men but would also "Americanize" the flood of immigrants migrating to
the city streets. Most reform efforts tried to bring order to urban chaos by
teaching impressionable urbanites proper behavior. Sunday Schools, Bible
tract societies, YMCAs, and settlement houses represent only a few of the
attempts to stabilize the city. To ameliorate the problems stalking youths
on city streets, reformers tried to redeem urban society by reforming the
rising generation of urban dwellers.[1]

The first "urban" generation in Mormon history presented LDS social
leaders with similar problems—anomie, misbehavior, and maladjustment.
Much of the impetus behind the Mormon recreation program stemmed from
the social conditions apparent in LDS-dominated urban areas, particularly
Salt Lake City. Instead of following the "settlement-house" pattern, where
reform was brought to the city, Mormon leaders favored a "rugged life"
model that stressed outdoor experience. Like other contemporary reformers, from Theodore Roosevelt to Robert Baden-Powell, Progressive-Era
Mormons looked to nature to solve the social and spiritual problems besetting urban youth.

The Church of Jesus Christ of Latter-day Saints was born on the American frontier. Never in western New York, nor Ohio, nor Missouri, nor Illinois had the Saints experienced urban living on a wide scale. Even in
Nauvoo, Illinois, which boasted a population of fifteen thousand in 1845,
the Mormon settlement was situated at the very western border of the organized United States.[2] Following the Mormon migration of 1847, most LDS
members found themselves far removed from urban pressures for the remain-
der of the nineteenth century. Mormons were farmers living in small communities.[3] Not much had changed the LDS lifestyle since Joseph Smith left
his father's farm in Palmyra, New York, to organize the religious movement
in 1830. As the twentieth century dawned, however, Mormons and their
leaders faced the unprecedented task of controlling a new generation of
"urban" members of the church—young men and women who had never
lived off the land and were personally unacquainted with the hardships
suffered by early church members. These urban youth represented a new

challenge to LDS leaders—one that required new techniques to teach young Mormons the lessons not only of their "frontier" religion but of "frontier" life as well. The products of frontier living—emotional and spiritual hardihood, independence, self-reliance, and hard work—would need to be created by new methods. By utilizing the Boy Scout movement and other nature-based programs, including a large program of camping for young women, LDS leaders hoped to transmit the lessons of the pioneer past to the next generation of church members.

Soft in the City

In the early years of the twentieth century, a series of jeremiads by Mormon leaders warned that young men, lured by the luxury and ease of urban life, were becoming soft. Noting how far the young men of Utah had fallen from the example of their hardworking forebears, one writer made clear the link between urban life and indolence. After a conversation in which the superintendent of a large smelting plant had remarked that Utah boys were lazy and weak compared to the pioneers, the author admitted: "The remarks embarrassed me—a Utah boy myself—and I found no explanation for this condition, which I trust, is not general." Though not yet widespread throughout the church, adolescent inactivity, according to the author, "exists only in those localities where mechanical industry is beginning to invade the easy-going rural districts of our state. Even this observation . . . is a reproach to our young men, for, it should be remembered, Utah has for its emblem the hive of busy bees—the very motto of Industry."[4] A scant six years after the state motto and seal had been created (Utah gained statehood in 1896), the motto of "Industry" resonated only in rural areas. Urban locales—replete with "mechanical industry"—already seemed far removed from the swarm of busy bees inhabiting the state seal.

In a similar article six months later, young men again were condemned for rejecting the work habits and occupations of their pioneer forefathers. "The growing disposition of young men in our communities to shirk the arduous duties and drudgery incident to the learning of a skillful trade is very regrettable," read one of a series of "Talks to Young Men." "Many of the founders of our cities and towns were tradesmen, as well as financiers, and by reason of the success which their energy reaped, have reared their sons far more luxuriously than they themselves were reared." Whereas many of his contemporaries hailed the effects of progress caused by the struggle to survive in a Darwinian world, this author located a decline in LDS stock due to the ease of middle-class life in the city. "This comfortable environment has developed, in the rising generation, tastes for 'nicer' vocations; and the workshop is abandoned for the office, the bank, or the bar. The tendency toward professional callings has been stronger than it should have been during the past decade, and a return to the bench and workshop would today be proper for the majority of our young men." Free from the lessons taught by hard work, the youth of the church had fallen from the lofty heights attained by their fathers. In his final flourish, the author pled: "It will require grit and determination to lay aside habits for true character, and to put aside fine clothes and white linen, and put on overalls and jumper, and get to work in dust and grease and smoke, but that's the sure way to make men."[5] The city—and the ease of its occupations—robbed young Mormon men of their masculinity, their true character. Effete occupations in the emerging professions seemed to be feminizing adolescent males, clothing their manhood in white linen and lace.

Church president Joseph F. Smith echoed the fears regarding degenerate youths and their fascination with the professions. During the church's General Conference in April 1903, Smith spoke of "the need of teaching the young people to be producers, mechanics and artisans, rather than mere followers of the learned professions." He encouraged manual training for young men and learning in the domestic sciences for young women, "so that they may be able to produce something for the general welfare." Without belittling "scholastic attainments, such as the schools and universities lead the youth to acquire," Smith extolled the virtues not of mechanical vocations but of agricultural life. He "pointed out the need of knowing how to cultivate the soil to the best advantage, and of how to make articles needful for the comfort and convenience of the people, and of how to manage the practical affairs of home." "The nobility of practical labor, and the contentment arising therefrom," he contended, "will be more clearly manifest among the people."[6] The message emanated from many voices: the "young men of this community," according to another author, "had lost the vitality of their fathers." Like so many Puritan divines bemoaning the decadence of the second and third generations, modern-day Mormon Mathers recognized that the city had weakened the will of their boys.[7] No longer working on the farm, or behind the workbench, young Mormon men had succumbed to the ease offered by urban professions. "These young men are always on the lookout for 'soft snaps.' They shun difficulties. They abhor hard work. They swarm our business colleges, studying how to become bookkeepers and stenographers."[8] The loss of vitality signaled not only diminished masculinity but a rise in flabby muscles and mushy morals as well.

Other Mormon leaders coupled the denigration of urban life with a glorification of life on the farm. One can hear the echoes of a Jeffersonian agricultural attitude[9] in the words of Milton Bennion, a professor of philosophy at the University of Utah, who asserted, "'Cities are the graves of the human species.' These words of Rosseau may be extravagant, but they are not wholly devoid of truth. The city not uncommonly becomes the grave of a whole family in the course of a few generations. On the other hand," Bennion advised, "the farms steadily renew the population of the country districts, and at the same time pour a stream of recruits into the cities to renew and invigorate business and professional life."[10] Bennion's comments capture the problem and the solution for Progressive Mormons—the vice and laxity of the cities were best countered by the virtues of agricultural life.

In opposition to the corruption and depravity of the city, rural life was characterized as clean and healthy, even redemptive. According to Frank J. Hewlett, the former president of the Salt Lake City Council, farm life offered an antidote to all of the ills that plagued young men in the city. "Were it possible to send out boys on a farm a part of the summer," Hewlett recommended, "it would result to their advantage, both physically and morally. During their spare moments, they could study nature in the mountains, streams and valleys. They could study the flowers, birds and insects in their native environments. There is no young man that is so busy but he can devote a few minutes each day to the study of a book, and absorb every point that is for his intellectual benefit."[11] To Hewlett and others, it appeared so simple—to take the city out of the boy, you needed to take the boy out of the city. Physically, morally, intellectually, even temperamentally, nature mitigated the problems caused by growing up in the city. Though the bucolic rural conditions found in Hewlett's purple prose may have never existed on most American farms, his argument resonated with many urban dwellers. As Richard R. Lyman, the First Assistant Superintendent of the Young Men's Mutual Improvement Association, claimed, "Our greatest men and our best citizens as a rule grow up on the farm."[12]

Even before Hewlett called for young men to go back to the farm (at least during summer vacation), Mormon authors had begun to construct a poetic point of view that connected rural life and spiritual and physical well-being. An early articulation of this perspective appears in the poem "Beyond the City," written by Grace Ingles Frost in 1906:

> Beyond the city where the hay,
> Newmown, with fragrance fills the breeze
> That from my brow drives care away,
> And ends in song among the trees.

Beyond the city and its toil,
It makes my heart forget its pain,
To watch the farmer till the soil,
Or gather in the ripened grain.
Beyond the city! That is where,
I fain would rest when life is done,
Within the shadows of the hills,
Until he comes—the Holy One.[13]

In her poetic voice, Frost expands on the vision espoused by Frank Hewlett. Describing the city with words like "hum," "want," "sin," "toil," and "pain" and detailing a rural life of breezes, setting suns, and fresh-cut hay, Frost's Manichean dichotomy might as well compare heaven and hell. The poet intimates that the triumphal return of Christ will occur in the "shadows of the hills," where farm folk reside "beyond the city." God seems closer in the country—surely even He must be more comfortable where the sky is blue and the air clean. W. P. Kinsella's fictional Shoeless Joe Jackson was right—heaven is a lot like Iowa.[14]

Perhaps the crescendo of the artistic glorification of farm life appeared in Evan Stephens's 1918 paean to "The Farmer Boy." The author of many LDS hymns and the conductor of the Tabernacle Choir from 1890 to 1916, Stephens unabashedly celebrates the Jeffersonian yeoman ideal transplanted to the prairies of the far West:

I sing of the lad that tills the soil,
With the tan upon his face,
With his sturdy limbs, grown by honest toil—
Counting labor no disgrace, Counting labor no disgrace.
Ah yes I sing of the farmer boy,
And the joys that bless his life.
He has health and wealth free of such alloy,
As the city's noise and strife, As the city's noise and strife.[15]

Tan farm lads produce not only foodstuffs but sturdy limbs by honest toil. It is difficult to imagine a Progressive-Era LDS psalm dedicated to "The Street Urchin" or "The Boy on the Corner."

Others followed Frost's artistic trajectory in painting an arcadian portrait of rural America. Nephi Anderson's fictional story "The End of the Rainbow" describes not only heroic Roni Jones's flirtation with the city but the Mormon urban experience generally. Following the unsuccessful courtship of a young woman in a nearby city, Roni returns to his country home and waxes sentimental about his surroundings.

How good, thought he, to get home again; to see the unsullied blue of the sky, instead of the blackness of the chimney smoke; to smell the sweetness of all things growing, instead of the stench of mills, and mines, and streets; to hear the twitter of birds, the drone and chirp of insects, the soft whisperings of willow tops, instead of the clatter of paved streets, and the roar and rattle that men make when they crowd together into cities. He took long breaths of the air, and how good it was! He had been away nearly six months, but it seemed an age of wear and tear and confusion. His coming out of it all into this big, free, open country, was like being born again into a new world.[16]

Anderson's vision of Jones's journey might well stand in for the Mormon urban experience. Latter-day Saints, like Jones, had not sojourned in the city long, but to many, "it seemed an age of wear and tear and confusion." Urban amenities that typically earned praise garnered only criticism from Anderson's pen—even paved city streets clatter and roar! Surely, in Anderson's estimation, the sullied cities were not fit for the courtship of the Saints.

Though farmland played a significant role in the Mormon vision of rural beauty, many Mormon artists found anticity inspiration in the mountains that ramparted many of the valley cities of Utah. To partake of the cleansing power of nature, one did not have to reside on a farm, but it was necessary to leave the city. What life in the city had dissipated, nature's canyons could restore. In the words of Annie D. Palmer:

With the call of the canyon my hunger returns,
That old school-time hunger that toil never earns;
The hunger that flavors each morsel just right,
And comes without coaxing, noon, morning, and night.
The games 'round the bonfire, the story, and song,
With the call of the canyon come crowding along.

With the call of the canyon come memories sweet
Of the dawning of love with its chapter complete;
Of the timid response when my love was declared,
And her modest reserve in confessing she cared—
How I loved in the canyons to stroll by her side.
To the deeds of the grove where the feather-ferns hide.

While the canyon is calling, I quicken my pace,
And clasp her again in a loving embrace;
Still just as angelic, as modest, as fair,—
And we plan a short rest from life's hurry and care
With our girls and our boys in a canyon retreat,
Where the gladness of nature our gladness will greet.[17]

Love blooms best in a clean, virginal natural setting where the sin of the city is washed off "on the river's cool bank." However, unlike the fictional Roni Jones's return to the farm, refreshment from the city's canyons did not require a permanent relocation. Rather, individuals and families could take a temporary "retreat" from the city and return revitalized to their urban lives. The concept of a temporary retreat would become central to the Boy Scout and Girls' Camp programs instituted by the church.

Recapitulating the Pioneer Past

In addition to solving urban social and spiritual problems, retreating into nature was seen as a way to bridge the generational gap that separated third- and fourth-generation Mormons from church founders. The earliest LDS leaders—including the church presidents Brigham Young and John Taylor as well as respected apostles like Heber C. Kimball—had benefitted from membership in Joseph Smith's inner circle. Their proximity to the prophet not only provided intense spiritual and personal growth but also gave them legitimacy among the Mormon faithful. Appealing to the memory of martyred Joseph was an easy way to rally church members. Throughout the nineteenth century, church leaders could relate personal experiences with the prophet: Brigham Young had been Smith's appointed successor; John Taylor stood by the prophet when he was felled by the mob at Carthage jail; Wilford Woodruff was set apart as an apostle in 1839; and Lorenzo Snow first met the prophet in 1831. Joseph F. Smith, church president during most of the first two decades of the twentieth century, represented the last link to the prophet's inner circle and the persecution that drove the Saints west. Born at Far West, Missouri, in 1838 to Hyrum (Joseph's older brother) and Mary Fielding Smith, Joseph F. Smith, as a child, had known the prophet and had experienced severe tribulation traveling across the plains with his widowed mother. He would be the last LDS Church president to be able to speak of the early persecutions in the first person. Smith's successor, Heber J. Grant, was born in Utah in 1856.[18]

The corrosion of the physical and spiritual mettle of young Mormon men caused by the city seemed compounded by their chronological remoteness from the Prophet Joseph Smith. Spiritual slack loosened the taut rope that had led Mormons through the darkest days of the church's early existence. It was feared that the rising generation—free from the privations of Mormonism's early days and personally unacquainted with the luminaries of the church's founding—did not contain the spiritual fortitude to move the church into the twentieth century. Not having passed through the refining fires of transcontinental migration and without personal memory of the prophet or his immediate successors, young Mormons possessed few of the experiences that had fortified church leaders from the beginning. To resurrect the tradition of pioneer hardihood, Mormon leaders turned to nature activities, particularly the Boy Scouts, to provide a frontier experience, if only by proxy.

Mormon efforts to "use" their history did not begin with camping trips and Boy Scout meetings. The closing decades of the nineteenth century saw a rush by Mormons to reclaim their pioneer past. In the 1880s, in an effort to revive and spread the story of Joseph Smith's theophanic First Vision, the LDS artist C. C. A. Christensen painted huge murals depicting the event. Displaying the canvasses throughout Utah and Idaho, Christensen ushered in a new era of reverence for the Prophet Joseph. In the following decade, Mormons organized a number of historical societies, including the Genealogical Society of Utah in 1894, the Utah Society of the Sons of the American Revolution the next year, and the Utah State Historical Society and the Sons and Daughters of the Utah Pioneers by the end of the century. Likewise, emphasis was placed on male members of the church tracing their priesthood authority and keeping records regarding ordinations and other church ordinances. Missionaries were instructed to keep diaries detailing their daily events, and Mormons who owned pioneer diaries were asked to donate the historical materials to the church or at least allow church historians to copy them. Furthermore, around the turn of the century, the church purchased important early Mormon history sites, including the Solomon Mack home in Vermont and the Carthage jail in Illinois, sites commemorating the beginning and the end of the Prophet Joseph Smith's life.[19] Because the number of Saints able to remember the important events in LDS history was diminishing, the church went to great lengths to create an "institutional memory" to replace the personal memories of the dying pioneer generation.

The "founding" period of the church—stretching from Joseph Smith's First Vision to the forced migration to the Great Basin—was receding farther into the past. A virtual death watch was instituted in the *Improvement Era,* marking the passing of each known pioneer who had crossed the plains in the original 1847 migration. News capsules typically included information like "Ezra Shoemaker, of Manti, died in Salt Lake City, Oct. 1. He was born in Adams Co., Ill., March 20, 1843, and came with his parents, to Utah, in 1847. For the last seventeen years he was second counselor to Lewis Anderson, president of the South Sanpete stake."[20] In September 1922, on the seventy-fifth anniversary of the pioneer trek, a search of church members located 125 living pioneers from the 1847 crossing.[21] Two years later, in May 1924, the "last of the original pioneers who entered Salt Lake Valley, July 24, 1847, under the leadership of Brigham Young," died in Shelley, Idaho. Lorenzo Sobieski Young, only seven years old when he crossed the continent, died at age eighty-four.[22] No Latter-day Saint had the power to bring back the pioneer dead. It was hoped, however, that by initiating young men in nature experiences, the spirit of the pioneers, in physical hardihood and spiritual strength, could be revived. To resuscitate the flagging pioneer tradition, Mormon leaders turned to an organization that built boys' character and instilled discipline through experiences in the great outdoors. The Boy Scout program would help solve the problems of urban life and would also connect Mormon boys to their pioneer past.

According to the reminiscences of one of the original Mormon Boy Scouts, the first Scout troop in the LDS Church was organized in October 1910 by the Waterloo Ward in the Salt Lake Granite Stake.[23] The impetus for sponsoring the Boy Scouts came from a young English immigrant, Thomas George Wood, who had recently settled in the area. Wood "called to the attention of the ward's Bishopric that the Deacons and Teachers would like to go on hikes." Wood had done some research on Scouting while in England and had purchased a British Scouting manual. Under the authorization of Bishop Asahel H. Woodruff, Wood organized a Scout troop sponsored by the YMMIA of the Waterloo Ward. The group quickly enrolled fifty young men between the ages of twelve and eighteen. Though it was difficult for Wood to devise programs that would maintain the interest of all of the boys, the new Scoutmaster worked hard to learn the rudiments of the Scout program in addition to his study of "nature, the birds, trees, stars, campcrafts, out-door cooking and the virtues of manly living." Regular meetings took place in the basement of the Waterloo chapel immediately following the YMMIA lesson. Many of the early Scout activities remained popular throughout the twentieth century: preparation of a Scout pack, nature study, first aid, knot tying, learning scout laws, and performing good turns. Activities like marching drills and delivering wood to needy persons rounded out the troop's activities. Outdoor adventures such as hikes to Black Mountain and outings to Mountain Dell and Saratoga Springs offered prime opportunities for nature study and transported the young men out of the city, at least temporarily.[24]

Not all church leaders, however, were convinced of the need for any youth organizations beyond the MIA. Elder B. H. Roberts, in charge of a committee investigating the possibility of adding Scouts to the MIA's program, reported the committee's findings: "We are already provided with both sufficient and efficient organization to cover the field of activities proposed by 'scouting.'" Moreover, the committee believed that "to create new scout units, or to confederate with other organizations would likely result in dividing the interests of the junior members of our associations, and perhaps wean them from love and loyalty to their organization founded through the inspired leaders of our Church, for which there would be and *could* be no compensating returns."[25] This announcement, made in April 1911, seemed to foreclose future Scout units within the church.

Proponents of Scoutcraft, however, refused to admit defeat. Following B. H. Roberts's announcement, one prominent church recreation leader— Eugene L. Roberts, the director of physical training at Brigham Young University—placed his arguments for Scouting in front of the Mormon people through the pages of the *Improvement Era*. Keenly aware of the desire of many young men to join the Scouting ranks, Roberts articulated a stance that placed Scouting activities squarely within the confines of LDS thought.[26] In calling for a Scout-like "Boy Pioneers of Utah" (not expressly connected to the Boy Scouts organization), Roberts enunciated the major reasons that Mormon boys should become Scouts—to save them from the sins of the city streets and to teach young men the lessons of pioneer life. In the October 1911 *Improvement Era*, Roberts turned his attention to the burgeoning city and modern life. Those living the "artificial life" of the cities suffered from a "perceptible degeneracy" that spawned various reform movements to "offset the unfortunate results and to reclaim mankind for the natural and the sane." Even the Mormon farmer had been robbed of his "verile [sic] physical manhood and healthy mentality" by the advent of labor-saving farm machinery.[27]

To Roberts, the answer to urban degeneration appeared in the tenets and activities of movements such as the Boy Scouts that "aim to correct the deformities, as it were, of civilization, and give the boys of the world a healthy point of view in life." Though many of the principles espoused by the Boy Scouts applied to the circumstances in Mormon Utah, Roberts recognized that a program tailored specifically to Mormon ends would be more acceptable to the young men of the faith and to the church's hierarchy. Contending that the Boy Scout organization contained "features which do not apply to conditions in Zion, and it lacks much that is apparently needed in this community," Roberts declared, "We need an organization of our own colored with our own 'Mormon' ideals and fitted to our 'Mormon' environment."[28]

The main problem besetting Mormon youth centered around the descent of the rising generation from the faithfulness of their pioneer forefathers. Roberts described the fears of many LDS leaders:

It was but yesterday that our fathers were engaged in various pioneer struggles. They made themselves a magnificent generation through their terrific fight against the desert and adverse circumstances. No one can read of their physical hardships and religious trials without being fired with admiration. But their work is finished; they have made the desert bloom and built up a commonwealth; and their sons, lolling in comparative luxury, are gradually forgetting their debt to their fathers. The pale, city-bred boy, who has never camped on the deseret [sic], nor seen the wilds, who has never tramped over the hills, nor "roughed" it, cannot truly sympathize with the struggles of his father. He reads or listens to stories picturing the pioneer life, but he cannot appreciate; he imagines, but not clearly; thrills, but not deeply; is interested, but not enthusiastically.

Urban life had destroyed the pioneer spirit that formed the core of Mormon identity. The lessons of their fathers failed to reach the ears of city youth, drowned out by factory whistles, street cars, and commercial amusements. Admitting that the "pioneer life is gone," Roberts feared the worst: "A generation hence and the sons and daughters of the pioneers may be just as shallow and frivolous and indifferent as the weaklings on the streets of New York, removed several generations from their pioneer ancestors."[29]

The way to fend off the seemingly inevitable generational declension was found in a Boy Scout–like movement that would "bring the youth of Zion into [a] close and lasting relationship with [their] fathers and forefathers!" Proposing the creation of the Boy Pioneers of Utah, patterned after Brigham Young's organization of the original pioneers, Roberts was the first to add a Mormon flavor to the Boy Scout movement. A Mormon group would "embrace all the salient features of the Scouts with more or less the same code of honor, the same activities, and with the same purposes in general." The Boy Pioneers, however, would "aim to preserve the memory of the pioneers, and to teach reverence and sympathy for their religious struggles." By camping out and spending time in nature, boys would recapitulate the pioneer past and learn to imitate not only the harsh conditions of the frontier but also to "follow [the pioneer] code of moral teachings." In sum, Roberts predicted that the quasi-Scouting association would solve both of the major problems facing the church's urban youth by offsetting the effects of city life and promoting a revivification of the pioneer spirit. The Boy Pioneers provided the answer to the church's city-bred declension. "If such an organization did no more than stimulate a healthy enthusiasm and create a loyal admiration of these noble pioneers, who blessed these westerns deserts with their God directed efforts," wrote Roberts, "it would justify itself." Moreover, as a "lasting monument to the memory of the pioneers," the Boy Pioneers would assume significant religious importance by becoming "a veritable 'passover' in preserving the story of their pilgrimage across the plains and their subsequent struggle with the desert."[30]

Roberts's efforts to bring Scouting within the Mormon fold of recreation proved successful. It appears that the arguments found in "The Boy Pioneers of Utah" even affected B. H. Roberts, previously one of Scouting's staunchest opponents within the church. Whether the idea of the Boy Pioneers appealed to Elder Roberts's love of the Mormon past or his concern about the Mormon future, Eugene Roberts's ideas seemed to have changed B. H. Roberts's mind. Not long after Eugene Roberts made his case, B. H. Roberts published an article in the *Deseret News* calling for the church to join the national Boy Scout organization.[31] Whatever the reason for the change in policy, the MIA General Board adopted the name "M.I.A. Scouts" to cover the outdoor activities being pursued by young men in the church. Membership was limited to boys from twelve to eighteen years of age.[32] The church affiliated with the Boy Scouts of America the next year, in 1913.

The rigorous life of outdoor activities struck a resonant chord among church members who had long venerated the memory of pioneer hardships. As the LDS Church initially rallied behind the Scouting program, the main emphasis was not on instilling patriotism or teaching useful nature skills; rather, Scouting served as a proxy "pioneer" experience that taught young Mormon men the physical and spiritual skills of their forebears. To train young men for the future, Mormon leaders turned to a new program that was firmly rooted in the past. The general YMMIA leader Lyman R. Martineau introduced the MIA Scout program to church members by recalling the accomplishments of the Mormon pioneers: "The great movement of the Church from Illinois and Iowa to these mountains in 1847, and the years immediately following, developed among both men and women the highest art of scoutcraft, perhaps, that has been found among any pioneers in the history of our country. Loyal to country and to their religion, hardy and persevering, they made thousands of shining examples of choicest citizenship, brave, wise, and God-fearing." If the early Saints practiced a protoform of Scouting, surely young men in the twentieth century could benefit by pursuing similar activities. And rugged outdoor activities were at the heart of Scouting. Scout leaders like Martineau hoped that by replicating pioneer conditions, modern Scouts could learn pioneer lessons.

Although all frontier conditions could not be duplicated, urban Scouts made the most of the hardships at their disposal. Quoting from the Scout *Handbook for Boys*, Martineau praised the vigorous programs that required a Scout to be "systematically taking exercise, playing games, running, and walking. It means that he must sleep enough hours to give him the necessary strength, and if possible to sleep very much in the open, or at least with the windows of his bedroom open both summer and winter. It means also that he should take a cold bath often, rubbing dry with a rough towel. He should breathe through the nose and not through the mouth. He should at all times train himself to endure hardships." The list of Scout "hardships"— cold beds and cold baths, rough towels, and flared nostrils—reflects the sometimes humorous methods by which character was to be built. Though church leaders never linked dry, hard skin with hard-and-fast morals, the notion persisted that even self-imposed or contrived hardships could lead to physical and spiritual growth.[33] If pioneer trials defied duplication, hardships would have to be created to test the boys. In city homes, boys could triumph over frontier conditions—even if they had to let the cold air in themselves.

Fittingly, one of the first major projects initiated by MIA Scouts involved the organization of a "Pioneer Trail Party," which hiked from Echo Canyon to Salt Lake City to commemorate the original pioneer trek and to call attention to the need for an automobile road along the route. Throughout the hike, church leaders like B. H. Roberts related pioneer stories to the boys and pointed out remnants of the pioneer experience, like the canyon fortifications of 1858. In Echo Canyon, the group sang "with spirit and feeling heretofore unexperienced in their lives" the hymn of the original pioneers, "Come, Come, Ye Saints." Lessons were taught using pioneer artifacts, including a banner containing all of the names of the original 1847 company, made by the Relief Society at Winter Quarters. Many boys examined an old buckskin coat that had been worn by Thomas Bullock on the original trek. When the group stopped for lunch at the Henefer meetinghouse, church leaders, including President Anthon H. Lund, Francis M. Lyman, and Orson F. Whitney, delivered "stirring pioneer and patriotic speeches." Some of the boys, however, thought these orations "lasted a long time" and were relieved when lunch was finally served. At each camping location on the trek, a post was constructed with the inscription, "Mormon Pioneer Trail, 1847—M.I.A. Scouts passed here July, 1912." These markers reified the connection between the 1847 pioneers and the Boy Pioneers of the Progressive Era. The re-creation of the pioneer march exemplified the goals of urban LDS Scouts to "obtain inspiration for the admirable work of the pioneers, to enjoy a pleasant outing, and to get some education in nature, discipline, and history." Hiking along the pioneer route introduced the young men to trail life and reminded them of the adversities faced by early Mormons. Calling for an auto route to parallel the trail—the introduction of modern transportation as another tool to recapture the past—seemed a perfect fit for a group of urban boys living (temporarily) in the tradition of their ancestors.[34]

In addition to recapitulating their pioneer past, Scout programs helped young Mormon men become upstanding citizens. Surrounded by temptations in the city, Scout groups offered an outpost where citizenship, loyalty, and discipline received prime importance. Extolling the ability of Scouting to reform wayward boys and direct rudderless urban youth, the social critic Jacob Riis explained that Scout programs were "getting at the boy on his own ground, setting him to do the things he ardently wants to do, but, in our cities with their twisted social conditions, doesn't know how to do." The problem, according to Riis, was that "every boy has in him a little savage and a potential good citizen. The question is which is to get the upper grip; . . . Give him the street and the gutter for a playground, rob him of his play, and he joins the gang and learns the lessons that do not lead to respect for authority or property. . . . The savage has come uppermost, and he lives the law of the jungle." If society, however, offered the boy a leisure-time alternative through Scouting, the disrespectful urban savage could change his stripes and would "adopt the Scout law to be dutiful, obedient, helpful, and clean, with the same enthusiasm." Though the city Scout and the city savage started from the same point, "it [was] the way they work out that makes the difference."[35] Involvement in Scouting brought the best out in boys, according to Riis and others. The organization had the ability to uplift boys and direct them toward positive behavior.

In an article outlining the merits of athletics and Scout work in the church, the LDS Scout leader Oscar A. Kirkham quoted a poem that cut to the heart of Riis's message:

> Here's to the Apache of the street!
> Lawbreakers of today, lawmakers of tomorrow;
> Builders of cities; kings and princes of America—
> My boy, your boy, everybody's boy,
> God bless them all![36]

Scouting would take the "Apache of the street" and, as the editor of the *Improvement Era* described, direct the "exuberant spirit of the boys" in the proper direction. As Scouts, boys learned "to love nature in the open, care for themselves and their comrades, to render first aid to the injured, find their way in the mountains and forests; and, above all, the youngsters are taught wholesome discipline, and a tenderness for the weak, a respect for the rights of others, reverence for good men and women, good things and places."[37] Discipline and respect—the lack of which seemed to form the core of most urban "savages"—distilled into the young man naturally from participation in Scouting programs. Urban reformers and Mormon leaders agreed on that potential.

Scout leaders within and outside the LDS faith commented on the ability of the program to take "'the boy at that time of his life when he is beset with the new and bewildering experiences of adolescence and divert his thoughts therefrom to wholesome and worth-while activities.'"[38] The positive potential of Scouting appeared boundless. According to the national commissioner of the Boy Scouts, Ludvig Dale, in a speech delivered at MIA annual conference in June 1915, Scouting translated the "desires and the ideals and the ambitions of the average, normal boy into controlled action" and showed him "what to do, and [kept] him so busy that he [hadn't] the time to don't." In Dale's estimation, the program not only led to "clean minds, clean hearts, efficient hands" but ultimately resulted in a "better city, better state, and a better nation." LDS leaders surely nodded in agreement. Dale, however, went even further, claiming that participation in the Scouting program could have averted the war raging in Europe: "What would have happened, if fifty years ago there had been boy scouts? I could see French boy scouts, and English boy scouts sending a message to their brother boy scouts in Germany; how we regret that you, brother boy scouts, should be at enmity, because we have learned to be imbued with sentiments of patriotism and good feeling, and we hope that the war will soon be over, never again to come, because of the boy scouts. These are the kind of principles the boy scouts are learning."[39] Though critics feared that the uniformed, disciplined Scouts contributed to the type of jingoistic nationalism that led to the conflict, Scout leaders maintained an undaunted faith in the organization's ability to uplift the behavior of young men throughout the world.

Mormon leaders hoped Scouts would foster a dual citizenship that combined state and church. As the MIA Scout commissioner John Taylor advised parents, a good scout was not only a better son and a better citizen, he was also a "better member of the Church."[40] The spiritual aspects of Scouting had concerned LDS leaders from the beginning. Before allying the MIA Scouts with the national Boy Scout organization, church leaders received assurances from the national BSA council that the church would be allowed to select the leaders of LDS troops. Furthermore, the national council promised church leaders that they could use the Scout program "in whatever manner best served the purposes of the Church and with a distinct provision that Scout leaders would be permitted to make whatever religious application they desired in conducting the program." Non-LDS boys who participated in Mormon-sponsored troops, however, were not required to participate in any LDS religious rituals.[41] When Oscar A. Kirkham announced that the church had "joined the national organization in this great movement for the salvation of boys," he was surely framing the issue in both social and spiritual terms.[42]

Initially, Scout work was conducted in addition to the regular MIA weekly program. Even before the MIA Scouts affiliated with the national organization, Lyman Martineau promised that Scout involvement would not replace the standard work of the YMMIA. In fact, he believed that "scoutcraft will add enthusiasm and loyalty to the regular work of Mutual Improvement and other organizations."[43] Shortly thereafter, however, an infectious enthusiasm for Scouting had overtaken the MIA program of religious study. Where once Scout activities had supplemented religious learning, it was decided that "religious training definitely would be included through application of the spiritual teachings of the Boy Scout program from the L.D.S. viewpoint."[44] Scouting was not only a method to teach young men about the pioneer past, it was also used to teach LDS theology as well. Norman Geertsen poetically described the spiritual values required "To Be a Scout":

> To be a Scout—oh, what an aim!
> To live a life; to play the game;
> To do each day that kindly deed;
> To help some worthy soul in need.
>
> To be a Scout and hike along
> The mountain path and lilt a song.
> To make a bed where winds have trod,
> Makes man and boy both think of God.[45]

Geertsen's poetic image captures the vision that prompted the LDS Church to turn wholeheartedly toward Scouting: young Mormon men (and their fathers) leaving the city to hike mountain paths in a virtual recapitulation of the pioneer experience. Along the way, they not only gain a profound respect for nature but also turn their thoughts to God. Another LDS poet, Ivy Houtz Woolley, concluded that the eventual reward of Boy Scout service would be eternal splendor:

> Oh, boy band, oh, joy band,
> Your laws are heaven's laws:
> When living by your noble code,
> Who could on sin's brink pause?
> Oh, boy band, oh, joy band,
> Press forward heart and soul,
> Climb on and on, for on the heights
> Awaits your sought for goal.[46]

Mormon Scouts, at least in Wooley's formulation, follow in the footsteps of the ancient prophet Moses, who scaled Mount Sinai to find God in a burning bush. The twentieth-century "joy band" of Boy Scouts—situated as latter-day "youth of Israel"—likewise find God by trekking to the mountain tops.

Though LDS Church officials used the Scouts to inculcate Mormon values, representatives of the Boy Scout organization championed the positive aspects of troops sponsored by religious bodies. During a visit to Salt Lake City, Chief Scout Executive James E. West categorically advocated mixing religion and Scouting: "A scout is reverent. He is reverent toward God. He is faithful in his religious duties, and respects the convictions of others in matters of custom and religion. Because of the deep concern in the religious instruction of the youth of America, we have very definitely advocated the troop being organized in connection with the church, so that there might be given to the boys of that troop all of the influence, all of the traditions, which stand back of that church."[47] Church and MIA officials could not have agreed more. Scouting quickly became an effective recruiting and teaching tool refined in particular ways to meet the social and spiritual needs of Mormon youth.

By 1915—only five years after Waterloo Ward had sponsored the first Scout troop in the church—more than three thousand young men participated in LDS-sponsored Scouting activities. From 1915 to 1921, the number of Mormon Scouts increased nearly fourfold. Despite the fact that the church had officially affiliated with the Boy Scouts of America in 1913, a considerable number of wards and stakes continued to sponsor Scouting activities without actually registering their boys with the national organization. For example, statistics for 1918 show that 3,705 boys had registered with official BSA troops, while another 2,162 participated in LDS scouting activities beyond BSA recognition. The next year, 4,528 registered with the national organization, and 3,708 participated in local, unaffiliated programs. From 1915 to 1922 (not including 1919), the number of Scouts registered with the BSA increased at an annual rate of 19.5 percent. For 1918, there were more Scouts in Utah, in proportion to the population, than in any other state. For every 137 people in the Beehive State, there was one Scout.[48] And by 1923, every stake in the church, with the exception of Colonia Juarez in northern Mexico, sponsored at least one registered troop.

Whenever possible, LDS leaders integrated Scouting with the existing programs of the YMMIA. By modifying Scouting methods—often by creating special requirements for Scouts and their leaders—the church tailored Scouting to suit its own needs. Interested in more than just preaching about the pioneer traits fostered by the organization, MIA officials ensured that Scouting involvement deepened Mormon religious beliefs and increased allegiance to the church. Not surprisingly, like athletics, Scout activities became a device that leaders employed to increase attendance at MIA meetings. MIA leaders of the Ogden, Utah, Ninth Ward, suffering from sparse attendance, decided that "Scout work was [their] only salvation" and concentrated their recruiting efforts along Scout lines. Within about a year, enrollment in the ward association had increased from five boys to nearly one hundred, according to the Scoutmaster Robert E. Wilson.[49] Scout work played such an important religious role in the lives of many young Mormon men that one MIA leader proposed that Mormon Scoutmasters be allowed to focus on that particular work without the distraction of additional church responsibilities. The MIA Scout commissioner John Taylor agreed: "A man who can guide twenty or thirty boys in their play and recreation and . . . impress upon them the necessity of giving service to their church, and living in conformity with the principles of the gospel, is doing a sufficiently valuable work that should entitle him to some relief from other ward duties."[50] Taylor deemed the spiritual survival skills taught by Scoutmasters to be sufficiently important to warrant their undivided attention. Like Sunday School teachers, Scoutmasters preached conformity to church standards and deserved respect as religious role models.

In the spring of 1922, Apostle George Albert Smith outlined a method to ensure that church-sponsored Scouting activities strengthened activity in the youth auxiliary rather than competed with it. Speaking for the YMMIA General Superintendency, Smith requested that local Scout leaders be "men of faith, integrity, and ability" and that at least one member of the ward MIA presidency play an active role on the Scout committee. Stake superintendents were instructed to meet regularly with Scout leaders to ensure that "the spirit and atmosphere of the gospel [was] maintained in scout work." To spiritualize weekly Scout meetings, Smith advised local leaders to make the MIA *Junior Manual* a prominent part of the session. Reminding leaders that the Boy Scout program remained an appendage of the MIA auxiliary, the apostle asked stake superintendents to "call the scout men together and impress upon them that scouting is but an aid to the Y.M.M.I.A., in which we are striving to teach the principles of the gospel of Jesus Christ. . . . All scout leaders are, of course, Y.M.M.I.A. officers, and should be brought into conference with the other association officers at all times."[51] As one component of the association's diverse offerings, Scouting provided an effective way to train young Mormon men to follow gospel teachings.

Just as athletics was used as a lever to induce young men to comply with the Word of Wisdom, Mormon officials required Scouts and their leaders to obey the principles of the dietary code. The 1925 *YMMIA Hand Book* prescribed that under the MIA's leadership, "no person shall be chosen a scout official who uses tobacco." Noting that Scouts promised to keep themselves physically clean, the handbook prohibited young Scouts from using the illicit substance as well. However, when a Scout showed an "inclination to try to overcome the habit, and his actions are consistent with his promise to try," he was to remain in the troop and receive encouragement from Scout leaders. If, however, the boy "wilfully disregards his promise, and does not try to discontinue the habit within a reasonable time," the offender should be suspended from the organization until his behavior conformed to the MIA's policy of abstinence. Following the boy's expulsion, the Scoutmaster must "continue his efforts with the scout until he has accomplished a reform."[52] In Scouting, like athletics, the church found a malleable method of social control. At times, the threat of expulsion acted as a "stick" to punish wayward young men, while on other occasions the lure of fun and fraternity within the organization acted as a "carrot" to entice the boy to modify his behavior.

Not every requirement in the Boy Scout handbook comported with church standards, however. When elements of Scouting conflicted with LDS essentials, Scouting had to give way. For instance, Scout leaders needed regular reminders that the physical, outdoor aspects of Scouting were not in line with Mormon standards for the Sabbath day. In associations that met on Sunday nights, Scouts could participate in lectures or recitations on Scout subjects. Talks on first aid, the Scout laws, and nature received official sanction. Physical activities, such as bandaging, signaling, drills, knot tying, or Scout demonstrations, however, did not pass church muster and had to be performed on other nights. These activities were prohibited "in order that nothing may be introduced that will tend to undermine the boys' respect for sacred Sabbath."[53] Even the Scout "cheer"—venerated for "bringing the boys together, making each one feel more closely related to the others"— was to be eliminated or performed silently on Sunday. Scouts were directed to sing familiar melodies as a substitute.[54] Sabbath-day hiking was also prohibited. When several Scout groups sponsored hiking excursions that began on Saturday afternoon and continued over Sunday, the question arose whether this was appropriate for Mormon youth groups. Even if outdoor religious exercises were held on the Sabbath, the General Board concluded, "we do not feel at liberty to sanction any 'hikes' that include any portion of the Sabbath day." Sunday hikes challenged a long-standing slogan of the YMMIA: "We stand for a Sacred Sabbath and a Weekly Half Holiday."[55] In this case, Scouting yielded to the Sabbatarian principles of the church.

Other more fundamental Scout activities likewise clashed with Mormon sensibilities. The *YMMIA Hand Book* for 1925 requested that LDS Scouts and Scout officials not participate in the traditional Scout hand clasp. In its place, LDS Scouts substituted the American handshake. Additionally, Mormon scouters were instructed to use the phrase "Scout Promise" instead of "Scout Oath." Scouting rituals—including the official induction ceremony and advancement from one class to another—could be made "very impressive" but should remain "simple and dignified." "Ceremonies" were not to be used.[56] Though the reasons were never fully articulated, it is not difficult to understand why church leaders drew the line at taking "oaths" and participating in secular Scouting ceremonies. Ceremonial aspects of Scouting were likely passed over in deference to the sacred ceremonies performed in Mormon temples. Perhaps it was feared that an association with Scouting ceremonies might diminish the impact of the holy activities within the temple. Scriptural injunction also proscribed the taking of "oaths." In the Sermon on the Mount, Christ warned his followers: "Swear not at all; neither by heaven; for it is God's throne: Nor by the earth; for it is his footstool: neither by Jerusalem; for it is the city of the Great King. . . . But let your communication be, Yea, yea; Nay, nay: for whatsoever is more than these cometh of evil."[57] The Book of James insists that all who make superfluous oaths will "fall into condemnation."[58] Biblical literalism trumped any attraction to the secular ceremonies and oaths of the Boy Scouts. In the early years of Mormon Scouting, when religious imperatives clashed with BSA programs, Mormon leaders remained selectively loyal to the national program.

Aligning with the Boy Scouts helped Progressive-Era church leaders combat two of the most disturbing trends of the early twentieth century—the effects of urbanization on young Mormon men and the loss of pioneer fortitude in the rising generation. Though the seemingly relentless process of urbanization could not be stopped by hiking in the canyons or taking cold baths, Boy Scouts provided an inoculation against the perceived effects of living in the city. By taking the boy temporarily out of the city and introducing a respect for nature and the past, it was hoped that Boy Scouts would turn young Mormon men into modern boy pioneers. Like the half-way covenant in Puritan New England, Mormon leaders used the Boy Scouts to increase the connection between the religious organization and members of the third and fourth generation who seemed to be falling away from church tradition.[59] Scouts maintained the interest of young men in the church and helped pave the way for the church to thrive in new urban surroundings.

Summer Camps and Working Women

The social pathologies that attended city life did not affect boys alone. Though Scouting provided one avenue of relief for Mormon boys, LDS girls likewise needed a program to save them from the sins of the city. The main concerns regarding urban young women did not center on the declension from a heroic past; rather, the increasing numbers of working women and the mounting monotony of their employment in offices and factories led church officials to institutionalize nature programs that removed girls from the confines of the city. By building spacious and well-appointed summer retreat homes, stakes throughout the church conscientiously advocated nature activities as a means to mitigate the storm and stress of city life for young women. These summer homes were not merely a feminized version of the pioneer recapitulations of the Boy Scouts. Instead, the homes provided physical and spiritual recuperation for city-bound working women by offering an affordable resort location in the canyons around Salt Lake City and picturesque spots elsewhere. As one pamphlet described the summer programs at the Girls' Camp in Logan Canyon, the camp brought "rest, recreation, and inspiration" to Mormon women usually mired in the workaday stresses of urban life.[60]

Summer homes were not the first attempt to get LDS young women into the Great Outdoors. In 1913, the YLMIA adopted the Campfire Girls program as the main element of their summer activities. The relationship, however, quickly soured when the Campfire organization rejected the modifications proposed by the Young Ladies' auxiliary. Following a year of experimentation, the YLMIA created its own program (the Bee-hive Girls), which bore a "'direct application to our Church and western home.'"[61] The brief flirtation with the Campfire Girls indicated the YLMIA's interest in nature-based activities in an environment that the church could control.

The regular YMMIA and YLMIA season—where young men and women met weekly for classwork and activities—lasted from September to June. In agricultural areas with abundant farm work throughout the summer months, this schedule allowed adolescents to stay at home and help on the farm. In urban areas, however, when school released students for the summer, the increased leisure time was spent playing rather than working. Filling the long summer days became a primary concern for church youth leaders. Scouting kept young men busy tying knots and camping. Young women in the church, however, were left with more mundane tasks to occupy their lazy days. Outdoor meetings, MIA reading-course books, book reports, needlework, and handicrafts did not keep young women interested during the summer months. Girls needed something else to do. Following the example of the successful Scouting initiatives, several stake YLMIA leaders devised a summer camping program to keep the girls involved during the annual summer break.[62]

In addition to the lull of the summer months, other urban factors motivated YLMIA officers to look to nature for social and spiritual salvation. The YLMIA presidency of Salt Lake City's Liberty Stake, sponsors of the first LDS girls' summer home, explained their rationale for constructing the "Liberty Glen Camp" located beyond the city's borders in the south end of the Salt Lake Valley. They wrote that the "conditions surrounding our girls have greatly changed within the past few years," primarily because "scores of [girls] are now engaged in offices, department stores, and factories, and others are in school." Because these young women enjoyed more spending money than previous generations, "many of them feel compelled through fashion's demands to dress better, and to expend their money more freely than in previous years." The article surmised that because working girls spent their money so frivolously, they rarely had the necessary funds to spend their vacation days at a reputable summer resort. Even when young women in their teens and early twenties possessed the means to relax at a resort location, they "ordinarily return[ed] more exhausted from the strenuous conditions of such a life than they were before they left home." To aid these working women, the officers of Liberty Stake's YLMIA decided to "provide a place where the girls could enjoy nature's luxuries to the fullest extent; and at the minimum cost."[63]

The Liberty Glen Camp—named for the sponsoring stake and the beauty of the surrounding countryside—was located on the farm of James Godfrey, about one mile east of the Salt Lake suburb of Murray. This location provided not only plenty of clean drinking water but also an "abundance of fresh food direct from the farm." Liberty Glen did not offer a rigorous outdoor survival experience like the Boy Scouts but was a retreat where urban women could recharge their physical and spiritual batteries. Just beyond the shadows of the city's spires, the summer camp was only twenty minutes from the nearest streetcar line and five minutes from Godfrey's home. Easily reached from the city, the camp presented "every feature of one remotely situated from civilization." Though removed from the comforts of the city, these civilized women enjoyed civilized accommodations. Cots with clean straw mattresses—made up with sheets, pillows, and pillowcases brought by the camper—provided a nightly resting place within the spacious sleeping house (20 x 40 ft.). Electric lights and access to Godfrey's telephone reminded campers of their close connection to the outside world. The presence of a piano, donated by the Consolidated Music Company, made sure the girls had "many of the conveniences of the home" amid "all the luxuries of an outdoor life." During the summer of 1912, each camper paid approximately three dollars for her summer stay at Liberty Glen. Most campers paid the fee in cash; others provided bread, fruit, and butter to cover their costs.[64]

Underneath an American flag waving atop a forty-foot pole, the activities at Liberty Glen were largely unorganized. Each day, a different group of three campers received assignments to cook, wash the dishes, and clean the campsite. All other campers used their time as they chose. During a week's stay at the camp (the sessions ran from Saturday to Saturday so "those going home would be ready for work Monday morning"), young women fished, hiked, and swam in addition to their camp chores. A special day each week was set aside as "Mother's Day," when visitors were entertained with bonfires, candy pulls, concerts, and open-air dances. Despite its name, other visitors on Mother's Days included fathers, ward authorities, and friends. Campers roundly considered these days the highlight of the week's activities.[65]

At Camp Atoka, the girls' summer camp for which the most information exists, campers participated in activities much like their sisters at Liberty Glen. Located in South Fork Canyon and operated by the Ogden Stake, Atoka summer campers enjoyed the freedom to plan most of their own activities. Hiking, wading and swimming in the river, and campfires at night kept the girls busy. Anna Saunders Easthope, a camper at Atoka during the middle part of the century, remembered playing records on an old Victrola as well as reading a book on the lives of Madame Chiang Kai-shek and her sisters.[66] Camp rules at Atoka were simple, if not always obeyed:

1. Lights out at 10:30 p.m.
2. Clothes should be modest.
3. Keep the camp clean.
4. Strictest: don't go out on the highway and hitch rides.
5. Don't leave the camp boundaries without permission.
6. Always say morning and evening prayers.
7. American flag is raised in the morning and retrieved by sundown.[67]

Parents' night—complete with campfire and a program of storytelling, readings, skits, musical numbers, and sing-alongs—provided a chance for families to get together and enjoy the natural setting. On Sunday, entire wards journeyed up to South Fork to hold sacrament meeting and testimonial services with the girls. Not all activities at Atoka, however, were quite so proper.

Periodically, fights broke out among campers. On one occasion, two young women "punched and slugged it out" after one camper had dragged her muddy feet across a freshly mopped floor. Often campers taped their initials on their backs and suntanned. The pale initials announced to others that the owner of a monogrammed back had been to camp. During a costume contest one year, a camper pulled her bathing suit down to her waist and tied a huge sunbonnet across her chest. Dancing in front of her peers, the girl's nude appearance shocked the audience.[68] Atoka, it seems, was a place where fun and faith, revelry and reverence went hand in hand.

These outdoor activities prompted many of the participants to wax poetic about their experiences. One example, dedicated to the founders of the Liberty Glen Camp, captures the force of nature as it revealed itself on the edges of Salt Lake City:

> Twittering birds and rippling brooklets
>   Mingle with our cheerful song,
> While the merry peals of laughter
>   With the breezes float along.
> Round the camp-fire, songs and stories
>   Crown the pleasure of the day,
> Gentle moonbeams guard our slumber,
>   Happy girls of M.I.A.
> We have wandered in the meadows,
>   We have waded in the streams;
> We have banished care and sadness
>   And have dreamed the sweetest dreams.
> Life has been a round of pleasure
>   In this glen of Liberty;
> May the peace that here attends us
>   With its founders ever be.[69]

In light of such soaring sentiment, it is easy to imagine that the girls of Liberty Glen had been camping on a grandiose Hudson River School canvas rather than a twenty-minute walk from a Salt Lake streetcar suburb. To working women cloistered in the artificial canyons of city corridors, the fresh air and sweeping landscapes at Liberty Glen not only supplied a change of scenery but allowed them to recuperate from the long workdays of the preceding year.

The success of the Liberty Glen experiment encouraged other stakes to construct summer retreats for their young women. In Logan Canyon, the YLMIA of Logan Stake raised a cobblestone and log structure that could accommodate sixty campers. Built nearly a decade after Liberty Glen, the MIA home in Logan Canyon more closely resembled a commercial resort than a church camp. Twelve huge cobblestone pillars rounded the building, providing structural integrity and an imposing facade. Inside, three immense exposed logs supported the upstairs sleeping quarters. Thirteen windows (screened and with wooden blinds) offered a "splendid view" in all directions from inside the cabin. Complete with dining room, cozy living room, kitchen, and small hospital, the facilities created a beautiful backdrop for evenings of "songs, stories, games, fun, and laughter." Modern lavatories (containing showers, basins, and toilets) completed the home's creature comforts. Paid for by fund-raising efforts, including a carnival, apron bazaar, and vaudeville show, the home supplied a location where "girls will be chaperoned and well cared for and given a happy outing—a rest, a change, a bit of wholesome recreation that every girl should have every year."[70]

By the summer of 1924, five summer homes were operating, and four more had been planned. Mutual Isle in Provo Canyon boasted a swimming pool and interesting rock formations; American Fork's Mutual Dell was close to Timpanogos Cave as well as a hiking trail to the nearly twelve-thousand-foot peak of Mount Timpanogos; the MIA Girls' Summer Home at Lakota on Bear Lake in northern Utah was praised for its boating facilities and horseback riding.[71] The crown jewel of the girls' summer camp system was located twenty miles up Big Cottonwood Canyon—the MIA Girls' Summer House at Brighton. Operated by the four Salt Lake City stakes and built in 1922, the Brighton home stood on the south rim of Silver Lake Basin at the base of Mount Wolverine and Mount Milicent. An imposing structure, the log home stood three stories high and measured 140 x 40 feet. The main floor contained a long, spacious dining room and a reception hall. At each end of the building a "big cheery" fireplace welcomed cold campers after an evening swim. The upper floors housed sleeping apartments complete with good beds and comfortable mattresses. More than one hundred girls could be accommodated at once. The Brighton home set the standard for other LDS summer camps. As one report affords, "No one who loves the great out of doors will find a resting place more attractive" than the Brighton home.[72] Few would have disagreed.

The primary philosophy underlying the construction of elaborate summer homes was voiced in 1924 by Emily H. Higgs of the YLMIA Summer Camp Committee. Writing for the committee, she asserted that "joy, rest, recreation and companionship under beautiful conditions is the rightful heritage of every girl whether rich or poor." Although it sounds like Higgs and others may have wanted to democratize (or socialize) the availability of the summer resort experience, that was only part of their message. Leaders wanted girls to leave their stifled lives in the city and "to live for a time free and apart from the confusing influences and petty irritations which daily routine may impose." The camps, however, were more than a respite from the hurly-burly of life in the city. YLMIA leaders believed that the natural beauty surrounding the camps would turn girls away from the city as well as elevate their thoughts heavenward. One Summer Camp committee member instructed the girls to keep "A Log of the Camp" and record the week's outstanding events. The list of probable topics included "happenings in which God's providence is manifested," which would help the "M.I.A. girls of the future [to] catch a glimpse of the faith and wholesome sweetness, the charm of the girls of today."[73]

Claire N. Hulme, the chairperson of the Summer Home Committee in the Cache and Logan Stakes, provided the purest pronouncement regarding the ability to commune with the divine through nature. "The consciousness of God is a gradual growth with most of us," Hulme contended, and "we understand best the power and goodness of the Creator of all by acquaintance with and appreciation of His works." Hulme proposed that "through sleeping among the tree-tops, as we do in our camp, with the stars shining upon our beds, there are moments when the most thoughtless girl realizes, if but dimly, the wonder and glory of it all. And she sighs to feel that the least things of Nature are apt to be greater than the noblest of man's achievement." Bombarded by the concerns of the city and faced only with the marks of "man's achievement," girls met little opportunity to find God on city streets. It was only "living in the canyon for a time" that could produce this "attitude of mind and make the heart responsive to the greatest, though the invisible, things in life, such as love, justice, and service." According to Hulme, this "renewal of the spirit" was possible only through the "subtle charm of nature." Hulme concluded that camping opened the girls' minds to spiritual concerns better than any other activity. "It is so apparent to us that our home has brought not only joy, but ethical and spiritual values into the lives of hundreds of girls, that we pronounce camping, under proper conditions, one of the very finest activities an association can provide for its membership."[74]

By building large, comfortable homes in beautiful natural settings, leaders of the Young Women's auxiliary institutionalized nature programs as part of the organization's offerings. Working women—mired in urban offices and factories—received an annual opportunity to rest and recuperate in a resort-like setting at a minimal cost. Moreover, because they could leave their everyday concerns behind, young women enjoyed an unparalleled opportunity to commune with their Creator in the great outdoors.

A Natural Bridge across the Generation Gap

The Boy Scouts and Girls' Camps furnished the bulk of outdoor activities for Progressive-Era Mormon adolescents. Another noteworthy outdoor social activity was also instituted in the first decades of the twentieth century—annual Fathers and Sons camping excursions. As early as 1919, the YMMIA made provisions for a summertime camp outing for all fathers and sons in the church. Under the administration of local stakes and wards, camping offered an excuse for boys and their fathers to spend time together. Little direction was given to local officials: "Have a vacation, do something different, get close to your boys, go out into the open country and play, sing, rest, and worship." As long as campers stayed in the open for at least three days and avoided resorts that "interfere[d] with the camp social spirit," it was thought that the intergenerational camping experience would be "one of the most pleasurable and profitable of the season."[75]

In the following years, the list of prescriptions and proscriptions increased, but the rationale behind the church-sponsored camping trip remained simple—by getting boys and their fathers together in a natural setting, they would grow closer. Men could impart wisdom to their sons; boys could learn from the experience of fathers. Church leaders recognized the detrimental effects of absentee fathers who spent long hours in offices and factories. Because too many fathers spent the majority of their time away from the family, many adolescent males had grown up without fatherly advice and direction. After asking fathers, "Are you chums [with your son]? Or merely acquaintances?" a model invitation responded, "Some fathers are too busy to discharge their most important responsibility—the proper rearing of their children. Every boy NEEDS the companionship of his father."[76] In fact, the need to cultivate a father's influence in his son's life was felt so sharply that mothers were to be left at home during this trip. "While some might think that it would be splendid to have the mothers along, this one annual outing is being taken for those wholesome effects that can come only from the association of fathers and sons."[77] The 1927 pamphlet added that "every mother should be happy to know that her son has the intimate companionship of her husband for a few days, sleeping in the same blankets, receiving his counsel and advice."[78] By institutionalizing an annual gender-exclusive outing for fathers and sons, the YMMIA sought to foster intergenerational connections and counteract the corrosive effects of modern life on young men. In making the annual outing a camping trip, organizers hoped to capitalize on the spiritual and social recuperative powers of nature, as the Boy

Scouts and Girls' Camps had looked to the great outdoors to return civility to city-bound boys and girls.

YMMIA leaders had lofty expectations for the tripartite combination of fathers, sons, and the outdoors. The pamphlet describing the Fathers and Sons outing for the summer of 1925 captured the organizer's high hopes. "Fathers and Sons outings offer great opportunity for fellowship and companionship between father and son," began the pamphlet. "The great out-of-doors is a natural setting in which this purpose may be best accomplished. While the period is very brief, lasting perhaps from three to ten days, yet because of the close relationships which it brings—in sleeping, eating, hiking, playing, fishing, enjoying one another; great opportunities are offered for the formation of lasting friendships." Father-son friendships meant a generational détente—a warming of familial relationships that allowed sons to see their fathers in a new light and provided fathers with a chance to teach their offspring important lessons.

Most significantly, the outdoor setting cleared the way for fathers to approach their sons about spiritual topics. "The campfire is a real opportunity for spiritual growth," argued YMMIA leaders, because "when father and son sit on the same log by the camp-fire, a warmth of real companionship is established. The hour is a sacred one." Spending time with his son, away from the city's commotion, permitted a father to gain a "better understanding" of his boy and opened an avenue to "counsel with him about the pit-falls that might prove dangerous." Home, farm, and business responsibilities were also more easily discussed among the beauties of nature. Boys needed to learn from their fathers, and fathers needed to reclaim the patriarchal role with their sons. Far away from the din of urban siren songs, both generations needed to be reminded that "the best leader for a boy to follow is his own father."[79]

But boys did not follow their fathers into the wilderness simply to sit at their feet and learn the lessons of life. Camp leaders were to ensure "that there shall be opportunities for fun as well as for serious thought" during their summer sojourn. Every boy, the pamphlet advised, possessed a "natural desire to go to places, to see things, to get out of doors into the big world." As part of the "great environmental urge," boys heard the "call of the open spaces, of the towering peaks, of the lakes and streams and the woods." There was more to discover in "God's great wonderland" than Dad's discourses alone. Moral messages played a key role, but Fathers and Sons outings were meant to be fun. Hiking, fishing, boating, and stories told around a glowing campfire made up only a portion of the camp's amusement. On Boy's Day, the young men treated their fathers like favored guests by taking over all camp chores, including cooking, cleaning, and entertainment. For Dad's Day, the pattern reversed. A day of sports—including a variety of activities so that all could participate—kept the campers busy playing horseshoes or mass volley games. In many camps, a stage built from a hayrack provided the backdrop for an evening of dramatic and comedic sketches. "Pioneer Night" found the group around a campfire listening to a "noted pioneer" from the local area whose stories might "stimulate interest in a program of inspirational pioneer incidents."[80] And no camp was complete without the singing of songs around the fading embers of the fire. Most acclaimed were the parodies of popular tunes, including a song written by George H. Brimhall and sung to the tune of "Old Oaken Bucket." The verses illustrate the high hopes surrounding the yearly camping trips:

> The castles I built in my mind for the future;
>> The jolly good times that our gang always had;
> The yearnings I felt for a closeness with nature;
>> And then the great outings I had with my dad.
>
> The long-wished for outings; the joy-giving outings;
>> The heart-clinching outings I had with my dad.
>
> I've been with good fellows, and some that were "yellows,"
>> Been thrown midst the lure of the tempters of men;
> But there was one lever, that held me up, ever,
>> When I might have fallen again and again.
> The thought of my mother—yes, there was another;
>> And when it arose—then I could not be bad.
> Its presence o'er-whelmed me; when memory compelled me,
>> To think of the outings I had with my dad.
>
> The long-ago outings; the heart-clinging outings;
>> Those soul-saving outings I had with my dad.[81]

Other songs celebrated "the Dad who thinks enough of his boy to take the time for a game of ball" over the father who was "so very busy making 'cash.'"[82]

What the city had torn asunder—boys from their busy working fathers— a few days camping in the country might put back together. Almost from the start, Fathers and Sons outings proved popular. In the summer of 1923, more than eight thousand fathers and sons satisfied the "environmental urge" by spending several days together in the great outdoors.[83] Judging from the widespread acceptance of the outings (they continue in the church today), the great expectations of intergenerational reconciliation has been at least partially fulfilled.

As Mormon life moved into the cities of twentieth-century America, LDS leaders instituted a number of programs designed to relocate Mormons (at least temporarily) to the frontier setting, where pioneer values had flourished. "Rugged life" movements like the Boy Scouts taught young men the skills of frontier survival and reconnected an urban generation with its pioneer past. For the young women of the church, annual pilgrimages to rural "resorts" built by the church offered a respite from their worldly labors. Camping in the great outdoors also brought fathers and sons together in a setting far removed from their urban homes. As the burgeoning conservation movement groped toward an understanding of the value of the American wilderness, Mormons were institutionalizing outdoor activities as a vital part of their social and spiritual programs.[84] Written in 1906, before most of the church's nature programs had been created, the first lines of Grace Ingles Frost's poem "Beyond the City" capture the movement's essence and provide a fitting epitaph:

> Beyond the city's busy hum,
> Beyond its want, its sin and care,
> I linger at the set of sun,
> And feel that God is nearer there.[85]

Notes

1. For one view of the social anomie caused by unabated urbanization in the mid-nineteenth century, see Karen Halttunen, *Confidence Men and Painted Women: A Study in Middle-Class Culture in America, 1830–1870* (New Haven, Conn.: Yale University Press, 1982). The most comprehensive discussion of urban reform efforts is found in Paul S. Boyer, *Urban Masses and Moral Order in America, 1820–1920* (Cambridge, Mass.: Harvard University Press, 1978). A first-person account from one reformer appears in Jane Addams, *Twenty Years at Hull-House* (1910; rpt., Urbana: University of Illinois Press, 1990).

2. See Glen M. Leonard, *Nauvoo: A Place of Peace, a People of Promise* (Salt Lake City: Deseret Book; Provo, Utah: Brigham Young University Press, 2002). Leonard estimates that approximately fifteen thousand Mormons lived in the Nauvoo region (179).

3. For more on small-town Mormon life, consult the following articles from Ronald W. Walker and Doris R. Dant, eds., *Nearly Everything Imaginable: The Everyday Life of Utah's Mormon Pioneers* (Provo, Utah: Brigham Young University Press, 1999): Ronald W. Walker, "Golden Memories: Remembering Life in a Mormon Village," 47–74; Dean L. May, "It Takes a Village: Social Character in Rural

Settlements," 75–88; Richard Neitzel Holzapfel and David A. Allred, "A Peculiar People: Community and Commitment in Utah Valley," 89–115. See also Richard H. Jackson, "The Mormon Village: Genesis and Antecedents of the City of Zion Plan," *BYU Studies* 17 (1977): 223–40; Dean L. May, "The Making of Saints: The Mormon Town as a Setting for the Study of Cultural Change," *Utah Historical Quarterly* 45 (Dec. 1977): 75–92; Dean L. May, *Three Frontiers: Family, Land, and Society in the American West, 1850–1900* (New York: Cambridge University Press, 1994); Lowry Nelson, *The Mormon Village: A Study in Social Origins* (Provo, Utah: Research Division, Brigham Young University, 1930).

4. "Talks to Young Men: I. Industry—Its Bearing on Success," *Improvement Era* 6 (Nov. 1902): 55.

5. "Talks to Young Men: VIII. A Trade," *Improvement Era* 6 (June 1903): 603–4.

6. "Editor's Table—Seventy-third Annual Conference of the Church," *Improvement Era* 6 (May 1903): 545.

7. For more on the struggles facing Puritan New England, see Edmund S. Morgan, *Visible Saints: The History of a Puritan Idea* (Ithaca, N.Y.: Cornell University Press, 1963).

8. "Talks to Young Men: V. The Same Is Damned," *Improvement Era* 7 (Mar. 1904): 367. The author, however, did qualify his condemnation by adding, "Not that I would be understood as implying that all bookkeepers and stenographers are shirkers; for as a class they are honorable enough, when they enter their profession from right motives."

9. For more on the Jeffersonian agrarian worldview, see Drew R. McCoy, *The Elusive Republic: Political Economy in Jeffersonian America* (New York: W. W. Norton, 1982).

10. Milton Bennion, "To the Young Men on the Farm," *Improvement Era* 12 (Mar. 1909): 371. Not all Mormon leaders, however, preached a return to the farm. President Franklin S. Harris of Brigham Young University argued against the need to flee the city. From an economic perspective, Harris wrote, "The decrease in the relative number engaged in agriculture is looked on by some as being a bad condition, and they are all the time talking about 'back to the farm' and of keeping the boys on the farm. As a matter of fact, the condition that has developed is probably the most wholesome that could exist, because, in these days of machinery, it is possible for one farmer to produce as much as several farmers could previously, and this leaves the other workers free to manufacture such commodities as will raise the general standard of living. . . . So that rather than to mourn at the fact that there are relatively fewer farmers, we should really welcome this condition, since it means that those who are farming will have a much better opportunity to make a living wage than if the old high percentage of farmers were maintained." See Franklin S. Harris, "Changes in Occupation," *Improvement Era* 27 (Mar. 1924): 428.

Earlier in the century, others had argued that rural dwellers were often so removed from the church's influence that they fell away. Specifically, Apostle Matthias F. Cowley warned about shepherd boys who began smoking when they were "away from home and the benefits of an elevating and refining influence which usually attends home life; and away from the social, spiritual, and intellectual influences which attach to every well-regulated ward throughout the Church." Though sheep herders presented an atypical example, it was clear that rural areas were not free of vice and sin. See M. F. Cowley, "Counsel to Boys Engaged in Isolated Labor," *Improvement Era* 7 (Mar. 1904): 364.

11. Frank J. Hewlett, "What of the Boy in Summer Time?" *Improvement Era* 11 (May 1908): 534.

12. Richard R. Lyman, "Reclamation," *Improvement Era* 27 (Apr. 1924): 505. Lyman's text had originally been delivered at the Seventeenth Annual International Farm Congress at Kansas City.

13. Grace Ingles Frost, "Beyond the City," *Improvement Era* 9 (Sept. 1906): 881.

14. See W. P. Kinsella, *Shoeless Joe* (New York: Ballantine Books, 1982), 16.

15. Evan Stephens, "The Farmer Boy," *Improvement Era* 21 (Jan. 1918): 250–51. For a more complete description of Stephens's career and life, see D. Michael Quinn, *Same-Sex Dynamics among Nineteenth-Century Americans: A Mormon Example* (1996; rpt., Urbana: University of Illinois Press, 2001), 231–42.

16. Nephi Anderson, "The End of the Rainbow," *Improvement Era* 13 (June 1910): 699.

17. Annie D. Palmer, "The Call of the Canyon," *Improvement Era* 18 (May 1915): 661.

18. For additional biographical information on church presidents, see Leonard J. Arrington, ed., *The Presidents of the Church* (Salt Lake City: Deseret Book, 1986).

19. For a more complete account of the church's attempts to recapture the past, see James B. Allen and Glen M. Leonard, *The Story of the Latter-day Saints,* 2d ed. (Salt Lake City: Deseret Book, 1992), 452–53.

20. *Improvement Era* 26 (Nov. 1922): 92.

21. LeRoi C. Snow, "Pioneer Celebration," *Improvement Era* 25 (Sept. 1922): 1020.

22. "Passing Events," *Improvement Era* 27 (May 1924): 707.

23. There has been some dispute about which was the first Scout troop to be organized by the church. One history of Scouting in Canada claims that the Aetna Troop in Cardston deserves the honor. "In the year 1910," according to Edward H. Hansen and Glen A. Hansen, "King Edward VII made a decree to organize the Boy Scouts of Great Britain throughout the British Empire. It was in the fall of 1910 that the Boy Scouts of Great Britain came to the Cardston district to find sponsors and get Scouting started here. They had no luck in Cardston at this time, but the group received a warm welcome in the Aetna Ward by Bishop Nathan W. Tanner. He was so full of love and concern for his people that he eagerly accepted this new program which appeared so promising for the young men. . . . He went right to work to get Scouting started in the Ward. He called James Henry Tanner to be the first Scoutmaster of the First Aetna Troop which was the first Scouts sponsored by the Church of Jesus Christ of Latter-day Saints." See Edward H. Hansen and Glen A. Hansen, "Scouting in Aetna and Cardston District," 1. The typescript is located in the LDS Historical Department, Salt Lake City.

24. Richard Strong Best, "History of Troop 1, Boy Scouts of America, Salt Lake City, Utah, Waterloo Ward, LDS Church, 1910–1916" (Farr West, Utah: R. S. Best, 1984), 1–3, 10. The self-published reminiscences can be found in L. Tom Perry Special Collections, Harold B. Lee Library, Brigham Young University, Provo, Utah.

25. "The Boy Scout Movement in Utah," *Improvement Era* 14 (Apr. 1911): 542.

26. Roberts's reasons for publishing his views in the *Improvement Era* appear in his personal files located at L. Tom Perry Special Collections, Harold B. Lee Library, Brigham Young University, Provo, Utah. Roberts explained the impact of Elder B. H. Roberts's decision: "This report was keenly disappointing to a rather large group of young men, I was one of these. At the conclusion of the meeting I returned to Provo and immediately began to write an article in defense of scout activities. In this article I took the stand that if the church is not ready to become a member of the National Organization it should create its own organization which might well be called THE BOY PIONEERS OF UTAH or some other appropriate name."

27. Eugene L. Roberts, "The Boy Pioneers of Utah," *Improvement Era* 14 (Oct. 1911): 1085, 1086. By at least one account, the Mormon pioneers and the seventeenth-century Pilgrims had a great deal in common. By forging a link with their own past, Mormons also created a connection with the first European settlers of New England. Preston Nibley made the connection: "There is truly a striking similarity in the coming of the Pilgrim Fathers to the Atlantic coast, in December 1620, and the march of the first body of 'Mormon' Pioneers to the shores of Great Salt Lake, in 1847. Both groups of people were in quest of a place where they could be free and independent, and worship God as their consciences dictated. For this inestimable privilege they were willing to forsake all that in a worldly way was near and dear to them, face the hardships and perils of a long journey, and endure the suffering which was sure to be theirs in the settlement of a new and strange country." Through the rigors of Scouting, Progressive-Era Mormons hoped to tap into the moral heritage of the Pilgrim-Pioneer continuum. See Preston Nibley, "The Pilgrim Fathers and the 'Mormon Pioneers,'" *Improvement Era* 15 (July 1912): 774.

28. Roberts, "Boy Pioneers," 1088, 1089.

29. Ibid., 1089.

30. Ibid., 1090, 1091, 1092.

31. Late in his life, Eugene Roberts reported that his *Improvement Era* article had directly influenced B. H. Roberts's change of heart. In an unpublished passage found in his personal collection, Eugene Roberts noted: "Having completed the article I took it to President George H. Brimhall of the Brigham Young University for his appraisal. The president was enthusiastic and asked for a copy. This he took to Salt Lake City. Whatever sequence of events followed I have never been told. However, not long after President Brimhall took my article to Salt Lake City Elder B. H. Roberts published in the *Deseret News* a long and convincing argument in defense of Scoutcraft in which he proposed that the church join with the National Boy Scout Organization. . . . Just what part [my article] played in causing the church committee to reverse its decision I don't know and most probably never will know. Presi-

dent Brimhall insisted it was the direct cause. However, it is more than likely that I had some influence." See Eugene L. Roberts Collection, L. Tom Perry Special Collections, Harold B. Lee Library, Provo, Utah.

32. "Mutual Work—M.I.A. Scouts," *Improvement Era* 15 (Jan. 1912): 287.

33. L. R. Martineau, "M.I.A. Scouts," *Improvement Era* (Mar. 1912): 359, 357, 361. The desire to equate twentieth-century Scouts with pioneers of the nineteenth century occurred outside of the United States as well. In January 1926, when the church organized a Scouting troop in Hamburg, Germany, the legend of the Mormon pioneers migrated across the Atlantic. Describing the German group, it was recorded: "A spirit of cooperation, not unlike that of the pioneers of Utah, prevails among these pioneers of Scouting in this land." See Aaron C. Taylor, "Mutual Work—M.I.A. Scout Work in Hamburg, Germany," *Improvement Era* 30 (Feb. 1927): 381.

34. "Over the Pioneer Trail," *Improvement Era* 15 (Sept. 1912): 1033–34, 1036, 1038.

35. Jacob A. Riis, "The Boy Scouts," *Improvement Era* 17 (July 1914): 871. Riis's essay first appeared in the 24 October 1913 edition of *The Outlook*.

36. Quoted in Oscar A. Kirkham, "Mutual Work—Athletics and Scout Work," *Improvement Era* 19 (Feb. 1916): 375.

37. "Editors' Table—Boy Scouts," *Improvement Era* 17 (Mar. 1914): 385.

38. This phrase appeared on the MIA Scout application form. Quoted in "Mutual Work—Of Interest to Scouts," *Improvement Era* 17 (Aug. 1914): 996.

39. Ludvig Dale, "What Boy Scouts Must Know and Be," *Improvement Era* 18 (Aug. 1915): 922. The next year, the MIA Scout commissioner Dr. John H. Taylor defended church scouts against cries of militarism. "Have you the idea that the scout organization is military in its nature, and will teach your boys to kill and destroy? If such an idea were correct, you would be doing exactly right in keeping your boy out of it. . . . When the boy becomes a scout, to destroy life takes on new meaning; the birds, the insects, the animals, demand his protection, and become immune from useless and reckless destruction. The mission of the scout is to save life, not to destroy it." Taylor then discussed the uniform as a "serviceable suit" for Scout work as well as the necessity of drilling as a means of orderly transportation. See John H. Taylor, "For the Consideration of Parents," *Improvement Era* 19 (Jan. 1916): 239–40.

40. "Mutual Work—Boy Scouts—Organization and Purpose," *Improvement Era* 17 (Aug. 1914): 894.

41. George Q. Morris, "Thirty-five Years of Scouting in the Church," *Improvement Era* 51 (May 1948): 275.

42. Oscar A. Kirkham, "Mutual Work—What Can Be Done with the Boys, Brethren?" *Improvement Era* 17 (Mar. 1914): 489.

43. Martineau, "M.I.A. Scouts," 360.

44. Morris, "Thirty-five Years of Scouting," 312.

45. Norman Geertsen, "To Be a Scout," *Improvement Era* 32 (May 1929): 598.

46. Ivy Houtz Woolley, "The Boy Scouts," *Improvement Era* 27 (Feb. 1924): 380.

47. Oscar A. Kirkham, frontispiece, *Improvement Era* 26 (Apr. 1923).

48. See "Annual Report of M.I.A. Scouts, Year Ending May 31, 1918," *Improvement Era* 21 (July 1918): 833. Typically, the *Improvement Era* reported the annual growth of the Scout movement. In addition to the above report, see "Passing Events," *Improvement Era* 18 (Mar. 1915): 468; "Athletic and Scout Work—Progress of Scout Work," *Improvement Era* 18 (July 1915): 842; "Mutual Work—Athletics and Scout Work," *Improvement Era* 19 (July 1916): 849–50; "Mutual Work—An Analysis of the General Statistical Report of the Young Men's Mutual Improvement Association for the Year Ending March 31, 1921," *Improvement Era* 24 (Aug. 1921): 946–47; "Mutual Work—Dr. Taylor's Report of Scouting, 1922," *Improvement Era* 26 (Feb. 1923): 393. On the early participation of the church in Scouting, see David I. Macleod, *Building Character in the American Boy: The Boy Scouts, YMCA, and Their Forerunners, 1870–1920* (Madison: University of Wisconsin Press, 1983), 194–95, 198. Robert Peterson also notes that the LDS Church was the first religious organization to accept the Boy Scouts of America. See *The Boy Scouts: An American Adventure* (New York: American Heritage, 1984), 55.

49. Robert E. Wilson, "A Hike to the Yellowstone," *Improvement Era* 18 (June 1915): 706.

50. "Annual Report of M.I.A. Scouts, Year Ending May 31, 1918," 834.

51. "Mutual Work—The Scouts and the Y.M.M.I.A.," *Improvement Era* 26 (Mar. 1923): 484.

52. Edward H. Anderson, *Y.M.M.I.A. Hand Book: A Guide for Stake and Ward Officers of the Young Men's Mutual Improvement Associations for the Church of Jesus Christ of Latter-day Saints,* 7th ed. (Salt Lake City: General Board, 1925), 121.

53. "Mutual Work—Scout Work on Sunday Night," *Improvement Era* 17 (Aug. 1914): 894.

54. For the quotation, see "Scout Cheers or Yells," *Improvement Era* 17 (Dec. 1913): 186. The prohibition of the Scout cheer on Sunday night appeared in "Mutual Work—Suggestive Outlines for Y.M.M.I.A. Freshmen Class for December," *Improvement Era* 17 (Dec. 1913): 183. A far cry from the recommended familiar melodies, one cheer suggested by the MIA field secretary Oscar A. Kirkham dripped with patriotic enthusiasm: "Zing a Zing! Boom! Boom! Zing a Zing! Boom! Boom! M.I.A. Scouts, Boom! A-M-E-R-I-C-A, Boy Scouts! Boy Scouts! U.S.A."

55. "Passing Events—No Hiking on the Sabbath Day," *Improvement Era* 19 (Mar. 1916): 478.

56. Anderson, *Y.M.M.I.A. Hand Book,* 121.

57. Matthew 5:34–35, 37.

58. James 5:12.

59. On the halfway covenant, see Morgan, *Visible Saints,* 129–38.

60. *The Girls' Camp in Logan Canyon,* 2. This pamphlet is located in the LDS Historical Department, Salt Lake City.

61. Quoted in Scott Kenney, *The Mutual Improvement Associations: A Prelimi-*

nary History (Salt Lake City: Historical Department of the Church of Jesus Christ of Latter-day Saints, 1976), 17.

62. See Elsie Ellen Hogan Van Noy, "Young Ladies' Mutual Improvement Associations from April 1927 to December 1937," 1, LDS Archives. Van Noy had been the general secretary of the YLMIA during the period described in her memoir.

63. "Liberty Glen Camp," *Young Woman's Journal* 24 (Jan. 1913): 31.

64. Ibid., 31–33.

65. Ibid., 32–33.

66. Carol T. Hines, *Camp Atoka: A History, 1912–1980* (Reno, Nev.: By the author, 1987), 8.

67. Ibid., 12.

68. Ibid., 9.

69. "To Our President," *Young Woman's Journal* 24 (Jan. 1913): 34.

70. Amy Lyman Merrill, "M.I.A. Home in Logan Canyon," *Young Woman's Journal* 33 (May 1922): 292–93.

71. "Y.L.M.I.A. Summer Homes," *Young Woman's Journal* 35 (June 1924): 310–11.

72. Sasie Heath, "Brighton Home," *Young Woman's Journal* 34 (June 1923): 377–78.

73. "Y.L.M.I.A. Summer Homes," 311.

74. Claire N. Hulme, "Is Camping Worth While for Y.L.M.I.A.?" *Young Woman's Journal* 35 (June 1924): 313–14.

75. "Mutual Work—Father and Son's Outing," *Improvement Era* 22 (Apr. 1919): 549.

76. *Fathers and Sons Annual Outing, Summer of 1925* (Salt Lake City: General Board of YMMIA, 1925), 4.

77. Ibid., 5.

78. *Fathers and Sons Annual Outing, Summer of 1927* (Salt Lake City: General Board of YMMIA), 5.

79. *Fathers and Sons Annual Outing, Summer of 1925*, 3.

80. George H. Brimhall, "Outings with My Dad," in ibid., 9.

81. Ibid., 10.

82. Ibid., 11.

83. "Mutual Work—Fathers and Sons' Outings," *Improvement Era* 26 (Sept. 1923): 1067. For descriptions of a number of outings, see "Fathers and Sons' Outings, and other Y.M.M.I.A. Activities," *Improvement Era* 25 (Oct. 1922): 1052–60; "Fathers and Sons' Outings," *Improvement Era* 26 (Oct. 1923): 1142–48.

84. On the conservation movement in the United States, see Roderick Nash, *Wilderness and the American Mind,* 4th ed. (New Haven, Conn.: Yale University Press, 2001); Stephen R. Fox, *The American Conservation Movement: John Muir and His Legacy* (Boston: Little, Brown, 1981); Harold T. Pinkett, *Gifford Pinchot, Private and Public Forester* (Urbana: University of Illinois Press, 1970).

85. Frost, "Beyond the City," 881.

CHAPTER FIVE

To Make the Most of Leisure

Recreation Responds in a Depression Decade

> On the social side, when unemployment is widespread business becomes demoralized, social and industrial strife in the form of riots and strikes are prevalent and the social institutions on which our civilization rests—the home, school, church and form of government—are undermined and eroded by the dark fear and unrest that grips the people. From the standpoint of the individual, the effects of unemployment may be seen in the breakdown of self-respect and morale, and in the loss of regular habits and of health through the lack of proper living incentives, food, clothing, medical care and recreation.
>
> —A. S. CANNON, "Social Planning—And a Public Employment Service" (1934)

> It appears that, given freedom through leisure, the majority of men will accept one of three alternatives. They will let down and become a watcher of somebody else, they will be enticed to antisocial conduct which will be the beginning of a career of crime, or they will acquire interests which will react to the benefit of the individual and society as a whole. The answer to this problem is the answer to the question.
>
> Can man be trusted with leisure?
>
> —JAY B. NASH, "What Will You Do with Your Leisure Time?" (1933)

In the months following the stock market crash of 1929, as the United States entered the most severe economic crisis in its history,[1] Mormons in Salt Lake City staged an impressive festival to mark the centennial of the church's founding. The week-long celebration in April 1930 included the illumination of the Salt Lake Temple with floodlights and the presentation of B. H. Roberts's multivolume *Comprehensive History of the Church of Jesus Christ of Latter-day Saints*. A pageant written especially for the anniversary, "Message for the Ages," entertained thousands of church members and visitors in nightly performances for a month. Though church leaders recognized the gravity of the nation's economic situation, they also strongly believed that the celebration was a fitting way to close out the church's tumultuous first century and to symbolize its bright future. Turning their backs on the Depression, at least for a time, the Mormons celebrated. It would take more than an economic depression to deter the Saints from gathering together for friendship and fun.

The long-held perspective in the church that valued recreation for its educational and social benefits played a role in the Mormon approach to solving some of the problems of the Great Depression. The large-scale recreation programs of the 1930s act as a case study of the LDS recreation movement. Conscientiously employing organized recreation programs to offset increasing amounts of leisure time, church leaders in the 1930s used each of the major components of Mormon recreation developed in the first third of the twentieth century: a recreation ideology specific to the needs of Depression-era Mormons was developed; and programs in athletics and the great outdoors were emphasized. Mormon recreation programs flowered during the 1930s. Combining a diffuse methodology with a clearly defined mission to ameliorate the social problems caused by a failing economy, church leaders used every weapon in their arsenal to combat the increased leisure time facing LDS members during the Depression decade of the 1930s.

Controlling Leisure Time

From Joseph Smith's stick pulling and wrestling to evening dances held along the Mormon Trail, recreation historically played a conspicuous though informal social role for Mormons. Between 1900 and 1930, however, church-sponsored recreational activities gradually became an institutionalized element of Mormon group life, especially for the youth.[2] During these thirty years, the church developed a leisure-time ideology, officially affiliated with the Boy Scout program, built a large number of camps for Young Women, sponsored a variety of athletic events, supported the construction of the Deseret Gymnasium, and used athletic heroes to "sell" a new interpretation of the Word of Wisdom. By the advent of the Great Depression, a well-organized Mormon recreation program was an integral component of general church activity.

Regarding the economy, by 1930 Utah had been in the throes of depression for almost a decade. Slow economic growth, low per-capita income, and a steady migration from farm to city had combined to forestall recovery after the post–World War I economic downturn began in 1920. When the stock market crash touched off bank closures and economic collapse in 1929, Utah's Mormons, like residents of other western agricultural states, were pushed even closer to the brink. Within a year of the stock market crash, only 33.5 percent of the population of Utah was gainfully employed, a lower percentage than any other state except Mississippi. Declining agricultural and mining prices, excessive freight rates, weak labor organizations, a high birth rate, and a severe drought in 1931 exacerbated the downward spiral.[3] Given these conditions, it seems counterintuitive that recreation would be given high priority, yet such programs flourished during the Depression decade of the 1930s.

It is probable that church leaders, most of whom had reached a hardscrabble maturity in the late nineteenth century, would have preferred to see church members at work, yet the economy forbade this solution. The Depression created a vast number of unemployed and underemployed Mormons. Though massive unemployment was regarded as a temporary condition, Mormon leaders recognized that remarkable increases in industrial production had expanded "leisure time" permanently. Not fully subscribing to the aphorism that "idle hands are the devil's workshop," LDS officials believed that if the increasing amount of time spent away from productive work was not directed into socially and spiritually productive channels it would propel the undisciplined toward destructive and harmful activities. Perhaps recreational programs could fill the void.

Recreation Responds in the Depression Decade

At the MIA's annual June Conference in 1932, Oscar A. Kirkham, the executive secretary of the YMMIA and a Scouting executive, spelled out the relationship between mechanization and leisure: "We are grateful for the machine. It has raised the burdens from a million backs, but it has thrown out a challenge to us. We must provide for the enrichment of leisure time, and in order for us to do that we must have more than technique, more than a bundle of tricks; we must have spirituality."[4]

G. Ott Romney, the football coach at Brigham Young University and a respected physical education teacher, believed that the church had to teach its members "how to utilize [their] leisure time pleasantly and profitably" because "miraculous inventions and magic labor-saving machinery threaten to increase constantly and consistently the amount of leisure time which the average individual has at his disposal."[5] The main concern for Romney and others was not that leisure time had expanded so rapidly; rather, they worried about how it would be used. Along these lines, the LDS Business College advertised: "Make the most of leisure by enrolling for a business course."[6] Leisure time was a double-edged sword: depending upon how it was used, it could lead either to destruction or salvation. An unsigned editorial in the *Era* warned starkly, "Watch the leisure time. Through it you may either make or break for eternity."[7]

Thus the struggle for the control of leisure time was part of the larger conflict between good and evil. As a participant in that momentous battle, the church felt compelled to enter the fray. Under the general theme of "Building Latter-day Saints through Recreation," the MIA in 1932 enlisted recreation as a force for good in the lives of church members. Local leaders were instructed to take advantage of "'the opportunity of the hour,'" which was to "enrich leisure" and to "spiritualize recreation" through appropriate church-sponsored activities. One anonymous Mormon author looked heavenward for the guide to proper recreation: "Jesus said: Overcome evil with good. When the mind is filled with thoughts of beauty and an appreciation of the Creator through his creations, there is no place for that which is gross, ugly or debasing. Where there is clean, uplifting, joyous activity, evil cannot enter."[8] Harrison R. Merrill, the editor of the *Improvement Era*, also cited Jesus as the model of appropriate recreation: "Jesus stood for the enrichment of life—abundant life, abundant living. . . . He had but few years, but he lived them to the full. He was a social being enjoying his associations with his fellow men. He attended the wedding feast; He ate with publicans and sinners; He visited with his friends Martha and Mary and Lazarus. . . . How He dignified those social occasions."[9] Possessing the ultimate combination of earthly affability and supreme spirituality, Jesus made the most of every occasion. Adolescent Mormons were expected to do no less. The *Improvement Era* also published the idealistic comments of Dr. Ray O. Wyland, the director of education and relationships for the Boy Scouts of America. "Our recreation must be put on a higher level," he wrote, "for there is nothing that so much reveals what we are and there is nothing that so determines what we are going to be as the way we spend our leisure time. . . . Society will grow better if our recreation is wholesome."[10]

Although social improvement was a worthy goal, Mormon leaders also cared about the state of the soul and warned frequently against the dangers of forbidden recreation. Expounding on the "poison" of idleness, the prize-winning essay in a church scholarship contest painted a picture of men sitting in a "smoke-filled room . . . wasting their time, playing cards, rolling dice, smoking, profaning, and telling smutty stories." The moral of the story made clear the degenerative potential of improper recreation. "The social degradation we see all around us, the many wrecks and downfalls of the young people of our nation have been caused by an unprofitable, improper use of their idle moments. The leisure that is forced upon the world is tainted with bitterness and tragedy!"[11] Such warnings reinforced the value of church-sponsored recreation for faithful Mormons. Under the direction of the church, parents and youth could be sure that the rising generation would avoid potentially destructive forms of recreation, increase in spirituality, and improve society. Thus, church recreation was seen as an effective weapon against negative social forces and also as a strategy for promoting internal cohesion within the church. To construct this double-missioned recreation program, church leaders willingly and selectively shopped among the nation's experts on recreational theory and practice.

Recreation Combating Social Evils

Church leaders recognized that certain social and political forces were largely beyond their immediate control. These included juvenile delinquency, mass political and social movements, and other social temptations. Yet church leaders believed that the redemptive powers of recreation could at least partially relieve these ills.

Juvenile delinquency, like crime in general, had been on the rise in Salt Lake City since the 1920s and was an increasingly serious problem in the years of the Depression. Though the federal government had reported in 1931 that Salt Lake had "fewer major crimes in proportion to population than any other large city in the country," city residents (including LDS Church leaders) were often reminded that lawlessness was growing.[12] Creating uncommon concern in the halls of church and civic power, the uproar over delinquent adolescent behavior reached a crescendo in 1929 with the publication of *Boys and Girls in Salt Lake City*, written by Arthur L. Beeley, a sociologist at the University of Utah and a member of the YMMIA General Board. Beeley reported that the local juvenile court had handled more than five thousand cases of juvenile delinquency between 1923 and 1928. Citing cases of offenders as young as six years old, Beeley's study argued that existing youth programs were inadequate to counter the trend toward adolescent aberrance.[13]

Concern about destructive juveniles grew in the next few years. Writing in the *Improvement Era* in 1935, the Utah educator and YMMIA General Board member Philo T. Farnsworth referred to "This Thing Called Delinquency" as "one of our major problems" and enumerated specific types of delinquency: sexual misbehavior (both fornication and what he termed "perversions"), acquisitiveness (stealing, burglary), and actions caused by "wander lust" (truancy and running away from home). Farnsworth cautioned that in a society where adolescent crime is rampant, "every leader of boys should feel a double urge to prevent delinquency and to foster positive, constructive activities."[14] In the battle against delinquency, the church recreation program was designed to turn out healthy, well-adjusted adolescents, thus preventing rather than reforming delinquents. Concurring with Farnsworth that prevention offered the best cure for antisocial behavior, Claude C. Cornwall, a former member of the YMMIA General Board who had studied social psychology at New York University, encouraged youth leaders to get to the root of the problems: "If these causes can only be found and eliminated, the chances are that there will not arise any necessity for treatment of delinquent behavior. If it can be prevented, it just won't happen."[15]

Although Boy Scouts had been a major component of LDS recreation since the 1910s, Scouting during the Depression was accorded special rank as an alternative to antisocial behavior.[16] Because delinquency was primarily considered a male phenomenon (Beeley's offenders were boys by a ratio of more than six to one), church leaders worked to channel young men's energy into socially useful activities. Apostle Melvin J. Ballard spoke of the high expectations that the church placed on Scouting in "dealing with the boy in his leisure time." Calling on every boy to join that "appealing program," Ballard made explicit the link between Scout activity and decreasing delinquency. "Many boys are in the State Reform School but there isn't, I am told, a single Boy Scout among them." He warned, "If you do not have your boy active in Scouting, he will be active in some unsupervised program in the pool hall or some other place where he is acquiring bad habits in both thinking and acting." In a world filled with socially destructive amusements, Scouting helped a boy avoid "the pitfalls that are in store for him."[17] Later, the *Improvement Era* reinforced Ballard's point by reporting that a recent survey of juvenile delinquency in a large western city had discovered that 85.5 percent of the boys in its juvenile court system "never had the opportunity of participating in or belonging to any character building organization" like the Boy Scouts.[18]

Countering the gloomy forecast facing boys with no access to Scouting were numerous Scouting success stories. Oscar Kirkham told about a mining company that "sent a check for $250 to the Scout council stating that up until the organization of a Scout troop in the town, the company had to employ a watchman to keep boys from breaking windows, light globes, and otherwise injuring property; but since the establishment of a troop there, depredations had ceased; and therefore, the $250 a month formerly used to keep the boys out of mischief could now be used to aid them in their Scout program."[19] Scouting had succeeded in turning these boys from delinquents into model citizens. Scouting, at least to some church leaders, offered a potent antidote to juvenile delinquency during the Depression.

The LDS recreation program also checked the expanding forces of social unrest that might have led to a rise in socialism or communism among church members. According to G. Ott Romney, by making "adequate provision for the use of the individual's leisure time," society "takes out a splendid insurance policy to protect itself against the evils of restlessness, of anti-social activities, of the adoption of dangerous 'isms' and '-ologies' and of perverted tastes."[20] High-ranking church officials understood the growing attraction of communism for the unemployed and impoverished. A march organized by the Communist Party in Salt Lake City in 1931 and a violent 1933 labor strike in Carbon County brought the fear of collective social action close to home for church leaders and Utah residents.[21] As Apostle Joseph F. Merrill proposed, "All will agree that a happy, stable state of society cannot exist where idleness and want abound, for these are fertile fields in which discontent and revolution germinate and quickly grow."[22] In light of the dire economic circumstances of the 1930s, communism apparently appealed to some Mormons, a fact that disconcerted church leaders. President Heber J. Grant and his counselors issued a "Warning to Church Members" in 1936: "With great regret we learn from credible sources, governmental and others, that a few Church members are joining directly or indirectly, the Communists and are taking part in their activities." Grant called upon all church members "completely to eschew Communism" for "the safety of our divinely inspired Constitutional government and the welfare of our church."[23] Helpful countermeasures included recreational activities that promoted democracy and American values. Patriotic church functions, including a remarkable year-long celebration of the bicentennial of George Washington's birth, were undertaken to "bring into every home a reverential and patriotic feeling."[24] Recreation, it was thought, would stave off revolution and act as a "social-insurance policy" against unwanted political "isms" and "ologies" that might prove tempting.

Other cultural "isms" more closely related to recreation also appeared threatening to church leaders during the 1930s, particularly the growing influence of commercialism. The popularity of movie houses, professional sports, and commercial dance halls concerned church leaders because such businesses were outside the church's control. Fully aware, as one author noted, that they were "competing with . . . commercialized recreational activities," Mormon leaders tailored their activity programs to meet the popular amusements on their own terms.[25] In some cases, the church created programs to compete with specific commercial activities in a thinly veiled effort to destroy social activities that could not be controlled. For example, the church built a community center in St. George, Utah, because local authorities found the prospect of a commercial dance hall undesirable. Juanita Brooks, a St. George resident later known for her landmark series of Mormon biographies and history of the Mountain Meadows Massacre, wrote about this episode for the *Improvement Era* from her perspective as a mother and schoolteacher. Posing the question, "Whose Business is Recreation? The Profit-takers' or the Home-makers'?" Brooks reported in 1938 the success story of a group of concerned citizens led by local Mormon leaders and financed by general church funds who responded when "certain commercial interests planned to put up a hall just outside the city limits where it would be free of supervision by the city officials." LDS city leaders opposed the new building, fearing that it would harm "the morals of the young people." A committee of four local leaders—one from each of the local LDS congregations and one from Dixie College—decided that the most effective response was to build "a hall larger and finer than any private concern could afford to do, and to run it on a non-profit basis to cut out competition." With a large share of the capital coming from general church funds, a thirty-three-thousand-dollar recreation hall was constructed. By charging only five cents to attend dances at the hall, the LDS-financed recreation center ended the threat posed by the private dance hall.[26] Fearful of unsupervised recreation, Mormon officials in southern Utah used their greater resources to ensure that, in the words of the western essayist Wallace Stegner, young Mormons would dance "in the place where the priesthood [could] keep an eye on them."[27] At least in this case, it seems that Gentile "profit-takers" were bested by Mormon "home-makers" and their connections to church capital.

LDS recreation also took on another "ism"—the psychological theories of Sigmund Freud. Eugene L. Roberts, the former basketball coach at Brigham Young University and a professor in the physical education department at the University of Southern California, claimed that Freudian theories had "caused untold suffering." In place of Freudian self-expression, Roberts called for the reenthronement of the "ideal of self-control and self-development." He queried, "Can we show that such Freudian abandon to desire has only the misery of mental and spiritual conflict at the end of its trail?" The best opposition was a recreation program that placed "special emphasis upon the socially cooperative activities such as were indulged in by our forefathers." Working and playing together in groups, like early pioneer Mormons, could rebuild the sense of community that Roberts feared had been splintered by Freud's emphasis on individualism. Though not recreation's foremost target, the attack on Freudianism evidences the belief that wholesome recreation could remedy a variety of social problems.[28]

Recreation and Internal Cohesion

In addition to protecting against outside influences, a more important function of Mormon recreation programs was to foster internal cohesion. Promoting attendance at church-sponsored functions, encouraging obedience to church leaders and doctrines, and spreading the Mormon faith through missionary work comprised the primary day-to-day goals and accomplishments of recreational activities throughout the 1930s.

Like they had for decades, local leaders used recreational activities to persuade youth to spend their leisure time at the meetinghouse. Leaders noticed that boys (and boys continued to be their primary concern) who attended social outings during the week were more likely to attend Sunday meetings. Deseret Stake in Salt Lake City noted an increase of 800 percent in monthly stake priesthood meetings after an outing was announced.[29] "Contests" became popular devices to stimulate activity, and the *Improvement Era* reported dozens. In Ogden, Utah, the Aaronic priesthood challenged the Melchizedek priesthood to a contest based on attendance at weekly priesthood meetings, Sunday School classes, and sacrament meetings and fulfilling ward teaching assignments for a period of six months. Winners would feast on strawberries and cream, while the losers dined on Boston baked beans. In this case, the boys enjoyed watching the men (most of whom were their fathers) eating baked beans nearly as much as they enjoyed their own tasty desserts. But the point of this contest, like other church competitions of the period, was "to stimulate greater interest and enthusiasm among the young men."[30]

Athletic games provided the backbone of the male-centered recreational program. Throughout the decade, wards, stakes, and the general church held annual sports tournaments, the most popular of which (basketball) attracted over ten thousand participants each year. Young men spent countless hours practicing and playing in the tournaments. By using athletics and other contests to promote activity among church members, LDS leaders were not duping the boys into unwitting activity; they were providing suitable rewards for participation, and many boys found basketball games or strawberries reason enough to maintain a connection with the church.

Recreational activities also allowed young men and women to mingle socially and romantically. According to Wallace Stegner, "Even in the grave and decorous atmosphere of the Ward House, even in Sunday Meeting, the back rows were converted into a preserve for courting couples."[31] The Alberta Stake in Canada made a special effort to use romance to attract young men to church. Explaining their high attendance figures, the Albertans advised, "We are trying to stress the attendance of the 'teen' age girls at sacrament meeting . . . we think that if more of the girls would attend, this would assist in getting a larger attendance of the boys."[32] All wards and stakes held dances throughout the year, further fostering "wholesome" romantic associations. Unlike gender-exclusive athletic contests, dances offered the youth the opportunity to couple up and spend time together. Romance may not have been the primary motive behind church social functions, but once boys and girls became romantic couples, the church recreation program did its best to capitalize on the situation.

As was the case earlier in the century, the Boy Scout program was used as a tool to increase church attendance and promote adherence to church principles. Apostle Ballard argued that "the end of Scouting" was "to make that boy an active worker in the Priesthood, to prepare him for the service of God, the missionary field and his responsibility at the head of a home. If we fail in that we have missed the objective for which Scouting was introduced."[33] Although the Boy Scouts of America had long catered to Mormon needs, in February 1936 LDS Church leaders announced that henceforth the "religious, spiritual, and moral phases of Scouting" were to be emphasized. Church-sponsored Scout troops should supplement Scouting principles by requiring adherence to specific church teachings as a "definite part of Scouting." Before a boy could advance in Scouting he had to prove his worthiness to the presiding officers by providing a record of his meeting attendance. Non-LDS boys in church-sponsored troops were encouraged to participate in their own religious congregations. Though this announcement did not represent a sharp break with past policies, the new emphasis made Scouting concerns a distant second to the inculcation of religious values.[34]

The church also continued to use recreation to promote the Word of Wisdom. Despite lax enforcement in the past, by the 1930s adherence to the Word of Wisdom had become a barometer of a church member's worthiness.[35] Having noted the increasing numbers of both female and male smokers during the 1920s and troubled by the repeal of Prohibition in 1933, church officials reemphasized the advantages of abstention and looked to the sports world for examples of abstaining athletes.

Continuing a long-standing practice, the *Improvement Era* showcased celebrity sports personalities to encourage adolescents to avoid alcohol and tobacco. In so doing, it was following a national trend. As mass consumption expanded in the first quarter of the twentieth century, advertisers increasingly used endorsements by sports and entertainment figures to increase sales, especially among young people who were anxious to mimic celebrity behavior. In the 1920s and 1930s, celebrity endorsements of cigarettes and alcohol were especially popular and effective. The church countered with celebrity antiendorsements. The most conspicuous LDS celebrity in the church campaign during the 1930s was David Abbott Jenkins, a "superman of speed and endurance" widely known for setting world land-speed records in his race car, the "Mormon Meteor." "Ab" regularly appeared on the pages of the *Era* insisting that "the simple, clean and wholesome life" rewarded abstainers with "endurance, calmness, steady nerve and imperturbable poise of mind and body." Boasting that he had "never tasted liquor or tobacco and does not use other milder beverages such as tea or coffee," Jenkins claimed that his abstemious lifestyle had allowed him single-handedly to defeat teams of three and four in marathon cross-country auto races.[36] The familiar message was clear—abstention leads to athletic success. In language reminiscent of "worldly" ads, the *Era* portrayed other famous church athletes. Monte Pearson, the Mormon pitcher for the Cleveland Indians, reported overcoming a short-lived smoking habit. "I would not be in the majors today if I had continued to use tobacco," Pearson declared. "The men who stay for years [in the major leagues] and make great names for themselves are nearly always abstainers from tobacco and liquor."[37] Denunciations of alcohol use also came from non-LDS celebrities, including the famed football coach "Pop" Warner of Temple University.[38] No studies have ever appraised the effectiveness of such campaigns, but they no doubt contributed significantly to establishing a culture of abstention.

In addition to promoting church activity and doctrinal adherence, sports and recreational activities were used by Mormon missionaries to change the frequently negative image of Mormonism among prospective converts. Aware that door-to-door proselyting rarely succeeded and often demoralized the young missionaries, mission leaders turned to recreation as a nonconfrontational way to elicit interest in the church. In 1935, a missionary reported from England: "Baseball in Britain is proving a powerful instrument for breaking down barriers of prejudice that existed for nearly a century and for opening the way to hear the Gospel message." More than just providing a cultural service by introducing the American game to interested Britons, most missionaries gave sports lessons as an opening to instruct their fellow players in the spiritual doctrines of Mormonism. To that end, the apex of missionary baseball in England was not found in the reports of games played and championships won but in the realization that "scores of baseball friends, some of them players and league officials, are attending both auxiliary and sacrament meetings."[39] The goal remained the conversion of souls, but recreation provided an affable method to secure the goodwill and friendships that might translate into conversions.

The success of this program in Great Britain prompted other experiments throughout Europe and the United States. In Germany, a group of American missionaries instructed "likely candidates for the German Olympic Basketball team" in the fundamental skills of the game. Coaching sessions before large audiences were followed by an "interesting illustrated lecture dealing with Utah's renowned national parks," after which more than fifteen hundred LDS pamphlets were distributed to exiting spectators.[40] Other attention-getting activities included participation in a community play in Germany, a singing group (the Millennial Chorus) that performed over the British Broadcasting radio network, a variety of sports in the Netherlands, and the performance of American songs on Swedish television.[41] In the United States, a Goodwill Quartet canvassed the Midwest "with the hope of presenting to the people of this mission the Gospel through the medium of song."[42] Young Mormons in Civilian Conservation Corps camps were instructed to invite non-LDS camp members to church activities: "A wonderful missionary work can be accomplished by making all young men in your vicinity welcome to all M Men functions," which involved athletic programs and courses of instruction, both practical and spiritual.[43] All over the globe, LDS-led recreational activities attracted non-Mormons as a first step toward conversion.

Beyond promoting church participation, fostering adherence to church teachings, and proselyting, Mormon recreation also filled other social functions. Deseret Clubs in California colleges created a recreational environment where the "idealism of L.D.S. young people" would be safeguarded against the rampant "atheism" prevalent on many campuses.[44] Recreational programs also taught young people skills that might lead to employment. In 1935 the Deseret Gymnasium sponsored a summer program for 150 adolescent boys from Salt Lake City who were "denied the advantages of living and working on a farm" and, in addition to recreational games, trained them in a "commodious well lighted and equipped shop under technically trained and experienced teachers." One grateful parent reported: "We were glad to have our son go to the Gym Summer School to keep him out of mischief. Now that he has learned so much about the technique of airplane construction and flight, we believe he may have found his vocation for life."[45] Finding a suitable vocation represented no small feat in Depression-era America.

Learning from the "Experts"

Although the story of late nineteenth-century Mormonism is often told in terms of resistance to political and economic forces that gradually wore down the church's stubborn separatism, a focus on the unwanted intrusions fails to tell the whole story. Equally one-sided is the view that Mormonism capitulated completely to mainstream America. The church's contacts with the outside world were often complex and ambiguous. In designing and implementing LDS recreation programs throughout the twentieth century, church officials willingly turned to outside experts and professionals for ideas and techniques about recreation. However, they consistently used those techniques to strengthen Mormon community values rather than simply making a wholesale accommodation to non-Mormon groups or value systems. Rather than "selling out" to Gentile experts, LDS leaders were cautiously "buying into" ideas that would serve their own ends.[46] That trend continued into the 1930s.

Judging from published statements and instructions to stake and ward recreation leaders, the parameters of the church program were not drawn from prophecy, revelation, or prophetic direction but rather were established in accordance with prevailing professional notions of appropriate social activities for adolescents and young adults.

There were important precedents for such borrowings. Mormon artists had honed their skills at the Académie Julian in Paris before painting various temple murals during the 1890s. Mormon scholars studied theology at the University of Chicago Divinity School in the late 1920s and early 1930s, returning to teach in the fledgling seminary/institute program. Stephen L Richards, then a thirty-eight-year-old apostle, and Amy Brown Lyman, general secretary to the Relief Society General Board and later its general president, promoted professional social work within the church after attending a national social work convention in Kansas City in May 1918.[47] By going beyond their borders to acquire "worldly" learning, Mormon recreation leaders furthered the LDS acceptance of secular trends. Church leaders concerned about recreation during the Depression first turned to non-LDS experts to gain sufficient knowledge and then applied that knowledge selectively to further internal church goals, thus using secular learning to create programs that actually served as a "hedge against secular influences" and reinforced a "sense of community among the believers."[48]

Philo T. Farnsworth's series on "The Boy, His Nature, and His Needs," published in nine installments in the *Improvement Era* in 1934 and 1935, explained basic principles of adolescent psychology so that youth leaders could create effective local recreation and activity programs. Farnsworth did not conceal the sources of his ideas; rather, he included extensive bibliographies with most of his articles and quoted from such reputable academic sources as Ada H. Arlitt's *Adolescent Psychology* (1933), Fowler O. Brooks's *Psychology of Adolescence* (1930), and M. V. O'Shea's *The Child: His Nature and His Needs* (1924). Farnsworth argued that "the basis of success [in the youth program] is the intelligent understanding of the nature and the needs of these youths and the wisdom to plan a program of activities that inspires respect, promotes confidence, and results in meaningful and worthy social responses on the part of these youths."[49] Rather than quoting scriptures that focused on the sinful and fallen nature of humankind to explain personal and social problems, Farnsworth turned to psychology and sociology. In one article, he explained the effects of a "bad environment" and described how unsuitable books, pictures, and companions "warp the social and moral trends of growth" and lead to juvenile delinquency and "defective" personality types. These bad influences should be replaced by church social activities, including the Boy Scout program.[50] Another article warned against the "major dangers" of allowing youthful appetites to build up and recommended defusing such pressures by "the satisfaction which comes from athletic competition."[51] Farnsworth even instructed youth leaders in the rudimentary skills of "case social work"—what he called "the scientific approach to the solution of delinquency and to the problem of defective personality"—by directing leaders to probe "the social background" of the troubled child and then to create an appropriate program.[52] Whether any leaders actually implemented Farnsworth's ideas remains unknown.

Mormon recreation leaders also borrowed extensively from the National Recreation Association (NRA), an organization of philanthropists, playground workers, and other advocates of wholesome forms of social recreation. Founded in 1906 in Washington, D.C., as the Playground Association of America, the organization had become widely known for its success in staffing playgrounds and implementing new methods of play for urban children. Though never officially allied with the National Recreation Association, LDS recreation leaders frequently attended meetings, borrowed ideas, and mined the NRA's literature for suggestions.[53]

In July 1932, a delegation of ten members from the MIA General Boards, joined by delegates from several stakes, attended the First International Recreation Congress, sponsored by the NRA, in Los Angeles. LDS attendees reported that this exposure broadened "their concept of the meaning of recreation and their vision of its possibilities as a character building and spiritualizing force." They expressed gratitude "that the leisure-time program of the MIA measures up so completely to the ideals and methods presented by these national groups."[54] As the delegates reviewed the church recreation program they discovered much to make them proud, found reinforcement for their belief in the redemptive power of recreation, and redoubled their commitment to using recreation to solve institutional and personal problems. In November 1932, the theme for the monthly conjoint session of the ward MIAs was "Building Latter-day Saints through Recreation." Young men and young women gave presentations designed to "enrich leisure" and "spiritualize recreation" by describing the spiritual force of music, the educational value of drama, and the "esthetic and spiritual values in the dance."[55] It is likely that the National Recreation Association conference influenced this new emphasis.

Two months earlier, in September 1932, Elsie T. Brandley, associate editor of the *Improvement Era*, quoted from Judge Robert H. Scott's address to the National Recreation Association meeting: "'The boy who steals a base is not likely to be stealing an automobile.'" Brandley claimed that Scott's conviction that proper recreation would reduce juvenile crime had "long been an unformulated statement" behind Mormon recreation programs.[56] Brandley's use of expert judicial testimony exemplifies the LDS outreach to recreation specialists; the direct connection of Judge Scott's ideas and Mormon programs typifies the close relationship between recreation leaders and Mormon leaders.

National Recreation Association influence had earlier appeared in the *M-Men Guide* for 1931–32, a course of study for young men. Its author, J. Ruel Griffiths, an associate professor of physical education at the University of Utah, included a chapter on "Recreation" and a chapter-length biography of the founder of the National Recreation Association, Joseph Lee. Based on texts written by recreation authorities, the lessons stressed the importance of choosing wholesome social activities as part of a healthy lifestyle and recommended further reading in experts like Eduard Lindeman and the renowned sociologist Edward A. Ross for ideas and explanations.[57]

Other experts influenced the MIA's recreation plans. In 1933, at the invitation of the *Improvement Era*, Jay B. Nash—a professor of education at New York University, an admired member of the National Recreation Association, and a leading voice in the American Association of Leisure Time Educators—wrote on problems posed by increased leisure during the Depression.[58] One local MIA group took the advice of the dance sociologist Marla War Lamkin that "the modern dance is essentially a dance for two . . . [and] is usually stiff, formal, and unimaginative" and instituted new group dances that developed "friendliness and sociability." Other youth groups were invited to follow their lead in planning dances.[59]

There are even a few suggestions that the LDS recreational programs influenced recreation professionals. Eugene L. Roberts observed in 1933, "The leisure-time program of the Mormon church is the 'talk of the town' at present among the country's recreation leaders."[60] In April 1938, a convention of recreation leaders from the western states gathered in Salt Lake City where they witnessed music, drama, singing, and speeches prepared by local MIA groups.[61] However, *Recreation,* the monthly publication of the National Recreation Association, contains virtually no mention of LDS recreational programs during the 1930s.

The *Era* regularly reviewed professional and academic books on recreation and child psychology in its monthly column "On the Book Rack." Sample titles included Ethel M. Bowers's *Recreation for Girls and Women* (1934), Arlitt's *Adolescent Psychology* (1933), J. J. B. Morgan's *The Psychology of the Unadjusted School Child* (1936), Martin H. Neumeyer and Esther S. Neumeyer's *Leisure and Recreation* (1936), Ruth Lampland's *Hobbies for Everybody* (1934), and *Sports For Recreation* (1936), compiled by the Intramural Sports Department at the University of Michigan. In the August 1936 issue alone, three recreation titles—*Leisure and Recreation, Hobbies for Everybody,* and *Sports for Recreation*—were favorably reviewed. The titles were chosen because of their helpfulness to youth advisors struggling to make local programs more effective. "The Sunday School teacher and the expert in week-day religious education should rely on the psychology of the adolescence and childhood as fully as any other teacher," noted one analyst.[62] The reviewer of Arlitt's *The Adolescent* (1938) explained that "all leaders of Scouts, Explorers, Bee-Hive Girls, and Junior Girls should read and re-read this helpful volume."[63] By seeking guidance from so many "outside" voices, church youth leaders sought to augment and refine their existing approaches.

Although recreational activities largely formed the social foundation of the LDS Church during the 1930s, they were not the only concern of church leaders, nor was the ability of recreation to change lives and improve society the only method of behavior modification espoused by church officials. Apostle John A. Widtsoe went so far as to beatify toil: "Blessed is work, properly directed, unceasing work, throughout life! It preserves physical health and prolongs life. It adds to our material and spiritual possessions. . . . The fruits of idleness are sorrow and sin. The doctrine that men and women must be usefully employed while life lasts, if health permits, is fundamental in the philosophy of the Gospel. It is the first law of prosperity."[64] There was no substitute for work—either in the world or in the gospel. Linking long life with hard work, church president Heber J. Grant argued, "I do not know of anything that destroys a person's health more quickly than not working. It seems to me that lazy people die young while those who are ready and willing to labor and who ask the Lord day by day to do more in the future than they have ever done in the past, are the people whom the Lord loves, and who live to a good old age."[65] Going beyond the physical benefits of work, Grant reminded youth leaders and others that in directing their youthful charges, the "important thing for you is have a love of your work and to do your work under the inspiration of the Spirit of the living God."[66] Scholarly learning and expertise had their place in church recreation and social programs, but, according to Grant, providence trumped psychology, and the Spirit of God mattered more than sociology.

The increasing attention given to recreation programs was balanced by a never-slackening emphasis on the importance of work. Recreation provided a partial answer to delinquency and unemployment during the Depression, but hard work continued to be championed as the vital force ensuring social order. In church conferences throughout the decade, church leaders glorified the value of work, called for self-reliance, and implored all to give an honest day's work, especially those employed on relief projects. Recreation was a temporary solution to idleness, a necessary sweetener for youth, and an earned reward for serious toil.[67]

Recreation served important functions in the LDS Church during the Depression decade of the 1930s. Recreation programs provided the church with a device to fight against problems like juvenile delinquency and social unrest. Furthermore, recreation increased cohesion within the church and offered missionaries a unique and effective way to meet potential converts. For the historian, Depression-era recreation provides additional evidence of the LDS Church reaching beyond its borders to acquire and use expert advice and knowledge. Applying that knowledge to solve internal dilemmas, the church did not accommodate or "give in" to the outside world; instead, through the process of "creative adjustment," church recreation leaders employed knowledge from the outside world to preserve their unique way of life.

In many ways, the activities of the 1930s reflect the central role of the recreation program in the LDS Church. Building on the foundation created during the Progressive Era, church leaders took existing ideologies and activities and used them to attack the unique leisure-time problems caused by the social and economic dislocations of the Great Depression.

Notes

1. For background on the crash and the Depression, see John Kenneth Galbraith, *The Great Crash, 1929* (Boston: Houghton Mifflin, 1961); Lester V. Chandler, *America's Greatest Depression, 1929–1941* (New York: Harper and Row, 1970); T. H. Watkins, *The Hungry Years* (New York: Henry Holt, 1999).

2. Thomas G. Alexander, *Mormonism in Transition: A History of the Latter-day Saints, 1890–1930* (Urbana: University of Illinois Press, 1986), 140, explains the evolution of the Mutual Improvement Associations: "Essentially literary, educational, and theological societies in 1900, by 1930 they had become organizations with a basic athletic and recreational thrust."

3. For the most comprehensive treatment of Utah's economy during the Depression, see John F. Bluth and Wayne K. Hinton, "The Great Depression," in *Utah's History*, ed. Richard D. Poll et al. (Provo, Utah: Brigham Young University Press, 1978), 481–96. Also see Leonard J. Arrington, *Utah, the New Deal, and the Depression of the 1930s* (Ogden, Utah: Weber State College Press, 1983). Another useful source on the economic impact of the Depression on Utah is Wayne K. Hinton, "The Economics of Ambivalence: Utah's Depression Experience," *Utah Historical Quarterly* 54 (Summer 1986): 268–85.

4. "Broadcasting from the M.I.A. Annual Conference," *Improvement Era* 35 (July 1932): 529.

5. G. Ott Romney, "A Habit Worth Acquiring," *Improvement Era* 35 (Nov. 1931): 14.

6. *Improvement Era* 35 (May 1932): 443.

7. "Suggestions for the Summer Program," *Improvement Era* 35 (June 1932): 494.

8. "Sunday Evening Joint Sessions for November," *Improvement Era* 35 (Oct. 1932): 745–46.

9. Harrison R. Merrill, "We Stand for the Enrichment of Life," *Improvement Era* 35 (Oct. 1932): 707. Merrill may have been influenced by Bruce Barton's characterization of Christ in *The Man Nobody Knows: A Discovery of the Real Jesus* (Indianapolis: Bobbs-Merrill, 1925). Merrill's treatment of the Savior as a social being conforms almost exactly with Burton's description of Jesus as the "Sociable Man" (see Barton, *The Man Nobody Knows,* chap. 6).

10. Dr. Ray O. Wyland, "Youth—And the Needs of the World," *Improvement Era* 39 (Dec. 1936): 752.

11. Merrill Wood, "Enrichment of Life through Constructive Use of Leisure," *Improvement Era* 37 (May 1934): 281.

12. Thomas G. Alexander and James B. Allen, *Mormons and Gentiles: A History of Salt Lake City* (Boulder, Colo.: Pruett Publishing, 1984), 223.

13. Arthur L. Beeley, *Boys and Girls in Salt Lake City* (Salt Lake City: University of Utah Department of Sociology and Social Technology, 1929), esp. chap. 2.

14. Philo T. Farnsworth, "The Boy, His Nature, and His Needs," *Improvement Era* 38 (Mar. 1935): 178.

15. Claude C. Cornwall, "Crime Prevention Is Better Than Cure," *Improvement Era* 37 (May 1934): 267.

16. Boy Scouting had been integrated into the YMMIA program in 1913. Two years later, the YLMIA allied with the Campfire Girls but dropped the affiliation after one summer, replacing it with its own Beehive program. The LDS connection to the Boy Scouts continues today. See James B. Allen and Glen M. Leonard, *The Story of the Latter-day Saints*, 2d ed. (Salt Lake City: Deseret Book, 1992), 478; see also chap. 4 in this book.

17. Melvin J. Ballard, "Aaronic Priesthood Correlation and the Y.M.M.I.A.," *Improvement Era* 35 (May 1932): 423–24.

18. "Scouts," *Improvement Era* 40 (Apr. 1937): 251.

19. Weston N. Nordgren, "Boy Scouts in Camp," *Improvement Era* 35 (Nov. 1931): 20.

20. Romney, "A Habit Worth Acquiring," 14.

21. A short history of socialism in Utah in the first two decades of the twentieth century can be found in John S. McCormick, "Hornets in the Hive: Socialists in Early Twentieth-Century Utah," *Utah Historical Quarterly* 50 (Summer 1982): 224–40. For an example of the growing attractiveness of communism in Depression-era Utah, see Helen Z. Papanikolas, "Unionism, Communism, and the Great Depression: The Carbon County Coal Strike of 1933," *Utah Historical Quarterly* 41 (Summer 1973): 254–300; Bluth and Hinton, "The Great Depression," 484.

22. Joseph F. Merrill, "The Problem of Unemployment," *Improvement Era* 42 (Dec. 1939): 716, 765. Even more than communism, Merrill feared the growing power of unionism and the increasing distance between the interests of capital and labor.

23. "Warning to Church Members," *Improvement Era* 39 (Aug. 1936): 488.

24. "Mutual Messages," *Improvement Era* 35 (Jan. 1932): 170.

25. Ira J. Markham, "Building Boys to Latter-day Saint Standards," *Improvement Era* 42 (Oct. 1939): 618. Despite the pitfalls of commercialism, the church did not simply proscribe all commercial social activity—a wise form of moderation. Rather, the *Improvement Era* urged LDS consumers to make intelligent choices and, as an example, provided a long-running series of movie reviews, "Lights and Shadows on the Silver Screen," which ran throughout the decade. For one example, see *Improvement Era* 35 (Apr. 1932): 350. Steven J. Ross offers a compelling analysis of "alternative" uses of films in the pre-Hollywood era in *Working-Class Hollywood: Silent Film and the Shaping of Class in America* (Princeton, N.J.: Princeton University Press, 1998).

26. Juanita Brooks, "Whose Business Is Recreation? The Profit-takers' or the Home-makers'?" *Improvement Era* 41 (Oct. 1938): 597.

27. Wallace Stegner, *Mormon Country* (1942; rpt., Lincoln: University of Nebraska Press, 1981), 18.

28. Eugene L. Roberts, "The New Leisure," *Improvement Era* 36 (Feb. 1933): 204–6, 253–54.

29. Manton Moody, "Means of Success in Promoting Attendance of the Aaronic Priesthood," *Improvement Era* 35 (Mar. 1932): 301.

30. "Field Notes," *Improvement Era* 35 (Nov. 1931): 42.

31. Stegner, *Mormon Country,* 7.

32. "Improvement in Aaronic Priesthood Work," *Improvement Era* 36 (Sept. 1933): 688.

33. Ballard, "Aaronic Priesthood Correlation," 423–24.

34. "Religious, Spiritual, and Moral Phases of Scouting to be Emphasized," *Improvement Era* 39 (Feb. 1936): 114.

35. On the changing interpretations of the Word of Wisdom, see Alexander, *Mormonism in Transition,* chap. 13.

36. Nephi L. Morris, "Ab Jenkins—Superman of Speed and Endurance," *Improvement Era* 39 (Mar. 1936): 140. Jenkins was immensely popular in the church and in local politics. His restored "Meteor" is on permanent display in the basement of the Utah State Capitol.

37. "Would Not Be in the Majors Today If I Had Continued to Use Tobacco," *Improvement Era* 38 (Nov. 1935): 700. For another perspective on Monte Peterson, see John Lardner, "The Deacon's Dilemma," *Newsweek,* 24 Mar. 1938, 49. Not all admonitions to keep the Word of Wisdom were humorless, however. The *Era* reported that "another Word of Wisdom argument" was found in the "story of the dear old lady who said that she knew the Word of Wisdom was true because look what happened to the men who were involved in the Teapot Dome scandal." See *Improvement Era* 41 (Feb. 1938): 128.

38. Earlier in the century, other non-LDS celebrities had been enlisted in the campaign against tobacco use. Dan McGugin, the football coach at Vanderbilt University, claimed, "'in fifty years' experience in athletics, I have never known of a boy who became a confirmed cigarette smoker when young who ever really amounted to anything very much in his life later on.'" Qtd. in "The Effect of Tobacco on the Boy," *Improvement Era* 21 (Nov. 1917): 11. The railroad magnate E. H. Harriman chimed in, "I might as well go to a lunatic asylum for employees, as to hire cigarette smokers." See "The Tobacco Curse," *Improvement Era* 15 (Apr. 1912): 547.

39. Wendell J. Ashton, "Baseball and Mormons in England," *Improvement Era* 38 (Oct. 1935): 645, 649.

40. Melvyn M. Cowan, "Missionary 'Attention Getters': Basketball in Germany," *Improvement Era* 39 (Sept. 1936): 571–73.

41. Rulon Blunck and John T. Cardall, "Mormon Missionaries in the Meissen Cast," *Improvement Era* 40 (Sept. 1937): 572; Robert S. Stevens, "Broadcasting with the Millennial Chorus," *Improvement Era* 40 (Feb. 1937): 92–93; J. Paul Vorkink and Joseph P. Lambert, "Our Friend-Making Missionaries in the Netherlands," *Improvement Era* 41 (July 1938): 412; Gustive O. Larson, "Mormon Missionaries on Sweden's National Television," *Improvement Era* 42 (Feb. 1939): 90.

42. Franklin Y. Gates Jr., "A Missionary Goodwill Quartet," *Improvement Era* 40 (July 1937): 403.

43. "M-Men in C.C.C. Camps," *Improvement Era* 38 (Feb. 1935): 113.

44. Elden Ricks, "The Deseret Club Movement," *Improvement Era* 41 (Sept. 1938): 540, 562.

45. Weston N. Nordgren, "Capitalizing on the Urge to Do Something," *Improvement Era* 38 (Feb. 1935): 91, 123.

46. See Leonard J. Arrington and Davis Bitton, *The Mormon Experience: A History of the Latter-day Saints* (1979; rpt., Urbana: University of Illinois Press, 1992), 243–61. See also Allen and Leonard, *The Story of the Latter-day Saints,* 429–92; James B. Allen and Richard O. Cowan, *Mormonism in the Twentieth Century,* 2d. ed. (Provo, Utah: Brigham Young University Press, 1967), chaps. 2, 6, and 10; Alexander, *Mormonism in Transition;* Jan Shipps, *Mormonism: The Story of a New Religious Tradition* (Urbana: University of Illinois Press, 1985).

47. For a personal perspective from a Mormon scholar who attended the University of Chicago Divinity School, see Russel Swenson, "Mormons at the University of Chicago Divinity School," *Dialogue: A Journal of Mormon Thought* 7 (Summer 1972): 37–47; Alexander, *Mormonism in Transition,* 131; Alexander, "Between Revivalism and the Social Gospel: The Latter-day Saint Social Advisory Committee, 1916–1922," *BYU Studies* 23 (Winter 1983): 19–39; Linda Jones Gibbs, *Harvesting the Light: The Paris Art Mission and Beginnings of Utah Impressionism* (Salt Lake City: Church of Jesus Christ of Latter-day Saints, 1987); Martha Elizabeth Bradley and Lowell M. Durham Jr., "John Hafen and the Art Missionaries," *Journal of Mormon History* 12 (1985): 91–105.

48. Arrington and Bitton, *The Mormon Experience,* 261.

49. Philo T. Farnsworth, "The Boy, His Nature, and His Needs," *Improvement Era* 38 (Nov. 1935): 705.

50. Philo T. Farnsworth, "The Boy, His Nature, and His Needs," *Improvement Era* 37 (Mar. 1934): 180.

51. Philo T. Farnsworth, "The Boy, His Nature, and His Needs," *Improvement Era* 37 (Nov. 1934): 693.

52. Philo T. Farnsworth, "The Boy, His Nature, and His Needs," *Improvement Era* 38 (May 1935): 325.

53. A thorough history of the National Recreation Association appears in Richard F. Knapp and Charles E. Hartsoe, *Play for America: The National Recreation Association, 1906–1965* (Arlington, Va.: National Recreation and Park Association, 1979).

54. "Mutual Messages," *Improvement Era* 36 (Nov. 1932): 47–48. Oscar Kirkham, the executive secretary of the YMMIA, delivered an address at the conference session entitled "Recreation in Religious Groups." See "First International Recreation Congress Program," *Recreation* 26 (July 1932): 188–89.

55. "Sunday Evening Joint Sessions for November," *Improvement Era* 35 (Oct. 1932): 745–46.

56. Elsie T. Brandley, "Pioneers in Many Ways," *Improvement Era* 35 (Sept. 1932): 643.

57. *M-Men Guide: Course of Study and M-Men Gleaner Program for 1931–32* (Salt Lake City: General Board of the YMMIA, 1931), 89–98.

58. Jay B. Nash, "What Will You Do with Your Leisure?" *Improvement Era* 36 (Feb. 1933): 195–98, 220.

59. "Dancing," *Improvement Era* 40 (Nov. 1937): 705.

60. Roberts, "New Leisure," 254.

61. "Play Leaders Witness M.I.A. Recreation," *Improvement Era* 41 (June 1938): 372.

62. Billie Hollingshead, "On the Book Rack," *Improvement Era* 41 (Jan. 1938): 35.

63. Marba C. Josephson, "On the Book Rack," *Improvement Era* 41 (Nov. 1938): 678. Remarkably, even books dealing with effective methods of sex education were discussed, though probably directed at parents more than youth leaders.

64. John A. Widtsoe, "Waste," *Improvement Era* 41 (Nov. 1938): 672–73.

65. Heber J. Grant, "The President on Church Security," *Improvement Era* 40 (Mar. 1937): 131.

66. Heber J. Grant, "To Those Who Teach Our Children," *Improvement Era* 42 (Mar. 1939): 135.

67. Garth Mangum and Bruce Blumell, *The Mormons' War on Poverty: A History of LDS Welfare, 1830–1990* (Salt Lake City: University of Utah Press, 1993), 97–100.

CONCLUSION

Recreation Recedes

> The first impression I had of the Mormon Church was of what
> the Mormons called Mutual, which you know about. Every
> Tuesday night, down in the ward amusement hall, youth activi-
> ties go on, classes of one kind or another, Boy Scouts, Girl
> Scouts, all those other organizations that Mormons are very
> good at. I fell into that with great eagerness. . . . I've forgotten
> what ward, but . . . I liked it. That gave me a kind of hole to
> crawl in, and I liked it very much.
> —WALLACE STEGNER

The end of the Great Depression did not mean the end of LDS recreational
programs. Throughout the war years and continuing to the end of the twentieth century, Mormon recreational programs have taught young church
members what it means to be "Mormon." Wholesome entertainments and
rigorous athletic events continued to socialize generations of Mormons long
after the Progressive Era faded into the distant past. Although the programs
continued, the emphasis on nurturing wholesome forms of recreation diminished in importance. The New Deal era proved to be the high point of LDS-
sponsored recreation. Church leaders warned against particularly illicit
activities—like pornography and gambling—but the coherent approach that
applied early in the twentieth century all but disappeared. Leaders at the
close of the twentieth century returned to the ad hoc pronouncements that
had characterized the leadership of Joseph Smith and Brigham Young. As
the Church of Jesus Christ of Latter-day Saints expanded throughout the
world, church officials focused less on the games that integrated Mormons
into the American mainstream and more on maintaining cohesion within a
growing, worldwide church.

The circumstances accompanying global growth forced church leaders to
amend the recreation programs. Beginning in September 1971, the popular
all-church athletic tournaments and music and dance festivals were replaced
with regional tournaments and festivals staged in local areas. No explanation was given for the change in athletic programs; however, *Ensign* magazine reported that dance and music festivals were modified "to permit in-

creased participation at the local level."[1] Recreational activities are carried out on a local basis in the church today.

Though globalization concerns within the church played some part in the decline of church-sponsored recreation, the social concerns that had given rise to the recreation program—namely, the unacceptable activities in American cities—had largely fallen by the wayside after the 1940s. As Mormons joined many other Americans by moving into suburban settings where middle-class values reigned supreme, the city's siren songs sounded less ominous. In the 1940s, the population of Salt Lake County outside of the city boundaries grew from sixty-two to ninety-two thousand. The next decade saw the population of the county (exclusive of the city) double to 194,000. More importantly, as one demographic study of the suburban migration shows, it was "largely parents with young children who [were] leaving the city."[2] Although Boy Scout programs and annual Girls' Camps continued to keep youngsters busy, they were couched in terms less antagonistic to urban life. Rather, the lure of outdoor activities became the adventure that could be added to a lackluster suburban adolescence. Urban problems were far from solved, but the Mormon migration to suburbia made the inner cities seem less of a serious threat to the rising generation than they had been in the early years of the century.

Like the Boy Scouts and Girls' Camps, many of the programs that were started during the Progressive Era remain a part of the church at the beginning of the twenty-first century. Athletic programs (primarily basketball) continue to interest church members worldwide, and obedience to the Word of Wisdom remains linked with athletic excellence. Although not generally in well-organized programs, American missionaries persist in spreading the Gospel by participating in sports with potential converts. The Boy Scout program of the LDS Church provides the foundation for the Scout movement worldwide and continues to offer adolescent Mormon males an opportunity to learn the skills of outdoor survival and personal leadership.

Not all leisure-time programs enacted during the early years of the twentieth century have endured, however. The "new" Deseret Gymnasium that was constructed in the early 1960s—an athletic pillar of central Salt Lake City—was torn down in 1997 to make way for the Conference Center, which hosts semiannual conferences and other church events. No plans have been made for the construction of another church-sponsored gymnasium. Perhaps the most important departure from the foundation of Progressive-Era recreation has been a steady movement away from the overarching recreation ideology of the early twentieth century. Though based on the "scientific" principles of the seven urges of humankind, the comprehensive approach to religious recreation was a dead letter after the Depression. Whether due to a decreasing faith in the social sciences or an orthodox theological turn in the 1930s, the ideological backbone of the recreation programs disintegrated over the years and was never replaced. Following a pattern familiar to early church members, LDS officials considered recreational issues on a case-by-case basis, creating policies as circumstances warranted.

Additionally, the church recreation program was a casualty of the massive commercialization of recreation, sports, and leisure in the decades after World War II. As professional sports franchises came to dominate popular spectator sports and television became ubiquitous, interest in church-sponsored recreational activities waned. Although church sports continue, they no longer have the power to define the community. In Salt Lake City, church league champions can hardly compete with the popularity of the NBA's Utah Jazz.

In the final decades of the twentieth century, a major change occurred in how the church used athletics and recreation to teach young Mormons how to behave properly. While the institutionalized aspects of Mormon recreation diminished, the church enthusiastically celebrated the success of Mormon athletes, not only to prove the benefits of keeping the Word of Wisdom but to provide a connection between Mormons and the sports-mad American society. Athletics provided a mechanism to show real-world examples of Mormons succeeding in the wider society.

The rise of Brigham Young University's football team in the 1970s offers the best case study of the church increasing its visibility through sports. Countless articles chronicled the rise of BYU's football power—from the hiring of the now-legendary coach Lavell Edwards through the succession of quarterbacks from Virgil Carter to Gary Shiede to Jim McMahon to Steve Young to Ty Detmer. Those names are as familiar to many Mormons as the names of their contemporary church leaders. To non-Mormon sports fans, BYU quarterbacks are perhaps the most widely recognized Mormons, short of the Osmond family. Press coverage of BYU sports, and by extension the church, reached a crescendo when BYU was crowned the national football champion in January 1984. Though controversial (many believed that the University of Washington football team deserved the title), the championship galvanized Mormons and provided the church a measure of legitimation from the outside world.[3] When the BYU quarterback Ty Detmer won the 1990 Heisman Trophy (awarded annually to the most outstanding collegiate football player), BYU's rank in the top tier of football programs was ensured.[4]

BYU's rise to athletic prominence did come at a price, however. In 1992, *Sports Illustrated* dubbed the Cougars "the most hated team" in America and claimed that the football team was "loathed for its holier-than-thou attitude as well as for its relentless success." Though not entirely positive coverage, most BYU fans concluded that their new title was a compliment, no matter how backhanded.[5] By the end of the twentieth century, then, the most prominent athletic arm of the church no longer involved individuals playing sports. Instead, by promoting BYU's football team, even reporting football scores during the priesthood session of General Conference, church leaders relied on spectatorship rather than participation to inculcate values and morals through sports.

The last quarter of the twentieth century witnessed the rise of other prominent Mormon athletes on the American sports scene. The baseball slugger Dale Murphy won the National League's Most Valuable Player award in 1982 and 1983; Danny Ainge played for the Boston Celtics, where he was a member of two NBA championship teams; and Steve Young quarterbacked the San Francisco 49ers to to the Super Bowl title in 1994 and was named the game's Most Valuable Player. Countless other Mormons populate professional sports leagues in the United States. Their popularity has increased the visibility of the church, and many of the athletes are committed to spreading the Gospel through their fame.[6] For example, in an effort to teach young members of the church how to be Mormon, Young, Ainge, and Murphy spoke at a church fireside and described the lessons they had learned from their athletic achievements. The Progressive emphasis on participation may have waned, but the church still used sports and recreation to transmit values to the rising generation.

Though widespread participation in sports was no longer valued by the end of the century, the church continued to capitalize on the successes of church athletes beyond BYU's football team. For example, the Olympic gold medal gymnast and Mormon Peter Vidmar was invited to speak in the priesthood session of General Conference in April 1985. Delivered nearly fifty years after the Creed Haymond story linked abstinence and athletic achievement, Vidmar's talk reinforced the connection. He said, "I feel very blessed that at a young age I was taught the importance of keeping the Word of Wisdom. I committed myself to keeping that commandment." Vidmar then described an international meet in Germany, where he had won the vaulting competition. On the victory stand, Vidmar faced a dilemma when he received not only the gold medal, gifts, and flowers but a silver cup of wine, which the champion was to drink and pass to the next athlete. After some hesitation, a German competitor instructed Vidmar to "take a little sip" and hand the cup to the next athlete. Vidmar responded, "No, it's against my religion, and I can't even take a sip."[7] Somewhere, Creed Haymond and

Joseph Cannon must have been smiling. The settings had changed for Mormon athletes over the years, but the lessons remained largely the same.[8]

Though Mormons had long been part of the sports scene in the United States, the church attracted attention from the entire world when Salt Lake City hosted the 2002 Winter Olympic Games. Some commentators and local officials feared that the event would become the "Mormon games," but the church largely remained in the background as the games took center stage in February 2002. Many news organizations reported on the Mormon influence in Salt Lake in positive terms, and the church became just another part of the cultural background of the games rather than a lead story. In large measure, the church gained rave reviews by refusing to capitalize on the attention being showered on Salt Lake City. The church's stance also helped to distance the institution from the bid scandal that dogged the games.

During the Olympic Games, however, the church did not completely fade into the background. In fact, church leaders took the opportunity to teach athletically inspired lessons that would have rung familiar to the Progressive playground theorists a century before. As visitors flooded into Salt Lake City, the church staged an elaborate pageant, "The Light of the World," which used the stories of various Olympic athletes to illustrate the meaning of life and the measure of true achievement in the world. Based around the central character of the Mormon Olympic champion Alma Richards, the play celebrated athletic achievement not as an end in itself but as a means to gain true understanding and find spiritual direction. In the play's climactic scene, Richards has "forgotten who [he is]"—in essence, lost his sense of heritage, his "Mormonness." With pictures of his gold-medal-winning high jump projected above his head, Richards prays for answers from God and finds his peace in winning the gold medal. In case the message was not clear, the narrator told the audience: "The light in Alma Richards and in all of us is not the light of victory alone. It is the light by which we find our path and follow it to the end."[9] Almost a century removed from Alma Richards's medal-winning jump, the story rang as true as ever. Athletic achievement was not the ultimate goal, it was only one avenue to find the truth. Whether it was 1912 or 2002, recreation and athletics remained viable ways for the church to inculcate values and model proper social behavior.

If you listen to quiet conversations in the corners of LDS meetinghouses, older members of the church remember the important role that Mormon recreation activities played in the church communities of their youth. Tales of Gold and Green Balls, music competitions, and basketball often bring a fond smile to their creased faces. Such anecdotal evidence of the impact of

LDS-sponsored recreation abounds within the church today.[10] Other more traditional evidence regarding the success of Mormon recreation programs is difficult to locate. No contemporary sociological studies charted the reasons for church attendance among the young, nor did any intensive studies report the relative importance of recreation as compared to theology, family influence, or spiritual persuasion. If such studies exist, they remain locked in the LDS archives, hidden from the prying eyes of historians.

However, one short evaluation of the YMMIA's recreation program appeared in the sociologist Arthur L. Beeley's *Boys and Girls in Salt Lake City*, a survey of the recreational and leisure-time pursuits of boys and girls in the Mormon capital during the 1920s. After reviewing the efforts of YMMIAs throughout the Salt Lake valley, Beeley and his staff concluded that the program's success was ambiguous. They wrote, "In spite of the remarkable work done by this organization, there are several things which stand in the way of its even greater usefulness." Regarding particular goals, Beeley's group did not evaluate Mormon recreation on its own terms but compared it to the sociological ideal of a program that would meet the most needs of the most members. Nevertheless, the study's conclusions offer meaningful insight into the shortcomings of the program. First, the study located several problems in the area of leisure-time leadership, including a "need for more, well-trained recreation workers on part and full-time bases to augment the non-paid services of the present, exclusively volunteer personnel." Further, the sociological team called for an end to the "socially obsolete ward and stake boundaries which still obtain, and to organize the work and supervise it on a city-wide basis." Finally, another "handicap" of the YMMIA program lay in the fact that each ward and stake furnished their own leaders. The report concluded that "since some wards have an abundance and others a paucity of leaders, there should be free importation and exportation of leadership potential."[11] Though Mormon leaders had labored to create a recreation ideology and to transmit it to local leaders through recreation institutes, they often fell short of the mark, at least according to this group of contemporary sociologists.

The study's most meaningful critique of YMMIA recreation programs stressed the "need to extend the self-governing opportunities in all departments of the work." It appears that church officers often took a heavy-handed approach and did not countenance local translation of recreation programs. As the survey concluded, "The program of activities while rich in quality is nevertheless too rigid to be easily adapted to special circumstances. There is an unnecessary uniformity in such matters as (a) the order of the program, (b) the time of closing, (c) the subjects to be taken up."[12]

Though uniformity and regularity were two of the values at the heart of the recreation program, church administrators may have learned the lessons too well. If local needs had been given wider berth, perhaps a more responsive recreation program would have emerged.

Even Beeley's contemporaneous study, however, yields little useful analysis. Because *Boys and Girls in Salt Lake City* was concerned primarily with the social effects of Mormon recreation, it offered no suggestions about the religious and spiritual impact of recreation within the church. For the most part, the leisure-time programs were designed to influence Mormons within the fold while accruing the secondary benefit of propelling Mormons toward the cultural mainstream of Protestant America. In the end, the effect of the programs remains nestled in the lives of individuals who learned the rules of various games in addition to learning morals, values, and proper social roles. The purpose of LDS play was to make Mormons—a process that takes place in internal realms where measurements prove meaningless.

By studying Mormons at play, however, we learn more than just how Mormons were "made." Though the LDS community might not represent Americans in every particular, their experience is instructive regarding the moral vision of Progressive recreation reformers. The era's play experts had largely come out of the Protestant social gospel tradition and continued to be influenced by Christian morals. Despite the fact that some historians of the Progressive period—most notably, Roy Lubove and Robert H. Wiebe— have argued that reformers abandoned their moral visions when they dove headlong into bureaucratic methods, the Mormon experience refutes this notion. Though smitten with sociological expertise and "scientific" play philosophies, Mormon recreation leaders maintained their moral foundation. Recreation reform represented only one means to accomplish a more morally upright society. In the details, perhaps bureaucracy prevailed. But when the big picture comes into view, the purpose behind Mormon play was not professionalization or bureaucratization but moral regeneration.[13]

Notes

1. "Programs and Policies Newsletter," *Ensign* 1 (Sept. 1971): 76.

2. Paul A. Wright, "The Growth and Distribution of the Mormon and Non-Mormon Populations in Salt Lake City" (Master's thesis, University of Chicago, 1970), 96.

3. Coverage of the 1984 national championship includes Jack McCallum, "Beware of the Candy Men," *Sports Illustrated,* 17 Dec. 1984, 38–46; Gary Smith, "A Season for Spreading the Faith," *Sports Illustrated,* 1985 College and Pro Football Spectacular, 84–101.

4. See Richard Hoffer, "A Ty Vote for the Heisman," *Sports Illustrated,* 10 Dec. 1990, 52–57.

5. Douglas S. Looney, "Clean, Sober, and Insufferable," *Sports Illustrated,* 31 Aug. 1992, 67–70. BYU and the church also received negative coverage in the sporting press regarding the church's prohibition on blacks holding the priesthood. See William F. Reed, "The Other Side of 'The Y,'" *Sports Illustrated,* 26 Jan. 1970, 38–39.

6. For typical examples of the press coverage that Mormon athletes received, consult the following. On Danny Ainge, see Jack McCallum, "Thank Heaven for Danny," *Sports Illustrated,* 20 Apr. 1981, 50–56. On Dale Murphy, see Rick Reilly, "So Good, He's Scary," *Sports Illustrated,* 3 June 1985, 76–88; and Steve Wulf, "Murphy's Law Is Nice Guys Finish First," *Sports Illustrated,* 4 July 1983, 27. Typical of Steve Young coverage is Peter King, "Chief Worry," *Sports Illustrated,* 4 Aug. 1997, 54–57.

7. Peter Vidmar, "Pursuing Excellence," *Ensign* 15 (May 1985): 38.

8. For more on Haymond and Cannon, see chap. 3 in this book.

9. *Light of the World,* soundtrack recording (Intellectual Reserve, 2002).

10. One recent example is Claudia Lauper Bushman, "Growing Up Mormon in the Outland," Sunstone Symposium, 4 Aug. 2000, audiotape available at L. Tom Perry Special Collections, Harold B. Lee Library, Brigham Young University, Provo, Utah. Bushman describes growing up as a Mormon in California during the 1940s and 1950s, when the church was "less dominant but more active."

11. Arthur L. Beeley, *Boys and Girls in Salt Lake City* (Salt Lake City: University of Utah Department of Sociology and Social Technology, 1929), 90.

12. Ibid.

13. See Roy Lubove, *The Professional Altruist: The Emergence of Social Work as a Career* (Cambridge, Mass.: Harvard University Press, 1965); Robert H. Wiebe, *The Search for Order, 1877–1920* (New York: Hill and Wang, 1967). For a further treatment of the "morality" of Progressive play reform, see Don S. Kirschner, "The Perils of Pleasure: Commercial Recreation, Social Disorder, and Moral Reform in the Progressive Era," *American Studies* 22 (Fall 1980): 27–42.

BIBLIOGRAPHY

Primary Sources

Unpublished

Eugene L. Roberts Collection. L. Tom Perry Special Collections, Harold B. Lee Library, Brigham Young University, Provo, Utah.

Fifteenth Ward, Salt Lake Stake. Recreation Committee Minutes, 1925–1928. LDS Church Historical Department, Salt Lake City.

Hinckley, Bryant S. "History of Deseret Gymnasium," 12 January 1938. LDS Church Historical Department, Salt Lake City.

———. Letter to "Brother," 7 February 1912. Deseret Gym Records, LDS Church Historical Department, Salt Lake City.

———. Letter to Friend, undated. LDS Church Historical Department, Salt Lake City.

———. Letter to "Parents of Real Boys," undated. Deseret Gym Records, LDS Church Historical Department, Salt Lake City.

Letter from Parents' Department to Parents, 14 June 1912. Deseret Gym Records, LDS Church Historical Department, Salt Lake City.

Mortensen, H. C. Letter to "Friend," 1940. Deseret Gym Records, LDS Church Historical Department, Salt Lake City.

"The New Recreation Hall in Connection with the Twenty-seventh Ward Chapel," ca. 1927. LDS Church Historical Department, Salt Lake City.

Smith, Hyrum, and Bryant S. Hinckley. Letter to Bishops, undated. LDS Church Historical Department, Salt Lake City.

"Synopsis of Course in Social and Recreational Leadership." LDS Church Historical Department, Salt Lake City.

Unsigned letter, 1912. Deseret Gym Records, LDS Church Historical Department, Salt Lake City.

Untitled poem, 1935. Deseret Gym Records, LDS Church Historical Department, Salt Lake City.

Published

Adams, Samuel Hopkins. *My Business Partner, "Gym."* LDS Church Historical Department, Salt Lake City.

Allen, James X. "Consistency." *Improvement Era* 10 (July 1907): 747.

"Amusements." *New Englander* 26 (July 1867): 399–424.

Anderson, Edward H. "Events and Comments." *Improvement Era* 10 (Feb. 1907): 316.

————. *Y.M.M.I.A. Hand Book: A Guide for Stake and Ward Officers of the Young Men's Mutual Improvement Associations for the Church of Jesus Christ of Latter-day Saints.* 7th ed. Salt Lake City: General Board, 1925.

Anderson, Nephi. "The End of the Rainbow." *Improvement Era* 13 (June 1910): 699.

"Annual Report of M.I.A. Scouts, Year Ending May 31, 1918." *Improvement Era* 21 (July 1918): 833.

Ashton, Wendell J. "Baseball and Mormons in England." *Improvement Era* 38 (Oct. 1935): 645.

"Athletic and Scout Work—Progress of Scout Work." *Improvement Era* 18 (July 1915): 842.

Ballard, Melvin J. "Aaronic Priesthood Correlation and the Y.M.M.I.A." *Improvement Era* 35 (May 1932): 423–24.

Beeley, Arthur L. *Boys and Girls in Salt Lake City.* Salt Lake City: University of Utah Department of Sociology and Social Technology, 1929.

Bennion, Milton. "The Ethics of Church Fairs." *Improvement Era* 10 (Oct. 1907): 959.

————. "To the Young Men on the Farm." *Improvement Era* 12 (Mar. 1909): 371.

Blunck, Rulon, and John T. Cardall. "Mormon Missionaries in the Meissen Cast." *Improvement Era* 40 (Sept. 1937): 572.

Boynton, P. D. "Athletics and Collateral Activities in Secondary Schools." *Proceedings of National Education Association* (1904): 213–14.

Brandley, Elsie T. "Pioneers in Many Ways." *Improvement Era* 35 (Sept. 1932): 643.

Brimhall, George H. "Continuity in Character." *Improvement Era* 2 (Oct. 1899): 929.

"Broadcasting from the M.I.A. Conference." *Improvement Era* 35 (July 1932): 529.

Brooks, Juanita. "Whose Business Is Recreation? The Profit-takers' or the Homemakers'?" *Improvement Era* 41 (Oct. 1938): 596.

Camp Saratoga: Deseret Gymnasium Boys' Camp. Pamphlet, 1912. Deseret Gym Records, LDS Church Historical Department, Salt Lake City.

Cannon, A. S. "Social Planning—And a Public Employment Service." *Improvement Era* 37 (Sept. 1934): 538.

Cannon, Joseph J. "Speed and the Spirit." *Improvement Era* 31 (Oct. 1928): 1005.

Cannon, Lewis Telle. "Increasing Enrollment and Interest in the Mutuals." *Improvement Era* 16 (Oct. 1913): 1223.

Cheney, Rulon H. "Chapel in Ocean Park Dedicated." *Improvement Era* 26 (Nov. 1922): 46.

A College Senior. "Five Memories I'd Like to Have." *Improvement Era* 30 (Dec. 1926): 145.

Cornwall, Claude C. "Crime Prevention Is Better Than Cure." *Improvement Era* 37 (May 1934): 267.

Cowan, Melvyn M. "Missionary 'Attention Getters': Basketball in Germany." *Improvement Era* 39 (Sept. 1936): 571–73.

Cowley, M. F. "Counsel to Boys Engaged in Isolated Labor." *Improvement Era* 7 (Mar. 1904): 364.

Dale, Ludvig. "What Boy Scouts Must Know and Be." *Improvement Era* 18 (Aug. 1915): 922.

"Dancing." *Improvement Era* 40 (Nov. 1937): 705.

Dancing for Middle Aged Women. Pamphlet, n.d. Deseret Gym Records, LDS Church Historical Department, Salt Lake City.

Deseret Gym Digest: Promoted in the Interest of Health, Happiness, and Humor 1 (26 Apr. 1950). Deseret Gym Records, LDS Church Historical Department, Salt Lake City.

The Deseret Gymlet 1 (17 Apr. 1912): 1.

"The Deseret Gymnasium." *Improvement Era* 13 (Sept. 1910): 1048.

Deseret Gymnasium Season 1912–1913. Pamphlet, n.d. Deseret Gym Records, LDS Church Historical Department, Salt Lake City.

Dividends. Pamphlet, n.d. Deseret Gym Records, LDS Church Historical Department, Salt Lake City.

Done, Willard. "Our Work—Preliminary Programs." *Improvement Era* 7 (Mar. 1904): 390.

Driggs, Howard R. "The Library-Gymnasium Movement: Elements of Success in the Work." *Improvement Era* 13 (Mar. 1910): 441–45.

———. "The Utah Library-Gymnasium Movement." *Improvement Era* 12 (May 1909): 510–16.

"Editor's Table—Amusements." *Improvement Era* 14 (May 1911): 638–39.

"Editor's Table—Boy Scouts." *Improvement Era* 17 (Mar. 1914): 385.

"Editor's Table—Dress and Social Practices." *Improvement Era* 20 (Dec. 1916): 172.

"Editor's Table—Hints to the Editors." *Improvement Era* 14 (Sept. 1911): 1038.

"Editor's Table—Maori Agricultural College Team Again Champions." *Improvement Era* 21 (June 1918): 740.

"Editor's Table—On Who Can Entertain." *Improvement Era* 18 (June 1915): 736.

"Editor's Table—Physical Exercise and the M.I.A." *Improvement Era* 11 (Feb. 1908): 305.

"Editor's Table—President Heber J. Grant's Conference Message." *Improvement Era* 29 (May 1926): 679.

"Editor's Table—Seventy-third Annual Conference of the Church." *Improvement Era* 6 (May 1903): 545.

"Editor's Table—The June M.I.A. Conference." *Improvement Era* 26 (July 1923): 843.

"Editor's Table—The Spirit of Religion." *Improvement Era* 6 (Oct. 1903): 945.

"Editor's Table—Worship in the Home." *Improvement Era* 7 (Dec. 1903).

"The Effect of Tobacco on the Boy." *Improvement Era* 21 (Nov. 1917): 11.

"Encouragement for 'Busy' Men." *Improvement Era* 1 (June 1898): 621.

Ericksen, E. E. *Memories and Reflections: The Autobiography of E. E. Ericksen.* Ed. Scott G. Kenney. Salt Lake City: Signature Books, 1987.

"Events of the Month." *Improvement Era* 7 (Jan. 1904): 233.

"Events of the Month." *Improvement Era* 7 (June 1904): 634–35.

Farnsworth, Philo T. "The Boy, His Nature, and His Needs." *Improvement Era* 37 (Mar. 1934): 180.

———. "The Boy, His Nature, and His Needs." *Improvement Era* 37 (Nov. 1934): 693.

———. "The Boy, His Nature, and His Needs." *Improvement Era* 38 (Mar. 1935): 178.

———. "The Boy, His Nature, and His Needs." *Improvement Era* 38 (May 1935): 325.

———. "The Boy, His Nature, and His Needs." *Improvement Era* 38 (Nov. 1935): 705.

Fathers and Sons Annual Outing, Summer of 1925. Pamphlet. Salt Lake City: General Board of YMMIA, 1925.

Fathers and Sons Annual Outing, Summer of 1927. Pamphlet. Salt Lake City: General Board of YMMIA, 1927.

"Fathers and Sons' Outings." *Improvement Era* 26 (Oct. 1923): 1142–48.

"Fathers and Sons' Outings, and other Y.M.M.I.A. Activities." *Improvement Era* 25 (Oct. 1922): 1052–60.

Faust, James E. "The Enemy Within." *Ensign* 30 (Nov. 2000): 44–46.

"Field Notes." *Improvement Era* 35 (Nov. 1931): 42.

"First International Recreation Congress Program." *Recreation* 26 (July 1932): 188–89.

Frost, Grace Ingles. "Beyond the City." *Improvement Era* 9 (Sept. 1906): 881.

Gates, Franklin Y. "A Missionary Goodwill Quartet." *Improvement Era* 40 (July 1937): 403.

Gates, Susa Young. *Life Story of Brigham Young.* New York: Macmillan, 1930.

———, ed. "A Mother's Letters to Her Missionary Son: II—Letter Posted to Chicago." *Improvement Era* 8 (Mar. 1905): 352–57.

Geertsen, Norman. "To Be a Scout." *Improvement Era* 32 (May 1929): 598.

The Girls' Camp in Logan Canyon. Pamphlet, n.d. LDS Church Historical Department, Salt Lake City.

"Good Team; Noble Work." *Improvement Era* 27 (May 1924): 695–96.

Grant, Carter E. "Double Victory." *Improvement Era* 31 (Aug. 1931): 874–76.

Grant, Heber J. "The Place of the Y.M.M.I.A. in the Church." *Improvement Era* 15 (Aug. 1912): 873, 875–76.
———. "The President on Church Security." *Improvement Era* 40 (Mar. 1937): 131.
———. "Testimony—The Little White Slaver." *Improvement Era* 18 (Aug. 1915): 912–13.
———. "To Those Who Teach Our Children." *Improvement Era* 42 (Mar. 1939): 135.
Hamilton, Samuel. "The Physical Square Deal and the Cigarette Habit among Boys." *Improvement Era* 16 (June 1913): 817.
Handball, a Game for Men: A Lively Pastime Full of Brief Breezy Bits for Busy Business Men. Pamphlet, n.d. Deseret Gym Records, LDS Church Historical Department, Salt Lake City.
Handbook of the YLMIA and the YMMIA. Salt Lake City: General Boards of MIA, 1931.
Harris, Franklin S. "Changes in Occupation." *Improvement Era* 27 (Mar. 1924): 428.
"Health Value Explained by Gymnasium Head." Unattributed newspaper clipping, Deseret Gym Records, LDS Church Historical Department, Salt Lake City.
Heath, Sasie. "Brighton Home." *Young Woman's Journal* 34 (June 1923): 377–78.
Hewlett, Frank J. "What of the Boy in Summer Time?" *Improvement Era* 11 (May 1908): 534.
Hines, Carol T. *Camp Atoka: A History, 1912–1980.* Reno, Nev.: By the author, 1987.
Hoffer, Richard. "A Ty Vote for the Heisman." *Sports Illustrated,* 10 Dec. 1990, 52–57.
Hollingshead, Billie. "On the Book Rack." *Improvement Era* 41 (Jan. 1938): 35.
Howell, O. E. "Play with Them." *Improvement Era* 28 (May 1925): 668.
Hull, Thomas. "Events of the Month." *Improvement Era* 6 (May 1903): 558.
———. "Study Period and Activities." *Improvement Era* 25 (Aug. 1922): 920.
Hulme, Claire N. "Is Camping Worth While for Y.L.M.I.A.?" *Young Woman's Journal* 35 (June 1924): 313–14.
An Ideal Summer Course for Boys: He Goes Home Clean and Contented. Pamphlet, n.d. Deseret Gym Records, LDS Church Historical Department, Salt Lake City.
"Improvement in Aaronic Priesthood Work." *Improvement Era* 36 (Sept. 1933): 688.
Josephson, Marba C. "On the Book Rack." *Improvement Era* 41 (Nov. 1938): 678.
Journal of Discourses. 26 vols. Liverpool, England: Latter-day Saints Book Depot, 1854–86.
Kimball, Edward P. "Character of Music Programs for Joint M.I.A. Meetings." *Improvement Era* 25 (Jan. 1922): 274–75.
King, Peter. "Chief Worry." *Sports Illustrated,* 4 Aug. 1997, 54–57.
Kirkham, Oscar A. Frontispiece. *Improvement Era* 26 (Apr. 1923).
———. "Mutual Work—Athletics and Scout Work." *Improvement Era* 19 (Feb. 1916): 375.

———. "Mutual Work—What Can Be Done with the Boys, Brethren?" *Improvement Era* 17 (Mar. 1914): 489.

Kleinman, Bertha A. "In My Play." *Improvement Era* 30 (Apr. 1927): 531.

Larson, Gustive O. "Mormon Missionaries on Sweden's National Television." *Improvement Era* 42 (Feb. 1939): 90.

Lemon, Melvin. "How Hyrum Second Ward Built Its Recreation Hall." *Improvement Era* 28 (Aug. 1925): 976.

"Liberty Glen Camp." *Young Woman's Journal* 24 (Jan. 1913): 31.

"Lights and Shadows on the Silver Screen." *Improvement Era* 35 (Apr. 1932): 350.

The Log of the Vanguard Trail. Salt Lake City: Mutual Improvement Associations, 1931.

Looney, Douglas S. "Clean, Sober, and Insufferable." *Sports Illustrated,* 31 Aug. 1992, 67–70.

Lyman, Francis M. "Manhood." *Improvement Era* 7 (Jan. 1904): 175–78.

Lyman, Richard R. "A Man among Men." *Improvement Era* 30 (Aug. 1927): 872.

———. "Reclamation." *Improvement Era* 27 (Apr. 1924): 505.

Markham, Ira J. "Building Boys to Latter-day Standards." *Improvement Era* 42 (Oct. 1939): 618.

Martineau, L. R. "M.I.A. Scouts." *Improvement Era* (Mar. 1912): 357–61.

———. "Second Annual M.I.A. Field Day." *Improvement Era* 15 (July 1912): 859–60.

———. "Some Problems in Athletics." *Improvement Era* 15 (Oct. 1912): 1137.

McCallum, Jack. "Beware of the Candy Men." *Sports Illustrated,* 17 Dec. 1984, 38–46.

———. "Thank Heaven for Danny." *Sports Illustrated,* 20 Apr. 1981, 50–56.

McJackson, Jane. "The M.I.A." *Improvement Era* 24 (Mar. 1921): 406.

McKay, David O. "A Message to the Youth of the Land." *Improvement Era* 24 (Jan. 1921): 191.

Medical Gymnastics and Scientific Massage. Deseret Gym Records, LDS Church Historical Department, Salt Lake City.

Merrill, Amy Lyman. "M.I.A. Home in Logan Canyon." *Young Woman's Journal* 33 (May 1922): 292–93.

Merrill, Harrison R. "Playing the Great Collegiate Game Football." *Improvement Era* 34 (Jan. 1931): 147.

———. "Speck's Faith." *Improvement Era* 19 (Feb. 1916): 345–49.

———. "Utah Athletes Coming to Their Own." *Improvement Era* 31 (Aug. 1928): 820–25.

———. "We Stand for the Enrichment of Life." *Improvement Era* 35 (Oct. 1932): 707.

Merrill, Joseph F. "The Problem of Unemployment." *Improvement Era* 42 (Dec. 1939): 716.

Merrill, Lewis A. "Choosing an Occupation." *Improvement Era* 5 (Jan. 1902): 212.

"Messages from the Missions—Playing Ball." *Improvement Era* 27 (Mar. 1924): 457.

M.I.A. Handbook. Salt Lake City: General Boards of the MIA, 1928.

M.I.A. Recreation Bulletin No. 5. Salt Lake City: General Boards of the MIA, 1925.

Milne, E. J. "Ward and Gymnasium Hall." *Improvement Era* 12 (Dec. 1908): 162–63.

M-Men Guide: Course of Study and M-Men Gleaner Program for 1931–1932. Salt Lake City: General Board of the YMMIA, 1931.

"M-Men in C.C.C. Camps." *Improvement Era* 38 (Feb. 1935): 113.

Moody, Manton. "Means of Success in Promoting Attendance of the Aaronic Priesthood." *Improvement Era* 35 (Mar. 1932): 301.

"'Mormon' Standards Approved." *Improvement Era* 30 (Apr. 1927): 564–65.

Morris, George Q. "Thirty-five Years of Scouting in the Church." *Improvement Era* 51 (May 1948): 275.

Morris, Nephi L. "Ab Jenkins—Superman of Speed and Endurance." *Improvement Era* 39 (Mar. 1936): 140.

"The Mutual Improvement League." *Contributor* 11 (Sept. 1896): 691–92.

"Mutual Messages." *Improvement Era* 35 (Jan. 1932): 170.

"Mutual Messages." *Improvement Era* 36 (Nov. 1932): 47–48.

"Mutual Work." *Improvement Era* 14 (July 1911): 844.

"Mutual Work—A Day for Recreation." *Improvement Era* 14 (Dec. 1910): 183.

"Mutual Work—Alpine Stake Athletic Contest." *Improvement Era* 13 (Aug. 1910): 952–53.

"Mutual Work—A 'Mormon' School in Hawaii." *Improvement Era* 28 (Sept. 1925): 1101.

"Mutual Work—An Analysis of the General Statistical Report of the Young Men's Mutual Improvement Association for the Year Ending March 31, 1921." *Improvement Era* 24 (Aug. 1921): 946–47.

"Mutual Work—Annual Conference." *Improvement Era* 13 (July 1910): 858.

"Mutual Work—Appreciation for the M.I.A. Handbook." *Improvement Era* 29 (Oct. 1926): 1199.

"Mutual Work—Athletics and Scout Work." *Improvement Era* 19 (July 1916): 849–50.

"Mutual Work—Basket Ball." *Improvement Era* 7 (May 1908): 562–63.

"Mutual Work—Basketball Leads in M-Men Activities." *Improvement Era* 29 (May 1926): 621.

"Mutual Work—Basket Ball League." *Improvement Era* 24 (Apr. 1921): 662.

"Mutual Work—Boy Scouts—Organization and Purpose." *Improvement Era* 17 (Aug. 1914): 894.

"Mutual Work—Cardston High School Basket Ball Team." *Improvement Era* 28 (June 1925): 793.

"Mutual Work—Class in Athletics." *Improvement Era* 16 (Dec. 1912): 177.

"Mutual Work—Curlew Stake Champions." *Improvement Era* 29 (July 1926): 901.

"Mutual Work—Dr. Taylor's Report of Scouting, 1922." *Improvement Era* 26 (Feb. 1923): 393.

"Mutual Work—Father and Son's Outing." *Improvement Era* 22 (Apr. 1919): 549.

"Mutual Work—Fathers and Son's Outings." *Improvement Era* 26 (Sept. 1923): 1067.

"Mutual Work—February Class in Athletics." *Improvement Era* 16 (Feb. 1913): 392.

"Mutual Work—General M.I.A. Conference." *Improvement Era* 14 (Aug. 1911): 943.

"Mutual Work—Juarez M.I.A. in Championship Contest." *Improvement Era* 13 (June 1910): 762–63.

"Mutual Work—Leadership Schools for Recreation." *Improvement Era* 27 (Feb. 1924): 389.

"Mutual Work—Member of American Olympic Swimming Team." *Improvement Era* 27 (Aug. 1924): 1011.

"Mutual Work—M.I.A. Meetings and Theatrical Shows." *Improvement Era* 11 (Jan. 1908): 229–30.

"Mutual Work—M.I.A. Reading Room and Gymnasium in Logan." *Improvement Era* 13 (Mar. 1910): 469–70.

"Mutual Work—M.I.A. Scouts." *Improvement Era* 15 (Jan. 1912): 287.

"Mutual Work—M.I.A. Scouts." *Improvement Era* 15 (June 1912): 755.

"Mutual Work—M.I.A. Track Meet." *Improvement Era* 13 (July 1910): 851–54.

"Mutual Work—Of Interest to Scouts." *Improvement Era* 17 (Aug. 1914): 996.

"Mutual Work—Preaching the Gospel of Better Recreation." *Improvement Era* 27 (May 1924): 696.

"Mutual Work—Recreation Leadership Institutes." *Improvement Era* 28 (May 1925): 703.

"Mutual Work—Resolutions Respecting Weekly Half-Holiday." *Improvement Era* 15 (Aug. 1912): 860–61.

"Mutual Work—Saloon Becomes Gymnasium." *Improvement Era* 9 (Apr. 1916): 568.

"Mutual Work—Scout Work on Sunday Night." *Improvement Era* 17 (Aug. 1914): 894.

"Mutual Work—Suggestive Outlines for Y.M.M.I.A. Freshmen Class for December." *Improvement Era* 17 (Dec. 1913): 183.

"Mutual Work—The Daynes Trophy." *Improvement Era* 14 (July 1911): 848.

"Mutual Work—The Deseret Gymnasium." *Improvement Era* 13 (Feb. 1910): 381.

"Mutual Work—The Genuine Sport Spirit." *Improvement Era* 26 (May 1923): 668.

"Mutual Work—The New Traveling Secretary." *Improvement Era* 16 (June 1913): 833.

"Mutual Work—The Policy of the Y.M.M.I.A." *Improvement Era* 12 (Jan. 1909): 247.

"Mutual Work—The Scouts and the Y.M.M.I.A." *Improvement Era* 26 (Mar. 1923): 484.

"Mutual Work—The Third Y.M.M.I.A. Normal Training Class." *Improvement Era* 16 (Feb. 1913): 393.

"Mutual Work—The Tokyo-American Baseball Team." *Improvement Era* 15 (May 1912): 663–64.

"Mutual Work—Winning Ball Teams, Box Elder Stake." *Improvement Era* 25 (Dec. 1921): 178.

Nash, Jay B. "What Will You Do with Your Leisure Time?" *Improvement Era* 36 (Feb. 1933): 197.

Nelson, Lowry. "The University a Workshop for Leaders." *Improvement Era* 26 (Mar. 1923): 450.

Nibley, Preston. "The Pilgrim Fathers and the Mormon Pioneers." *Improvement Era* 15 (July 1912): 774.

"1935 Summer Activities Deseret Gym and Lion House." Deseret Gym Records, LDS Church Historical Department, Salt Lake City.

Nordgren, Weston N. "Boy Scouts in Camp." *Improvement Era* 35 (Nov. 1931): 20.

———. "Capitalizing on the Urge to Do Something." *Improvement Era* 38 (Feb. 1935): 91.

"Notes." *Improvement Era* 1 (Sept. 1898): 853.

"On Smoking." *Improvement Era* 16 (Nov. 1912): 90.

"Our Work—Amusements and Entertainments." *Improvement Era* 7 (Dec. 1903): 146–47.

"Our Work—Eleventh Annual M.I.A. Conference." *Improvement Era* 9 (July 1906): 738.

"Our Work—General M.I.A. Conference." *Improvement Era* 10 (July 1907): 760–61.

"Our Work—Obstacles." *Improvement Era* 9 (Nov. 1905): 72–73.

"Our Work—Seventh Annual Conference of Mutual Improvement Associations." *Improvement Era* 5 (July 1902): 727.

"Our Work—The Annual Conference of the Mutual Improvement Associations." *Improvement Era* 4 (Aug. 1901): 790–91.

"Our Work—The Annual Conference of the Young Men's and Young Ladies' Mutual Improvement Associations." *Improvement Era* 2 (Aug. 1899): 711.

"Our Work—To Stake and Ward Officers of the Y.M.M.I.A." *Improvement Era* 9 (Oct. 1906): 979.

"Over the Pioneer Trail." *Improvement Era* 15 (Sept. 1912): 1033.

Pack, Frederick J. "How the Impending Tobacco Crusade Can Be Avoided." *Improvement Era* 24 (Jan. 1921): 223.

Palmer, Annie D. "The Call of the Canyon." *Improvement Era* 18 (May 1915): 661.

Parents' Bulletin No. 1: Recreation and Play. Salt Lake City: Deseret Sunday School Union, 1914.

"Park Your Worries at the Deseret Gym." Advertisement, n.d. Deseret Gym Records, LDS Church Historical Department, Salt Lake City.

Parry, Edwin F. "On Choosing Life Models." *Improvement Era* 5 (Jan. 1902): 173.

"Passing Events." *Improvement Era* 18 (Mar. 1915): 468.

"Passing Events." *Improvement Era* 26 (Apr. 1923): 585.

"Passing Events." *Improvement Era* 27 (May 1924): 707.

"Passing Events." *Improvement Era* 28 (Apr. 1925): 616.

"Passing Events." *Improvement Era* 30 (Mar. 1927): 485.

"Passing Events—No Hiking on the Sabbath Day." *Improvement Era* 19 (Mar. 1916): 478.

Perry, L. Tom. "Run and Not Be Weary." *Ensign* 26 (Nov. 1996): 37–38.

Peterson, Elmer G. "Utah Invites the Nation: A National Summer School at Logan." *Improvement Era* 27 (Mar. 1924): 445.

"Play Leaders Witness M.I.A. Recreation." *Improvement Era* 41 (June 1938): 372.

"Programs and Policies Newsletter." *Ensign* 1 (Sept. 1971): 76.

"Raising Funds by Recreation." *Improvement Era* 23 (Sept. 1920): 1036.

"Recreation Halls." *Improvement Era* 27 (Apr. 1924): 576.

Reed, William F. "The Other Side of 'The Y.'" *Sports Illustrated,* 26 Jan. 1970, 38–39.

Reilly, Rick. "So Good, He's Scary." *Sports Illustrated,* 3 June 1985, 76–88.

"Religious, Spiritual, and Moral Phases of Scouting to Be Emphasized." *Improvement Era* 39 (Feb. 1936): 114.

Ricks, Elden. "The Deseret Club Movement." *Improvement Era* 41 (Sept. 1938): 540.

Riis, Jacob A. "The Boy Scouts." *Improvement Era* 17 (July 1914): 871.

Roberts, B. H. "Physical Development." *Improvement Era* 15 (Aug. 1912): 920.

———. "Sphere of Y.M.M.I.A. Activities." *Improvement Era* 16 (Jan. 1913): 191, 193.

Roberts, B. H., George H. Brimhall, and Benjamin Goddard. "The Boy Scout Movement in Utah." *Improvement Era* 14 (Apr. 1911): 542.

Roberts, Eugene L. "The Boy Pioneers of Utah." *Improvement Era* 14 (Oct. 1911): 1084–86.

———. "The New Leisure." *Improvement Era* 36 (Feb. 1933): 204.

Robinson, W. O. *The Church and Recreation: A Resumé of the LDS Recreation Program as Directed by the Mutual Improvement Association.* N.p., n.d.

Rockne, Knute. "A Good Word for Utah Athletes." *Improvement Era* 31 (Dec. 1927): 173.

Romney, G. Ott. "A Habit Worth Acquiring." *Improvement Era* 35 (Nov. 1931): 14.

"Scout Cheers or Yells." *Improvement Era* 17 (Dec. 1913): 186.

"Scouts." *Improvement Era* 40 (Apr. 1937): 251.

Smith, Gary. "A Season for Spreading the Faith." *Sports Illustrated,* 1985 College and Pro Football Spectacular, 84–101.

Smith, Joseph F. "Editor's Table—Social Doings." *Improvement Era* 20 (Jan. 1917): 259.

———. "Editor's Table—True Love." *Improvement Era* 14 (July 1911): 829.

Snow, LeRoi C. "Pioneer Celebrations." *Improvement Era* 25 (Sept. 1922): 1020.

Social Advisory Committee Newsletter 3 (12 July 1920).

Statistical Abstract of Utah, 1996 Centennial Edition. Salt Lake City: Bureau of Economics and Business Research, David Eccles School of Business, University of Utah, 1996.

Stephens, Evan. "The Farmer Boy." *Improvement Era* 21 (Jan. 1918): 250–51.

Stevens, Robert S. "Broadcasting with the Millennial Chorus." *Improvement Era* 40 (Feb. 1937): 92–93.

"Suggestions for the Summer Program." *Improvement Era* 35 (June 1932): 494.

Summer Days and Nights in Salt Lake City, Utah: Where and How to Spend Them. Pamphlet, n.d. Deseret Gym Records, LDS Church Historical Department, Salt Lake City.

"Sunday Evening Joint Sessions for November." *Improvement Era* 35 (Oct. 1932): 745–46.

"Talks to the Young Men: I. Industry—Its Bearing on Success." *Improvement Era* 6 (Nov. 1902): 55.

"Talks to the Young Men: V. The Same Is Damned." *Improvement Era* 7 (Mar. 1904): 367.

"Talks to the Young Men: VIII. A Trade." *Improvement Era* 6 (June 1903): 603–4.

"Talks to the Young Men—The Tendency to Deify Evil." *Improvement Era* 2 (Oct. 1899): 944–46.

Taylor, Aaron C. "Mutual Work—M.I.A. Scout Work in Hamburg, Germany." *Improvement Era* 30 (Feb. 1927): 381.

Taylor, John H. "For the Consideration of Parents." *Improvement Era* 19 (Jan. 1916): 239–40.

"Teacher-Training and Social Work." *Improvement Era* 23 (June 1920): 746.

"Timely Thoughts from the June Conference." *Improvement Era* 26 (Aug. 1923): 925.

Todd, Douglas M. "Our Work—The Annual Conference of the Mutual Improvement Associations." *Improvement Era* 3 (Aug. 1900): 714.

"To Our President." *Young Woman's Journal* 24 (Jan. 1913): 34.

Vacation School, Young Men's Christian Association. Pamphlet. Salt Lake City: LDS Church Historical Department, 1914.

A Vacation with Pleasure and Profit: The Deseret Gymnasium Summer School. Pamphlet. Salt Lake City: LDS Church Historical Department, 1922.

Vidmar, Peter. "Pursuing Excellence." *Ensign* 15 (May 1985): 38.

Vorkink, J. Paul, and Joseph P. Lambert. "Our Friend-making Missionaries in the Netherlands." *Improvement Era* 41 (July 1938): 412.

"Warning to Church Members." *Improvement Era* 39 (Aug. 1936): 488.

What the Gymnasium Means to Women and Girls. Pamphlet. Deseret Gym Records. Salt Lake City: LDS Church Historical Department, n.d.

Widtsoe, John A. "Waste." *Improvement Era* 41 (Nov. 1938): 672–73.

Wilson, Robert E. "A Hike to the Yellowstone." *Improvement Era* 18 (June 1915): 706.

The Wise—For Health on Exercise Depend. Pamphlet. Salt Lake City: Deseret Gym, 1911.

Wood, Merrill. "Enrichment of Life through Constructive Use of Leisure." *Improvement Era* 37 (May 1934): 281.

Woolley, Ivy Houtz. "The Boy Scouts." *Improvement Era* 27 (Feb. 1924): 380.

"Would Not Be in the Majors Today If I Had Continued to Use Tobacco." *Improvement Era* 38 (Nov. 1935): 700.

Wulf, Steve. "Murphy's Law Is Nice Guys Finish First." *Sports Illustrated*, 4 July 1983, 27.

Wyland, Ray O. "Youth—And the Needs of the World." *Improvement Era* 39 (Dec. 1936): 750–53.

"Y.L.M.I.A. Summer Homes." *Young Woman's Journal* 35 (June 1924): 310–11.

"Y.M.M.I.A. Champions." *Improvement Era* 27 (Aug. 1924): 1004.

Young, Levi Edgar. "Sociological Aspects of Mormonism." *Improvement Era* 23 (July 1920): 828–29.

Secondary Sources

Addams, Jane. *The Spirit of Youth and the City Streets.* New York: Macmillan, 1926. Reprint, Urbana: University of Illinois Press, 2001.

———. *Twenty Years at Hull-House.* New York: Macmillan, 1910. Reprint, Urbana: University of Illinois Press, 1990.

Alexander, Thomas G. "Between Revivalism and the Social Gospel: The Latter-day Saint Social Advisory Committee, 1916–1922." *BYU Studies* 23 (Winter 1983): 19–39.

———. "From Dearth to Deluge: Utah's Coal Industry." *Utah Historical Quarterly* 31 (Summer 1963): 235–47.

———. *Mormonism in Transition: A History of the Latter-day Saints, 1890–1930.* Urbana: University of Illinois Press, 1986.

———. *Things in Heaven and Earth: The Life and Times of Wilford Woodruff.* Salt Lake City: Signature Press, 1992.

Alexander, Thomas G., and James B. Allen. *Mormons and Gentiles: A History of Salt Lake City.* Boulder, Colo.: Pruett Publishing, 1984.

Allen, James B. *The Man—Brigham Young.* Provo, Utah: Brigham Young University Press, 1968.

Allen, James B., and Glen M. Leonard. *The Story of the Latter-day Saints.* 2d ed. Salt Lake City: Deseret Book, 1992.

Allen, James, and Richard Cowan. *Mormonism in the Twentieth Century.* 2d ed. Provo, Utah: Brigham Young University Press, 1967.

Allen, James B., Ronald K. Esplin, and David J. Whittaker. *Men with a Mission: The Quorum of the Twelve in Great Britain, 1837–1841.* Salt Lake City: Deseret Book, 1992.

Andrus, Hyrum L., and Helen Mae Andrus. *They Knew the Prophet*. Salt Lake City: Bookcraft, 1974.

Andrus, Ruth. "A History of the Recreation Program of the Church of Jesus Christ of Latter-day Saints." Ph.D. dissertation, University of Iowa, 1962.

Arrington, Chris Rigby. "The Finest of Fabrics: Mormon Women and the Silk Industry in Early Utah." *Utah Historical Quarterly* 46 (Fall 1978): 376–96.

Arrington, Leonard J. *The Changing Economic Structure of the Mountain West*. Logan: Utah State University Press, 1963.

——. *Great Basin Kingdom: An Economic History of the Latter-day Saints, 1830–1900*. Cambridge, Mass.: Harvard University Press, 1958. Reprint, Salt Lake City: University of Utah Press, 1993.

——. *Utah, the New Deal, and the Depression of the 1930s*. Ogden, Utah: Weber State College Press, 1983.

——, ed. *The Presidents of the Church*. Salt Lake City: Deseret Book, 1986.

Arrington, Leonard J., and Davis Bitton. *The Mormon Experience: A History of the Latter-day Saints*. New York: Alfred A. Knopf, 1979. Reprint, Urbana: University of Illinois Press, 1992.

Arrington, Leonard J., and Thomas G. Alexander. *A Dependent Commonwealth: Utah's Economy from Statehood to the Great Depression*. Provo, Utah: Brigham Young University Press, 1974.

Bachman, Danel W. "A Study of the Mormon Practice of Plural Marriage before the Death of Joseph Smith." Master's thesis, Purdue University, 1975.

Banner, Lois W. *American Beauty*. New York: Alfred A. Knopf, 1983.

Barker-Benfield, G. J. *The Horrors of the Half-Known Life*. New York: Harper and Row, 1976.

Barth, Gunther. *City People: The Rise of Modern City Culture in Nineteenth-Century America*. New York: Oxford University Press, 1980.

Barton, Bruce. *The Man Nobody Knows: A Discovery of the Real Jesus*. Indianapolis: Bobbs-Merrill, 1925.

Beal, Owen Franklin. *The Labor Legislation of Utah: With Special Reference to the Period of Statehood*. Logan, Utah: N.p., 1922.

Beecher, Maureen Ursenbach. "The 'Leading Sisters': A Female Hierarchy in Nineteenth-Century Mormon Society." *Journal of Mormon History* 9 (1982): 25–39.

Beecher, Maureen Ursenbach, and Lavina Fielding Anderson, eds. *Sisters in Spirit: Mormon Women in Historical and Cultural Perspective*. Urbana: University of Illinois Press, 1987.

Bennett, Richard E. *Mormons at the Missouri, 1846–1852: "And Should We Die . . ."* Norman: University of Oklahoma Press, 1987.

Best, Richard Strong. *History of Troop 1, Boy Scouts of America, Salt Lake City, Utah, Waterloo Ward, LDS Church, 1910–1916*. Farr West, Utah: By the author, 1984.

Bird, Glenn V. "The Industrial Workers of the World in Utah: Origins, Activities,

and Reactions of the Church of Jesus Christ of Latter-day Saints." Master's thesis, Brigham Young University, 1976.

Bitton, Davis. "These Licentious Days: Dancing among the Mormons." *Sunstone* 2
(Spring 1977): 16–27.

Black, William T. *Mormon Athletes.* Salt Lake City: Deseret Book, 1980.

Bluth, John F., and Wayne K. Hinton. "The Great Depression." In *Utah's History.*
Ed. Richard D. Poll et al. Provo, Utah: Brigham Young University Press, 1978.
481–96.

Boyer, Paul S. *Urban Masses and Moral Order in America, 1820–1920.* Cambridge,
Mass.: Harvard University Press, 1978.

Bradley, Martha Elizabeth [Sonntag], and Lowell M. Durham Jr. "John Hafen and
the Art Missionaries." *Journal of Mormon History* 12 (1985): 91–105.

Bradley, Martha Sonntag. "'The Church and Colonel Saunders': Mormon Standard
Plan Architecture." Master's thesis, Brigham Young University, 1981.

Brinley, Douglas E. "Recreation in the Mormon Church." *Recreation* 38 (July 1944):
195–98.

Buenker, John D. *Urban Liberalism and Progressive Reform.* New York: Charles
Scribner's Sons, 1973.

Bushman, Claudia Lauper. "Growing Up Mormon in the Outland." Oral presentation, Sunstone Symposium, 4 August 2000. (Audiotape available at the L. Tom Perry
Special Collections, Harold B. Lee Library, Brigham Young University, Provo, Utah.)

Cahn, Susan K. *Coming On Strong: Gender and Sexuality in Twentieth-Century
Women's Sport.* New York: Free Press, 1994. Reprint, Cambridge, Mass.: Harvard
University Press, 1995.

Cannon, Kenneth L., II. "Deserets, Red Stockings, and Out-of-Towners: Baseball
Comes of Age in Salt Lake City, 1877–79." *Utah Historical Quarterly* 52 (Spring
1984): 136–57.

Cavallo, Dominick. *Muscles and Morals: Organized Playgrounds and Urban Reform,
1880–1920.* Philadelphia: University of Pennsylvania Press, 1981.

Chandler, Lester V. *America's Greatest Depression, 1929–1941.* New York: Harper
and Row, 1970.

Cohen, Lizabeth. *Making a New Deal: Industrial Workers in Chicago, 1919–1939.*
New York: Cambridge University Press, 1990.

Cowley, Matthias F. *Wilford Woodruff.* Salt Lake City: Deseret News, 1909.

Daniels, Bruce C. *Puritans at Play: Leisure and Recreation in Colonial New England.*
New York: St. Martin's Press, 1995.

Davis, Allen F. *Spearheads for Reform: The Social Settlements and the Progressive
Movement, 1890–1914.* 2d ed. New Brunswick, N.J.: Rutgers University Press,
1984.

Derr, Jill Mulvay. "'Strength in Our Union': The Making of Mormon Sisterhood."
In *Sisters in the Spirit: Mormon Women in Historical and Cultural Perspectives.*
Ed. Maureen Ursenbach Beecher and Lavina Fielding Anderson. Urbana: Univer-
sity of Illinois Press, 1987. 153–207.

Derr, Jill Mulvay, and Ann Vest Lobb. "Women in Early Utah." In *Utah's History.* Ed. Richard D. Poll et al. Provo, Utah: Brigham Young University Press, 1978. 337–56.

Derr, Jill Mulvay, Janath R. Cannon, and Maureen Ursenbach Beecher. *Women of Covenant: The Story of Relief Society.* Salt Lake City: Deseret Book, 1992.

DeSantis, Vincent P. *The Shaping of Modern America, 1877–1916.* Arlington Heights, Ill.: Forum Press, 1973.

DeShazo, G. Newton. "A Review of Statements Made by Certain Leaders of the Church of Jesus Christ of Latter-day Saints Which Refer to Various Objectives, Activities, and Desirable Experiences Inherent in Well Organized and Properly Conducted Physical Education and Recreation Programs." Master's thesis, Brigham Young University, 1971.

Diner, Steven J. *A Very Different Age: Americans of the Progressive Era.* New York: Hill and Wang, 1998.

DuBois, Ellen Carol. *Feminism and Suffrage: The Emergence of an Independent Women's Movement in America, 1848–1869.* Ithaca, N.Y.: Cornell University Press, 1978.

Ellis, Richard R. "A Review of Statements Made about the Presidents of the Church of Jesus Christ of Latter-day Saints Which Refer to Their Personal Involvement in Physical Education and Recreational Activities." Master's thesis, Brigham Young University, 1975.

Embry, Jessie L. *Mormon Polygamous Families: Life in the Principle.* Salt Lake City: University of Utah Press, 1987.

Filene, Peter G. "An Obituary for the Progressive Movement." *American Quarterly* 20 (1970): 20–34.

Foner, Philip S. *American Labor Songs of the Nineteenth Century.* Urbana: University of Illinois Press, 1975.

Forbush, William B. *The Boy Problem: A Study in Social Pedagogy.* Boston: Pilgrim Press, 1907.

Fox, Stephen R. *The American Conservation Movement: John Muir and His Legacy.* Boston: Little, Brown, 1981.

Galbraith, John Kenneth. *The Great Crash, 1929.* Boston: Houghton Mifflin, 1961.

Gems, Gerald R. "Selling Sport and Religion in American Society: Bishop Sheil and the Catholic Youth Organization." In *The New American Sport History: Recent Approaches and Perspectives.* Ed. S. W. Pope. Urbana: University of Illinois Press, 1997. 300–311.

Gibbs, Linda Jones. *Harvesting the Light: The Paris Art Mission and Beginnings of Utah Impressionism.* Salt Lake City: Church of Jesus Christ of Latter-day Saints, 1987.

Graham, Otis L., Jr. *An Encore for Reform: The Old Progressives and the New Deal.* New York: Oxford University Press, 1967.

Guttmann, Allen, and Lee Thompson. "Educators, Imitators, Modernizers: The Arrival and Spread of Modern Sport in Japan." *European Sports History Review* 3 (2001): 23–48.

Hall, David Roy. "Amy Brown Lyman and Social Service Work in the Relief Society." Master's thesis, Brigham Young University, 1992.

Halttunen, Karen. *Confidence Men and Painted Women: A Study of Middle-Class Culture in America, 1830–1870*. New Haven, Conn.: Yale University Press, 1982.

Hanks, Maxine, ed. *Women and Authority: Re-emerging Mormon Feminism*. Salt Lake City: Signature Books, 1992.

Hansen, Edward H., and Glen A. Hansen. "Scouting in Aetna and Cardston District." LDS Church Historical Department, Salt Lake City.

Hansen, Klaus J. *Mormonism and the American Experience*. Chicago: University of Chicago Press, 1981.

Hardy, B. Carmon. *Solemn Covenant: The Mormon Polygamous Passage*. Urbana: University of Illinois Press, 1992.

Hardy, Stephen. *How Boston Played: Sport, Recreation, and Community, 1865–1915*. Boston: Northeastern University Press, 1982.

Harris, Carl V. *Political Power in Birmingham, 1871–1921*. Knoxville: University of Tennessee Press, 1971.

Hatch, Nathan O. *The Democratization of American Christianity*. New Haven, Conn.: Yale University Press, 1989.

Hicks, Michael. *Mormonism and Music: A History*. Urbana: University of Illinois Press, 1989.

Higham, John. *Strangers in the Land: Patterns of American Nativism, 1860–1925*. 2d ed. New Brunswick, N.J.: Rutgers University Press, 1988.

Hinton, Wayne K. "The Economics of Ambivalence: Utah's Depression Experience." *Utah Historical Quarterly* 54 (1986): 268–85.

Hofstadter, Richard. *The Age of Reform: From Bryan to F.D.R*. New York: Vintage Books, 1955.

Holbrook, Leona. "Dancing as an Aspect of Early Mormon and Utah Culture." *BYU Studies* 16 (1975): 117–38.

Jackson, Richard H. "The Mormon Village: Genesis and Antecedents of the City of Zion Plan." *BYU Studies* 17 (1977): 223–40.

Jensen, Richard J. *The Winning of the Midwest: Social and Political Conflict, 1888–1896*. Chicago: University of Chicago Press, 1971.

Jensen, Richard L. "The British Gathering to Zion." In *Truth Will Prevail: The Rise of the Church of Jesus Christ of Latter-day Saints in the British Isles, 1837–1987*. Ed. V. Ben Bloxham, James R. Moss, and Larry C. Porter. Solihull, England: Church of Jesus Christ of Latter-day Saints, 1987. 165–98.

———. "Immigration to Utah." In *Utah History Encyclopedia*. Ed. Allan Kent Powell. Salt Lake City: University of Utah Press, 1994. 270–73.

Jensen, Richard L., and William G. Hartley. "Immigration and Emigration." In *Encyclopedia of Mormonism*. 5 vols. Ed. Daniel H. Ludlow. New York: Macmillan, 1992. 2:673–76.

Johnson, Paul E. *A Shopkeeper's Millennium: Society and Revivals in Rochester, New York, 1815–1837*. New York: Hill and Wang, 1978.

Kennedy, David M. "Overview: The Progressive Era." *The Historian* 37 (May 1975): 468.

Kenney, Scott. "E. E. Ericksen—Loyal Heretic." *Sunstone* 3 (July–Aug. 1978): 16–27.

———. *The Mutual Improvement Associations: A Preliminary History, 1900–1950.* Salt Lake City: Historical Department of the Church of Jesus Christ of Latter-day Saints, 1976.

Kimball, Richard Ian. "'Somethin' to Do': Mormon Recreation in Kanesville, 1849–1852." *The John Whitmer Historical Association Journal* 15 (1995): 35–49.

Kinsella, W. P. *Shoeless Joe.* New York: Ballantine Books, 1982.

Kirschner, Don S. "The Ambiguous Legacy: Social Justice and Social Control in the Progressive Era." *Historical Reflections* 2 (1975): 69–88.

———. "The Perils of Pleasure: Commercial Recreation, Social Disorder, and Moral Reform in the Progressive Era." *American Studies* 22 (Fall 1980): 27–42.

Kleppner, Paul. *The Cross of Culture: A Social Analysis of Midwestern Politics, 1850–1900.* New York: Free Press, 1970.

———. *The Third Electoral System, 1853–1892: Parties, Voters, and Political Cultures.* Chapel Hill: University of North Carolina Press, 1977.

Knapp, Richard F., and Charles E. Hartsoe. *Play for America: The National Recreation Association, 1906–1965.* Arlington, Va.: National Recreation and Park Association, 1979.

Korman, Gerd. *Industrialization, Immigrants, and Americanizers.* Madison: State Historical Society of Wisconsin, 1967.

Kraut, Alan M. *The Huddled Masses: The Immigrant in American Society, 1880–1921.* Arlington Heights, Ill.: Harlan Davidson, 1982.

Lally, Robert C. "The Life and Educational Contributions of Charlotte Stewart." Master's thesis, University of Utah, 1950.

Lasch, Christopher. *The Culture of Narcissism: American Life in an Age of Diminishing Expectations.* New York: W. W. Norton, 1978.

Layton, Stanford J., ed. *Being Different: Stories of Utah's Minorities.* Salt Lake City: Signature Books, 2001.

Leonard, Glen M. *Nauvoo: A Place of Peace, a People of Promise.* Salt Lake City: Deseret Book; Provo, Utah: Brigham Young University Press, 2002.

Levine, Peter. *Ellis Island to Ebbets Field: Sport and the American Jewish Experience.* New York: Oxford University Press, 1992.

Lubove, Roy. *The Professional Altruist: The Emergence of Social Work as a Career.* Cambridge, Mass.: Harvard University Press, 1965.

MacLeod, David I. *Building Character in the American Boy: The Boy Scouts, YMCA, and Their Forerunners, 1870–1920.* Madison: University of Wisconsin Press, 1983.

Madsen, Carol Cornwall, and Susan Staker Oman. *Sisters and Little Saints: One Hundred Years of Primary.* Salt Lake City: Deseret Book, 1979.

Madsen, Carol Cornwall. "Mormon Women and the Struggle for Definition: The Nineteenth-Century Church." *Sunstone* 6 (Nov.–Dec. 1981): 7–11. Reprinted in *Dialogue: A Journal of Mormon Thought* 14 (Winter 1981): 40–47.

Mangum, Garth, and Bruce Blumell. *The Mormons' War on Poverty: A History of LDS Welfare, 1830–1990*. Salt Lake City: University of Utah Press, 1993.

May, Dean L. "A Demographic Portrait of the Mormons, 1830–1980." In *After 150 Years: The Latter-day Saints in Sesquicentennial Perspective*. Ed. Thomas G. Alexander and Jessie L. Embry. Provo, Utah: Charles Redd Center for Western Studies, 1983. 39–69.

———. "The Making of Saints: The Mormon Town as a Setting for the Study of Cultural Change." *Utah Historical Quarterly* 45 (Dec. 1977): 75–92.

———. *Three Frontiers: Family, Land, and Society in the American West, 1850–1900*. New York: Cambridge University Press, 1994.

McCormick, John S. "Hornets in the Hive: Socialists in Early Twentieth-Century Utah." *Utah Historical Quarterly* 50 (Summer 1982): 224–40.

McCoy, Drew R. *The Elusive Republic: Political Economy in Jeffersonian America*. New York: W. W. Norton, 1982.

Moore, R. Laurence. "Learning to Play: The Mormon Way and the Way of Other Americans." *Journal of Mormon History* 16 (1990): 89–106.

———. *Religious Outsiders and the Making of Americans*. New York: Oxford University Press, 1986.

———. *Selling God: American Religion in the Marketplace of Culture*. New York: Oxford University Press, 1994.

Morgan, Edmund S. *Visible Saints: The History of a Puritan Idea*. Ithaca, N.Y.: Cornell University Press, 1963.

Mormino, Gary Ross. "The Playing Fields of St. Louis: Italian Immigrants and Sport, 1925–1941." *Journal of Sport History* 9 (Summer 1982): 5–16.

Morris, Richard B., and Jeffrey B. Morris, eds. *Encyclopedia of American History*. 7th ed. New York: Harper Collins, 1996.

Mulder, William. *Homeward to Zion: The Mormon Migration from Scandinavia*. Minneapolis: University of Minnesota Press, 1957.

Nash, Roderick. *Wilderness and the American Mind*. 4th ed. New Haven, Conn.: Yale University Press, 2001.

Nelson, Lowry. *The Mormon Village: A Study in Social Origins*. Provo, Utah: Research Division, Brigham Young University, 1930.

Olsen, Steven L. "Celebrating Cultural Identity: Pioneer Day in Nineteenth-Century Mormonism." *BYU Studies* 36 (1996–97): 159–77.

Osborn, Gordon Norman. "An Historical Study of the All-Church Softball Tournament of the Church of Jesus Christ of Latter-day Saints." Master's thesis, Brigham Young University, 1961.

Painter, Nell Irvin. *Standing at Armageddon: The United States, 1877–1919*. New York: W. W. Norton, 1987.

Papanikolas, Helen Zeese. "The Great Bingham Strike of 1912 and the Expulsion of the Padrone." *Utah Historical Quarterly* 38 (Spring 1970): 121–33.

———. *The Peoples of Utah*. Salt Lake City: Utah State Historical Society, 1976.

———. "Unionism, Communism, and the Great Depression: The Carbon County Coal Strike of 1933." *Utah Historical Quarterly* 41 (Summer 1973): 254–300.

Peck, Gunther. "Padrones and Protest: 'Old' Radicals and 'New' Immigrants in Bingham, Utah, 1905–1912." *Western Historical Quarterly* 24 (May 1993): 157–78.

Peterson, Robert. *The Boy Scouts: An American Adventure.* New York: American Heritage, 1984.

Pinkett, Harold T. *Gifford Pinchot, Private and Public Forester.* Urbana: University of Illinois Press, 1970.

Poll, Richard D., et al., eds. *Utah's History.* Provo, Utah: Brigham Young University Press, 1978.

Powell, Allan Kent. *Next Time We Strike: Labor in Utah's Coal Fields, 1900–1933.* Logan: Utah State University Press, 1985.

Putney, Clifford. *Muscular Christianity: Manhood and Sports in Protestant America, 1880–1920.* Cambridge, Mass.: Harvard University Press, 2001.

Quinn, D. Michael. *Same-Sex Dynamics among Nineteenth-Century Americans: A Mormon Example.* 1996. Reprint, Urbana: University of Illinois Press, 2001.

Riess, Steven A. *City Games: The Evolution of American Urban Society and the Rise of Sports.* Urbana: University of Illinois Press, 1989.

———, ed. *Sports and the American Jew.* Syracuse, N.Y.: Syracuse University Press, 1998.

Riis, Jacob. *How the Other Half Lives: Studies among the Tenements of New York.* New York: Dover, 1971.

Roden, Donald. "Baseball and the Quest for National Dignity in Meiji Japan." *American Historical Review* 85 (June 1980): 511–34.

Rodgers, Daniel T. *Atlantic Crossings: Social Politics in a Progressive Age.* Cambridge, Mass.: Harvard University Press, 1998.

———. "In Search of Progressivism." *Reviews in American History* 10 (Dec. 1982): 113–32.

Ross, Steven J. *Working-Class Hollywood: Silent Film and the Shaping of Class in America.* Princeton, N.J.: Princeton University Press, 1998.

Shipps, Jan. "In the Presence of the Past: Continuity and Change in Twentieth-Century Mormonism." In *After 150 Years: The Latter-day Saints in Sesquicentennial Perspective.* Ed. Thomas G. Alexander and Jessie L. Embry. Provo, Utah: Charles Redd Center for Western Studies, 1983. 3–35.

———. *Mormonism: The Story of a New Religious Tradition.* Urbana: University of Illinois Press, 1985.

Skidmore, Rex A. "Mormon Recreation in Theory and Practice: A Study of Social Change." Ph.D. dissertation, University of Pennsylvania, 1941.

Smith, Joseph. *History of the Church of Jesus Christ of Latter-day Saints.* 7 vols. Ed. B. H. Roberts. Salt Lake City: Deseret Book, 1971.

Smith, Joseph Fielding. *Life of Joseph F. Smith.* Salt Lake City: Deseret Book, 1969.

Sonne, Conway B. *Saints on the Seas: A Maritime History of Mormon Migration, 1830–1890.* Salt Lake City: University of Utah Press, 1983.

Sorrell, Richard. "Sports and Franco-Americans in Woonsocket, 1870–1930." *Rhode Island History* 31 (Fall 1972): 117–26.

Spring, Joel H. *Education and the Rise of the Corporate State.* Boston: Beacon Press, 1972.

Stegner, Page, ed. *Marking the Sparrow's Fall: Wallace Stegner's American West.* New York: Henry Holt, 1998.

Stegner, Wallace. *Mormon Country.* 1942. Reprint, Lincoln: University of Nebraska Press, 1981.

Stegner, Wallace, and Richard W. Etulain. *Stegner: Conversations on History and Literature.* Rev. ed. Reno: University of Nevada Press, 1996.

Swenson, Russel. "Mormons at the University of Chicago Divinity School." *Dialogue: A Journal of Mormon Thought* 7 (Summer 1972): 37–47.

Taylor, P. A. M. *Expectations Westward: The Mormons and the Emigration of Their British Converts in the Nineteenth Century.* Ithaca, N.Y.: Cornell University Press, 1965.

Van Noy, Elsie Ellen Hogan. "Young Ladies' Mutual Improvement Association from April 1927 to December 1937." LDS Church Historical Department, Salt Lake City.

Van Wagoner, Richard S. *Mormon Polygamy: A History.* Salt Lake City: Signature Books, 1986.

Walker, Ronald W. "Heber J. Grant." In *The Presidents of the Church.* Ed. Leonard J. Arrington. Salt Lake City: Deseret Book, 1986. 211–48.

Walker, Ronald W., and Doris Dant, eds. *Nearly Everything Imaginable: The Everyday Life of Utah's Mormon Pioneers.* Provo, Utah: Brigham Young University Press, 1999.

Watkins, T. H. *The Hungry Years.* New York: Henry Holt, 1999.

Weeks, Genevieve C. "Oscar C. McCulloch Transforms Plymouth Church, Indianapolis, into an 'Institutional' Church." *Indiana Magazine of History* 64 (June 1968): 87–108.

Welter, Barbara. "The Cult of True Womanhood, 1820–1860." *American Quarterly* 18 (Summer 1966): 151–74.

Wesson, Karl E. "Dance in the Church of Jesus Christ of Latter-day Saints, 1830–1940." Master's thesis, Brigham Young University, 1975.

Widtsoe, John A., ed. *Discourses of Brigham Young.* Salt Lake City: Deseret Book, 1925.

Wiebe, Robert H. *The Search for Order, 1877–1920.* New York: Hill and Wang, 1967.

Wilentz, Sean. "A Scandal for Our Time." *American Prospect* 13 (25 Feb. 2002): 20.

Wright, Paul A. "The Growth and Distribution of the Mormon and Non-Mormon Populations in Salt Lake City." Master's thesis, University of Chicago, 1970.

INDEX

Adams, Samuel Hopkins, 74
Addams, Jane, 26, 40
Ainge, Danny, 188
Alberta (Canada) Stake, 171
Allen, Forest C. ("Phog"), 44
Allen, James X., 32
Almo, Idaho, 105
Alpine (Utah) Stake, 103
American Fork, Utah, 103, 150
Anderson, Lewis, 133
Anderson, Nephi, 130–31
Angell, Emmett D., 44
Arlitt, Ada H., 175
athletic programs, 170; purpose of, 94–98; success of, 99–101; ward, 102–7

Baden-Powell, Robert, 126
Baldwin, James Mark, 27, 94
Ballard, Melvin J., 46, 167
basketball, 61, 104–7, 170
Bear Lake, 150
Beehive Girls, 146
Beeley, Arthur L., 166, 190–91
Bennion, Adam S., 42
Bennion, Milton, 42, 129
Big Cottonwood Canyon, 150
Bisbee High School, 109
Black Mountain, 134
Book of Mormon, 21–22
Bowers, Ethel M., 177
Box Elder (Utah) Stake, 99, 101, 102
Boy Pioneers of Utah, 135, 136, 138
Boy Scouts of America, 51, 186; argument

for, 135–37; and church ideals, 135, 143–45; and citizenship, 139–40; during the Depression, 167–68, 171; formation of, 134–37; and frontier ideals, 135, 136, 137–38; and YMMIA, 141, 142–44
Bradley, Martha Sonntag, 60, 65
Brandley, Elsie T., 176
Brigham Young University, 42, 44, 187–88
Brighton, Utah, 150
Brimhall, George H., 34, 44, 154
Brooks, Fowler O., 175
Brooks, Juanita, 169
Bullock, Thomas, 138
Burke, Melvin Tolman, 115, 116, 117

Cache (Utah) Stake, 61
Calder's Park, 101
Camp Atoka, 148–49
Campfire Girls, 146
Camp Saratoga, 81
Cannon, A. S., 162
Cannon, Joseph J., 117–20
Cannon, Lewis Telle, 67, 99
Cardston (Alberta), 110, 157n23
Carter, Virgil, 187
Christensen, C. C. A., 133
Christie, Walter, 114
Church of Jesus Christ of Latter-day Saints: attitude toward recreation, 21–25, 33–35, 89–90; attitude toward work, 33–35; and Boy Scouts, 134–37, 144–45; celebrating rural life, 128, 129–32; changes in recreation, 185–87; compared to other

reformers, 4, 11–12, 14–15; during the Depression, 164–73, 177–78; and frontier experience, 126–27, 132–134, 155; and purpose of recreation, 12, 13, 38, 43; and recreation, 35–52, 163–64, 170–73; in transition, 2–3, 10–12; and urban life, 66–67, 127–29; and urbanization, 3, 28–30, 125–26; using outside experts, 39–41, 44–45, 174–78
Civilian Conservation Corps, 173
Colonia Juarez, Mexico, 107, 109, 142
Colonia Juarez (Mexico) Ward, 99
Cornwall, Claude C., 167
Cottonwood (Salt Lake) Stake, 110
Cowley, Matthias F., 156n10
Cranney, A. E., 61
Curlew Stake, 110

Dale, Ludvig, 140
Daynes Trophy, 104
Deseret Gymnasium, 60, 66, 71, 104, 186; and advertising, 57–58, 70, 72, 73–80; during the Depression, 173; and focus on businessmen, 57–58, 73–76; and gender roles, 72–82; physical facilities, 67–69; and vocational training, 80–81
Deseret (Salt Lake) Stake, 170
Deseret Sunday School Union, 39
Detmer, Ty, 187
Dewey, John, 27
Done, Willard, 90
Driggs, Howard R., 59
Druselius, Erland, 71–72, 75
Duchesne, Utah, 99
Duchesne (Utah) Stake, 99

Easthope, Anna Saunders, 148
Echo Canyon, 138
Edwards, Lavell, 187
Ensign (Salt Lake) Stake, 98, 104
Ensign Twentieth Ward, 104
Ericksen, Ephraim E., 46

Farnsworth, Philo T., 166–67, 174–75
Fathers and Sons' Outings, 51, 152–55
Forbush, William Bryon, 3, 40
Freud, Sigmund, 169–70
Frost, Grace Ingles, 129–30, 155

Gates, Susa Young, 23, 30
Geertsen, Norman, 141
gender roles, 3–4, 41–42, 43–44, 72; female, 76–80, 81–82; male, 73–76, 80–81
Gila College (Arizona), 110–11
Gilman, Charlotte Perkins, 44
Girls' Camp, Logan Canyon, 146
Girls' Camps, 146–51, 186
Glade, Earl J., 42
Glancey, Harry, 115
Godfrey, James, 147
Gowans, E. G., 39–40, 98
Granite (Salt Lake) Stake, 45, 134
Granite Stake Tabernacle, 60
Grant, Heber J., 132; addresses, 42, 91, 168, 178; and the Word of Wisdom, 108, 111, 114
Griffiths, J. Ruel, 176
Grouse Creek, Utah, 105
Gulick, Luther H., 40, 41
gymnasiums: and basketball, 104–7; and chapels, 64, 65; early, 58, 60; and libraries, 59, 61–62; as social centers, 58, 61–65, 88

Hall, G. Stanley, 27
Hamilton, Samuel, 113
Hanson, Ramm, 67
Harlem Globetrotters, 82
Harris, Franklin S., 44, 156n10
Harvard Stadium, 118, 119
Hawkins, Clarence J., 80
Haymond, Creed, 115, 116, 117–20, 188
Hewlett, Frank J., 129
Higgs, Emily H., 150
Hinckley, Bryant S., 67, 80
Holden, Utah, 103
Honeyville, Utah, 115
Hulme, Claire N., 151
Hyrum, Utah, 62
Hyrum (Utah) Second Ward, 62

Ivins, H. Grant, 100

Jenkins, David Abbott, 172

Kimball, Edward P., 93
Kimball, Heber C., 132

Kimball, Paul, 123n60
Kirkham, Oscar A., 164; and Boy Scouts, 139, 140–41, 167–68; and YMMIA, 39, 45
Kleinman, Bertha A., 21

Laie, Hawaii, 110
Lamkin, Marla War, 176
Lampland, Ruth, 177
Larson, Clinton, 116
Latter Day Saints University (LDSU), 66, 81
LDS Business College, 165
LDSU. See Latter Day Saints University
Lee, Joseph, 40, 176
Lehi Silver Band, 104
leisure time, increase of, 25, 163–64
Liberty Glen Camp, 147–48, 149
Liberty (Utah) Stake, 147
Lindbergh, Charles A., 112–13
Lindeman, Eduard, 176
Lion House, 58, 81
Lloyd, Rev. E. C., 100
Logan Canyon, 146, 149–50
Logan (Utah) Stake, 149
Lubove, Roy, 191
Luke, Clinton, 116
Lund, Anthon H., 138
Lyman, Amy Brown, 15, 174
Lyman, Francis M., 35, 138
Lyman, Richard R., 112–13, 129

Mack, Connie, 114
Mack, Solomon, 133
Malta, Idaho, 105
Manti, Utah, 133
Maori Agricultural College, 110
Martineau, Lyman R., 15, 102; and Boy Scouts, 137, 141; and YMMIA, 97–98, 101
McGugin, Dan, 114
McJackson, Jane, 92
McKay, David O., 42–43, 112
McKeever, William Arch, 40
McMahon, Jim, 187
Merrill, A. P., 67
Merrill, Earl, 115
Merrill, Harrison R., 116–17, 165
Merrill, Joseph F., 168

Merrill, Lewis A., 34
MIA Girls' Summer Home at Lakota (Bear Lake), 150
MIA Girls' Summer House (Brighton), 150
MIA Home (Logan Canyon), 150
MIA Scouts, 137, 138, 141
Millard (Utah) Stake, 103
Milne, E. J., 98
missionaries and sports, 100–101, 172–73, 186
Morgan, J. J. B., 177
Mortensen, H. C., 77
Mountain Dell, 134
Murphy, Dale, 188
Murphy, Edwin L., 99
Murray, Utah, 147
Mutual Dell (American Fork), 150
Mutual Improvement League, 58
Mutual Isle (Provo Canyon), 150

Nash, Jay B., 162, 176
National Recreation Assocation. See Playground Association of America
Nebeker, Anne, 37
Neumeyer, Esther S., 177
Neumeyer, Martin H., 177
Nibley, Charles W., 69
North Weber (Utah) Stake, 104

Oasis Ward, 103
Ocean Park, California, 84n19
Ogden, Utah, 170
Ogden (Utah) Ninth Ward, 143
Ogden Stake, 148
Olsen, Charles L., 92
Olympic Games (Winter 2002), 189
O'Shea, M. V., 175

Pack, Frederick J., 114–15
Palmer, Annie D., 131
Panaca, Nevada, 62
Parry, Edwin F., 34
Pearson, Monte, 172
Perry, Fred, 82
Peterson, Elmer G., 44
Playground Association of America, 28, 175
Pope, J. J., 70

Pope, Theodore, 65
Pratt, Parley P., 23
Preston, Idaho, 103
Progressive reformers: compared to LDS Church, 4, 11–12, 14–15; and sociology, 25–28
Provo Canyon, 150

recreation: and church supervision, 96, 98–99; and cohesion, 170–73; commercialized, 28, 39, 168–69, 187; and gender, 3–4, 41–42, 43–44, 72; ideology, 35–52; need for, 28–33, 166–70; and physical benefit, 46, 47; and social values, 5, 41, 46, 47, 62, 63, 90; and sociology, 25–28, 47–51; and spiritual growth, 38, 40, 46, 47. See also athletic programs
Richards, Alma W., 115, 116, 189
Richards, Stephen L, 42, 174
Richens, W. F., 105
Riis, Jacob, 26, 139
Roberts, Brigham H., 38, 134–35, 137, 138
Roberts, Eugene L., 135–37, 169, 177
Robertson, Lawson, 118
Rockne, Knute K., 44, 113
Romney, G. Ott, 111, 164, 168
Roosevelt, Theodore, 113, 126
Ross, Edward Alsworth, 40, 45, 176
Rowe, Owen, 117
rural life, 128, 129–32

Sabbath observance, 31–32, 144
Safford, Arizona, 110–11
Salt Lake City, Utah, 5–10; immigration in, 7–9; industrialization of, 9–10; social problems in, 28–33; urbanization of, 6–7, 28–30
Salt Lake Fifteenth Ward, 105–7
Salt Lake Stake, 104
Salt Lake Twenty-seventh Ward, 63–64
Samoa, 100–101
Saratoga Springs, 134
Scott, Robert H., 176
Shelley, Idaho, 134
Shiede, Gary, 187
Shields, Alma Budd, 116
Shoemaker, Ezra, 133
Simpers, Ernest, 105
Smith, Frederick, 23

Smith, George Albert, 53n26, 143
Smith, Hyrum, 22, 132
Smith, Hyrum M., 67
Smith, Joseph, 21–23, 29, 108, 132
Smith, Joseph F., 66, 108, 132; about the youth, 29–30, 32, 41, 98, 128
Smith, J. R., 62
Smith, Mary Fielding, 132
Snow, Lorenzo, 132
Social Advisory Committee, 41–47
Social Hall, 58
South Fork Canyon, 148
Standing, John E., 103–4
Stegner, Wallace, 88, 169, 170–71
Stephens, Evan, 130
Stewart, Charlotte, 42, 47
St. George, Utah, 169
Stone (Curlew) Ward, 110

Tanner, James Henry, 157n23
Tanner, Nathan W., 157n23
Taylor, John, 132
Taylor, John Harris (Scout commissioner), 38, 140, 143, 157n39
team sports, 95–101, 104–7, 172–73
Temple of Health, 57, 66, 67, 70, 83
Thomas, Elbert D., 100
Thompson, J. Henry, 105
Todd, Douglas M., 54n34
Tokyo, Japan, 100
Tunney, Gene, 82

University of Pennsylvania, 117–18
urban life, 6, 28–30, 66–67, 127–29
Utah Agricultural College, 34, 44

Vacation School, 81
Van Noy, Elsie Ellen Hogan, 82
Vidmar, Peter, 188

Wagstaff, Melvin G., 100–101
Wahlquist, John T., 1, 47
Wandamere Park, 69, 102
Warner, Glenn Scobey ("Pop"), 44, 172
Waterloo (Granite) Ward, 134
Watkins, E. W., 99
Weber (Utah) Stake, 37, 101
Weir, L. H., 44
West, James E., 142

Whitney, Orson F., 138
Widtsoe, John A., 177–78
Wiebe, Robert H., 191
Wilson, Robert E., 143
Winder (Cottonwood) Ward, 110
Withers, Billy, 82
Wood, Thomas George, 134
Woodruff, Asahel H., 134
Woodruff, Wilford, 2, 3, 22, 132
Woolley, Ivy Houtz, 141
Word of Wisdom, 3, 71; and athletic success, 109–12, 186, 187–88; and Boy Scouts, 143–44; and LDS celebrities, 115–20, 171–72; and non-LDS examples, 112–14, 172; scientific support for, 114–15; and team sports, 96, 107; in transition, 108–9, 171–72
Wyland, Ray O., 165

YLMIA. *See* Young Ladies' Mutual Improvement Association
YMMIA. *See* Young Men's Mutual Improvement Association
Yokohama, Japan, 100
Young, Brigham, 23–24, 89, 132
Young, Levi Edgar, 62
Young, Lorenzo Sobieski, 134
Young, Steve, 187, 188
Young Ladies' Mutual Improvement Association (YLMIA): and spiritual growth, 89, 93; and summer camps, 146–51; training courses, 37–38
Young Men's Mutual Improvement Association (YMMIA): athletic programs, 91, 95–101; and Boy Scouts, 141, 142–44; field days, 101–4; overseeing recreation, 35–36, 38; and spiritual growth, 89, 93; training courses, 37–38

Richard Ian Kimball is an assistant professor of history at Brigham Young University in Provo, Utah. His articles have appeared in the *Journal of Sport History*, *Mid-America*, and the *Utah Historical Quarterly*. In 1999 he was awarded the William G. and Winifred F. Reese Memorial Award for the best dissertation in Mormon studies.

SPORT AND SOCIETY

A Sporting Time: New York City and the Rise of Modern Athletics,
    1820–70   *Melvin L. Adelman*
Sandlot Seasons: Sport in Black Pittsburgh   *Rob Ruck*
West Ham United: The Making of a Football Club   *Charles Korr*
Beyond the Ring: The Role of Boxing in American Society
    Jeffrey T. Sammons
John L. Sullivan and His America   *Michael T. Isenberg*
Television and National Sport: The United States and Britain
    Joan M. Chandler
The Creation of American Team Sports: Baseball and Cricket,
    1838–72   *George B. Kirsch*
City Games: The Evolution of American Urban Society and the Rise
    of Sports   *Steven A. Riess*
The Brawn Drain: Foreign Student-Athletes in American Universities
    John Bale
The Business of Professional Sports   *Edited by Paul D. Staudohar and
    James A. Mangan*
Fritz Pollard: Pioneer in Racial Advancement   *John M. Carroll*
Go Big Red! The Story of a Nebraska Football Player   *George Mills*
Sport and Exercise Science: Essays in the History of Sports
    Medicine   *Edited by Jack W. Berryman and Roberta J. Park*
Minor League Baseball and Local Economic Development
    Arthur T. Johnson
Harry Hooper: An American Baseball Life   *Paul J. Zingg*
Cowgirls of the Rodeo: Pioneer Professional Athletes
    Mary Lou LeCompte
Sandow the Magnificent: Eugen Sandow and the Beginnings of
    Bodybuilding   *David Chapman*
Big-Time Football at Harvard, 1905: The Diary of Coach Bill Reid
    Edited by Ronald A. Smith
Leftist Theories of Sport: A Critique and Reconstruction
    William J. Morgan
Babe: The Life and Legend of Babe Didrikson Zaharias   *Susan E. Cayleff*
Stagg's University: The Rise, Decline, and Fall of Big-Time Football
    at Chicago   *Robin Lester*
Muhammad Ali, the People's Champ   *Edited by Elliott J. Gorn*
People of Prowess: Sport, Leisure, and Labor in Early Anglo-
    America   *Nancy L. Struna*

The New American Sport History: Recent Approaches and
  Perspectives   *Edited by S. W. Pope*
Making the Team: The Cultural Work of Baseball Fiction   *Timothy Morris*
Making the American Team: Sport, Culture, and the Olympic Experience
  Mark Dyreson
Viva Baseball! Latin Major Leaguers and Their Special Hunger
  Samuel O. Regalado
Touching Base: Professional Baseball and American Culture in the
  Progressive Era (rev. ed.)   *Steven A. Riess*
Red Grange and the Rise of Modern Football   *John M. Carroll*
Golf and the American Country Club   *Richard J. Moss*
Extra Innings: Writing on Baseball   *Richard Peterson*
Global Games   *Maarten Van Bottenburg*
The Sporting World of the Modern South   *Edited by Patrick B. Miller*
The End of Baseball As We Knew It: The Players Union, 1960–81
  Charles P. Korr
Rocky Marciano: The Rock of His Times   *Russell Sullivan*
Saying It's So: A Cultural History of the Black Sox Scandal
  Daniel A. Nathan
The Nazi Olympics: Sport, Politics, and Appeasement in the 1930s
  Edited by Arnd Krüger and William Murray
The Unlevel Playing Field: A Documentary History of the African
  American Experience in Sport   *David K. Wiggins and Patrick B. Miller*
Sports in Zion: Mormon Recreation, 1890–1940   *Richard Ian Kimball*

Reprint Editions

The Nazi Olympics   *Richard D. Mandell*
Sports in the Western World (2d ed.)   *William J. Baker*

The University of Illinois Press
is a founding member of the
Association of American University Presses.

———————————————————

Composed in 10/13 Sabon
with Sabon display
by Jim Proefrock
at the University of Illinois Press
Designed by Dennis Roberts
Manufactured by Thomson-Shore, Inc.

University of Illinois Press
1325 South Oak Street
Champaign, IL 61820-6903
www.press.uillinois.edu